What People Are Saying About
AMERICAN EVITA: LURLEEN WALLACE

"How much I love this book! American Evita is just so gripping, fascinating and engaging! Beautifully written, too. Its revelations are sensational. The way Janice Law puts words together makes me want to jump up and down cheering!"

Helen Anders
Former *Austin American Statesman*

"I couldn't put this book down! Wow! Law writes an enthralling analysis of Lurleen Wallace and Evita Perón, drawing fascinating parallels, illuminating their personal and political lives."

Helen Hester-Ossa
Former head of Copyright Publications,
U.S. Copyright Office, Library of Congress

"Great concept! Law braids stories rich with complexities of state and national politics and—perhaps most satisfyingly—marital politics."

Professor Angie Chuang
***Los Angeles Times* former staff writer**
Author: *The Four Words for Home*

"Janice Law gets into Lurleen's mind. Until now, no writing about Governor Lurleen Wallace has ever done that."

Donald Jansen, esq.
Houston

i

COVER PHOTO: Alabama First lady Lurleen Wallace on the road campaigning in 1967 for Alabama Governor, reaches down from a portable platform to shake hands with an admiring young girl and her grandmother or mother. Their identities are unknown. State trooper E.C. Dothard, one of her bodyguards, watches. An Alabama flag furles in the background of downtown brick buildings.

COVER PHOTO BOTTOM LEFT: Tuscaloosa, Alabama S.H. Kress & Co 5-10-25 Cent store (circa 1937) where George Wallace and Lurleen Burns first met in July 1942 when she worked at the store as a clerk.

Photos used with permission of Alabama State Archives and Tuscaloosa Public Library.

BACK COVER PHOTO: Evita Duarte Perón, circa 1951

American Evita: Lurleen Wallace

BY JANICE LAW

Narrative Nonfiction Biography

Copyright © 2015
By Janice Law
Published By Eakin Press
An Imprint of Wild Horse Media Group
P.O. Box 331779
Fort Worth, Texas 76163
1-817-344-7036
www.EakinPress.com
ALL RIGHTS RESERVED
1 2 3 4 5 6 7 8 9
ISBN-10: 1-940130-83-2
ISBN-13: 978-1-940130-83-5

This narrative nonfiction book is dedicated to the National Press Club; to Helen Hester Ossa and Roberta Shaffer of the Library of Congress; to Ilene Gutman of National Museum of Women in the Arts—and to myriad dazzling, talented women whose devoted assistance helped me establish and develop American Women Writers National Museum in Washington, D.C., whose mission is honoring and showcasing work of premier American women writers, historical and contemporary.

—Judge Janice Law

www.americanwomenwritersnationalmuseum.org
www.judgejanicelaw.com

TABLE OF CONTENTS

*"I believe that everything wants
a living place,
its home, if you will,
where it becomes what its essence is
at a certain time
and in a certain place."
—Anonymous*

INTRODUCTION

Governor Lurleen Wallace of Alabama and First Lady Evita Perón of Argentina were women in their time but were not women of their time.

Born in the same era on different continents, the trajectory of their high profile achievements, and the men they married, paralleled in astonishing chrysalis patterns.

． ． ． ． ． ． ． ．

When a white woman, Alabama Governor Lurleen Wallace, died of cancer in 1968 in the violent years of Civil Rights confrontations, Rev. Dr. Ralph Abernathy, black high profile activist of the Southern Christian Leadership Conference, issued a public statement: "A dark shadow has been cast across the horizon of America by the death of the Honorable Governor Lurleen Wallace," declared Rev. Abernathy, a Dr. Martin Luther King Jr. top lieutenant.

Her husband George C. Wallace famously vowed: "Segregation forever."

Public admiration of a black leader for the wife of an avowed segregationist was unimaginable in 1968 America.

But it did happen.

Like Alabama's Lurleen Burns Wallace, Eva Duarte Perón of Argentina was born in a rural village. Neither was a high school graduate. Both were nudged by opportunity and high-profile husbands who utilized the women as tools to augment the men's zealous political ambitions. Lurleen and Evita began as adjuncts in traditional supporting roles. But innate charisma, ability to endure psychological and physical hardship, and political discernment of each woman enabled her to gallop past her spouse in a mere six-year period.

• • • • • • • •

When the Alabama Constitution barred bombastic Governor George Wallace from a second term, in frustration—as a political Hail Mary pass—he decided to run his wife, Lurleen, as his proxy so he could continue running for president of the United States a second time.

George was confident that the wife he thought he knew would do what he told her to do. After Lurleen won an overwhelming victory still never equaled proportionately in America's political history, George was in for uncomfortable surprises from the former dime-store clerk.

In an astonishing dichotomy, her electoral support included a majority of the black vote in 1966 while Americans watched blacks and whites clash violently nightly on television news.

For the first time in Alabama history, racially integrated bands marched in her 1967 inaugural parade.

Lurleen emerged, chrysalis-like, from what George assumed was the mousy housewife he was confident he could puppeteer—becoming an indefatigable, graceful campaigner: an astute, independent politico who told George after she was elected in a historic landslide that she would make her own decisions as governor, thank you very much.

And, yes, rumors of an impending Lurleen-George divorce are true. There was even a formal separation agreement. Lurleen may have been a victim of domestic violence.

Exasperated at ex-governor George's post-inaugural hanging around, Governor Lurleen moved him and his toiletries out of *her* governor's office to a makeshift closet down the hall. "She just put his butt out of there. I thought it was the greatest thing I'd ever heard in my life," remembers her daughter Peggy, laughing.

At the 1967 White House, when George tried following her into the annual governors-only conference, she rebuked him in front of President Lyndon Johnson and the nation's all-male governor coterie.

He continued, uninvited, into the room anyway.

Rapidly, "Leen" became her essence – who she was all along. She immediately persuaded the Alabama Legislature to approve funds for mental health facility construction and reform of Alabama's ghastly dungeons, as well as creating state parks and junior colleges, while mothering three teenagers and a six-year-old as George pursued—and very nearly won—the presidency.

. . . .

In Argentina, 5,000 miles away, but in the same general time period, widower Colonel Juan Perón is so grateful to his mistress, radiant radio actress Evita, for using her influence with unions to spring Juan out of prison, that he marries Evita as payback.

Evita, whom Juan embraced as a politically savvy equal from the beginning, thwarted Argentina's macho culture and outsmarted the affluent women of leisure who derided her theatrical career and illegitimate birth and were dismissive of her accomplishments. By courting votes of the poor (*descamisados*) and obtaining voting rights for women, Evita came within a hair's breadth of becoming, in 1951, Argentina's first vice president: South America's first female elected as a high-ranking government official.

Both women married steely-eyed realists, power-obsessed expedient men who were only too willing to tailor their consciences to fit whatever fashion of the times ensured their political success.

Daring to, or persuaded to, defy gender conventionality of the epoch, each woman initially hung back from campaigning until personal charisma and once-closeted political acumen catapulted them both to literal center stage, leaving their husbands as astonished also-rans.

Within the always-unforgiving spotlight glare of public life, each woman inched out of the shadow of her already famous spouse, as they quickly eclipsed the men in separate cultures on separate continents, where females were valued solely in domesticity contexts.

At very young ages, 41 and 33, Lurleen Wallace and Evita Perón attained political immortality, while their initially higher-profile spouses, on whose tutelage the women rose to international renown, faded.

Like presidential candidate Hillary Clinton, who half a century later works as a shrewd political team with her husband ex-President Bill, Lurleen Wallace and Evita Perón understood the magnifying power of two skilled campaigners who happen to be married to each other, working in tandem.

"Campaigns imprison a candidate in a bubble. If the person he or she is laying next to every night shares the same daily campaign mode bubble, that can be very comforting and bring them closer," said one operative.

They can also become competitors.

．　．　．　．　．　．　．　．

Death, which arrived very early for both, had to fetch Evita and Lurleen as they slept. Were they awake, death would have faced an even fiercer fight.   .

Author's Note: Evita Duarte Perón was born in 1919. However, at some point, she subtracted two years from her age by altering her birth date to 1921. This creates confusion when noting her age at points in her life. Judge Law uses the 1919 birth date.

Also, Lurleen Wallace's children insist that she graduated from high school. Those claims have been left in where they are direct quotes or the equivalent. However, notwithstanding decades of controversy, neither they nor anyone else has ever produced any written proof that she was a high school graduate. Other circumstances indicate Lurleen did not graduate from high school.

CHAPTER ONE
DEER GUTS ON A BRASS DOOR KNOB

"Chance encounters, often with people we barely know, are frequently responsible for our biggest breaks or greatest happinesses."
—Invisible Links by Richard Koch

At 22 years old, bounding from a state highway department truck into S. H. Kress & Co 5-10-25 Cent store in July, 1942, in Tuscaloosa, Alabama, the tanned young lawyer, cigar jutting from his lips skyward, was slicker 'n deer guts on a brass doorknob.

He left the motor running partly because the ol' dump truck's battery was in such sorry shape that if he turned the ignition off, it might not come alive again, and partly because being in a hurry was his integral nature.

He was like the truck: never really turning off his motor. It kept running full speed. There were no stops. Refueling pauses only.

He always felt he lived in a hurry, as if someone punched a fast forward button on his life story then raced off bemused, leaving others to puzzle out and cope with the blurred, rushed images of who and what he was.

Alabama born, he and the ferocious, unrelenting mid-summer heat had reached a comfortable détente accorded by equals who've met their match.

He was a young man bent on a mission. Hair oil. He liked to apply it liberally, comb it through right-handed while slicking it back with the heel of his left hand until it showed glossy black in reflected light. Combining the greasy pompadour with residual

3

swagger from his undergrad amateur boxer days, he knew he was cool.

Yes, ma'am, right cool, too.

• • • • • • • •

Lurleen Burroughs Burns, a high school student working part time, noticed the ol' well-worn truck, like one her father drove for a nearby paper mill, as it roared up to Kress's plate glass windows in a cloud of summer dust.

Olive skin inherited from her paternal Creek Indian ancestors; pouty, full lips, and short auburn hair of the 15-year old girl behind the Kress's counter caught the man's long-practiced eye. People would later observe that there was a remarkable physical resemblance of their facial features.

When she stepped away from the counter to greet him as a customer, her perfectly shaped, bronzed, muscled legs accelerated his personal interest beyond his intended purchase.

"For a lil' ol' country girl, I think he just looked like a movie star to her, walkin' in Kress's door. Something big. A lawyer," a friend commented.

Given the ample social chasm yawning between their education, family background, sophistication, and age, a southern colloquialism might have termed them then a mule and thoroughbred.

The initial words between the two, spoken over the glass-sided, wood-framed notions counter, constituted one of those fateful meetings, a star-crossed pinpoint in time that altered dramatically the future of each, catapulting both into a tumultuous, national high-profile life way beyond Tuscaloosa and almost beyond imagining, their public personas forever etched in America's history.

After 10 months of courting scheduled around beginning his World War II military service, they were married in Tuscaloosa by a justice of the peace on May 22, 1943: Lurleen Burns, the pretty dime-store girl from a farm family in tiny rural Northport and George Corley Wallace Jr., the slicker 'n deer guts on a brass door knob lawyer fueled by ambition so powerful, so laser focused that it obliterated everything and everyone—even his family.

· · · · · · · ·

Because Lurleen was legally underage at 16, the law required her parents, Henry and Estelle Burroughs Burns, to give their written consent in order for the marriage to take place.

No photos were taken of their no-frills nuptials.

Although in their courting days, George ate many meals at Lurleen's farm home with her parents and her brother Cecil, he never introduced Lurleen to his college-educated family during their courtship. He did not tell his family about the marriage until after it occurred.

Their wedding eve meal was chicken salad sandwiches and Cokes eaten at H&W drug store lunch counter near Kress's.

Lurleen's mother was the only guest attending the brief ceremony. Throughout their lives, their son-in-law George remained a taste Henry and Estelle Burns never acquired.

Success in the unforgiving fishbowl of lives lived publicly would exact an exorbitant personal price from Lurleen and George Wallace: turbulent, fractious years together Shakespearean in theatricality and storyline; operatic in high drama on a national stage, ending in aching sorrow for each, almost Biblical in consequences.

George would come breathtakingly close in 1972 to being elected president of the United States. In 1967, Lurleen was elected the third woman governor in America.

At that time, she was America's only female governor.

International publications identified Evita Perón, at 32, as the most powerful woman in the world. A 1966 Gallup poll showed Lurleen Wallace, born September 19, 1926—Alabama's first female governor— as the sixth most admired woman in America.

The other most admired women, listed in order of ranking were: Jackie Kennedy, Lady Bird Johnson, Indira Ghandi, Queen Elizabeth II, U.S. Senator Margaret Chase Smith, Mamie Eisenhower, Helen Keller, Madam Chiang Kai-shek, and writer Nobel Prize winner Pearl S. Buck.

The same 1966 Gallup poll ranked George Corley Wallace, born August 25, 1919, as seventh most admired man.

CHAPTER TWO

NEVER LEAVE YOUR MAN UNATTENDED
(NUNCA DEJE A SU HOMBRE DESATENDIDO)

Although Eva Duarte was on the arm of short, plump, un-interesting Colonel Anibal Imbert, who provided her a comfortable apartment near Buenos Aires' fashionable Avenida Alvear neighborhood, her eyes never stopped scanning the star-studded crowd mingling on the stage at the January 22, 1944, gala to benefit earthquake survivors from San Juan, 500 miles west.

January is hot summer in South American climes.

Through dogged persistence since age 15—and some talent—Eva had become a household name, a familiar voice in the remotest rancherias. She had created a significant career as a radio actress, resulting in her joining the other entertainment personalities.

It was helpful to her future career prospects, too, that her escort, Colonel Imbert, as Minister of Communications, controlled Argentina's radio stations. Imbert, who wore his military uniform to work at the radio station and allegedly required employees to salute him as they passed him in the halls, approved Eva's idea for the gala charity fundraiser.

A year earlier, at 23, she had begun starring in a weekly television soap "My Kingdom of Love," where she portrayed famous women in history: Queen Elizabeth I, Madame Chiang Kai-shek, the Tsarina of Russia, and others. The program concept was hers.

Life was to imitate "art." In a few years, Eva became as famous as the women she dramatized.

. . . .

At a mere 24 years old, she would take the first step on her yellow brick road to world acclaim that very night in the warm open air of the Luna Park boxing arena. Although some credited Perón with the charity event idea, it was Eva Duarte who persuaded Imbert to host the fundraiser featuring the crème de la crème of theater, governmental, and military society.

Whether Eva pushed Imbert to host the gala because Eva knew Juan Perón was highly likely to attend — for the pre-meditated purpose of meeting Perón -- or whether meeting Juan was happenstance could be debated endlessly. Some said she had glimpsed Juan from afar at an event a few weeks earlier.

No matter.

. . . .

Like a roulette wheel ball stopping on the winning number, Evita's eyes halted at a tall man whom she recognized as the Army officer rumored to be the behind-the-scenes leader of the military junta who took over from the civilian government in a 1943 coup.

Colonel Juan Perón, 48, was a prime catch: widowed (so no inconvenient spouse or ex-spouse), handsome, educated, and politically powerful.

Libertad Lamarque, 37, a film star and established recording figure with a popular light soprano voice, was conversing with Colonel Perón as Eva watched a few feet away.

Eva excused herself from Imbert, quickly stepping over to Libertad, whom she knew from the film and radio crowd.

"May I be introduced to this charming man?" Eva asked. She wore a black dress, long gloves, and a white feathery hat.

Men notice women in hats, she had learned.

Libertad obliged. What else could Libertad say without painting herself as rude in front of an attractive single man who embodied actual power in the country where she sought to have her records publicized?

Then the program began.

Returning to Imbert's side momentarily, Eva kept her eyes on each star who, one by one, left the row of on-stage chairs to take the microphone and perform briefly. As the gala itinerary moved closer and closer to Libertad's musical portion, Eva again excused herself from Imbert's attentions, moving as near as she could to Colonel Perón without attracting undue attention.

. . . .

No lioness crouching downwind in the Serengeti grass unseen by the zebra herd thundering past— perfect muscles taut with anticipation at what was at stake in what she was about to attempt— could match Eva's intensity of purpose in those foretelling seconds.

Eva's eyes never left the momentarily vacant chair next to Perón, or Perón.

Eva understood, as ambitious, driven people do, that opportunity really does knock only once. Speed and quality of response constitute the difference between success and a lifetime of being ordinary.

Her resolute road from small town Los Toldos, the following years of struggle to bring herself to a circumstance where she could meet someone of the caliber of Juan Perón, ended this night in this place. This pinnacle was the juncture of her astute long-range planning and fate.

Beautiful Eva was. She knew that.

Even her detractors conceded that fact quickly and unequivocally. She was a great beauty in any culture.

She had skin the color and texture of magnolias.

But she knew she had to evince more than a pretty face to impress and retain the colonel.

Perón had had many beauties.

The moment Libertad Lamarque left her position beside Juan Perón to go to the microphone to perform, Eva quickly seated herself in Libertad's vacated chair beside Colonel Perón in the shadows outside the klieg lights circle.

It would be the last time either of them would shy away from a brightly lit stage.

Eva's time sequence was adroit, masterful.

Had she not first implemented the feint of Libertad's formally introducing her to Perón, Perón might have been wary of a stranger in a black dress, long gloves and a white feathered hat suddenly moving physically next to him. In some ways, Argentina was still a society of formalities.

She knew she had few precious minutes until Libertad Lamarque's return to claim her seat.

Eva's move to Buenos Aires when she was a bold 15-year-old, the ensuing years spent struggling for more and bigger parts on popular radio dramas, her career-enhancing friendships with men she did not love —Eva's mind flashed to all those days that brought her to this singular flutter of opportunity. She understood that everything—absolutely everything depended on what she could derive from these few moments with Perón on this warm spring evening.

"I put myself at Perón's side. Perhaps this drew his attention to me. When he had time to listen to me, I spoke up as best I could," she writes in her autobiography *La Razon de mi Vida* (The Purpose of My Life).

"If, as you say, the cause of the people is your own cause— however great the sacrifice—I will never leave your side until I die," she whispered to Juan above the sounds of Libertad Lamarque singing into the microphone a few feet away.

It was an opening sentence she had rehearsed silently. Now she heard herself saying it aloud to Juan Perón over the music.

. . . .

When Libertad finished her songs, turning back to claim what she thought would be her seat next to Perón, both Evita and Juan were gone.

11

Libertad was furious.

Imbert was dumped.

Eva Duarte and Juan Perón slipped away to a river island area called El Tigre frequented by wealthy Buenos Aires residents on the weekend, but serenely quiet at other times.

Romantic with the sound of halyards clanking in the soft wind off the river surface, treetops brushing a purple-black night sky with a soothing shush-hush sound, and the fragrance of purple jacaranda tree blossoms, El Tigre was ideal.

They made their own earthquake.

Evita, as she became known, would always refer to January 22, 1944 as her "marvelous day."

Perón, too, fondly remembered their initial meeting, writing in his memoir that Evita came into his life "as if brought by destiny."

Eva's practical advance planning—rather than capricious destiny—may have had more to do with their meeting.

The next morning, a government limousine dropped Eva at the radio station where she worked. Her days using public transportation were over.

In about a year, Eva Duarte would become Evita, the affectionate diminutive version of a name Argentines bestow on the much loved.

Like the July 1942 meeting of Lurleen Burns and George Wallace in the Tuscaloosa dime store, the 1944 Eva-Juan meeting was the genesis of a coupling that would be writ very, very large.

CHAPTER THREE
DEMURE DISCIPLINE

Twenty four years after meeting brash and driven George in Kress's, Lurleen Wallace, 40, stood at the podium on the top step outside the state capitol building in Montgomery on January 16, 1967, in front of 250,000 people, the biggest attendance at a single event in Alabama history at that time.

For decades, she had stood as dutiful wife at many podiums on behalf her peppery, orotund husband, the outgoing governor whom she was replacing.

This time, for the first time, she was standing up for herself as governor—at *her* inauguration.

Lurleen, perceived by skeptics as an Eliza Doolittle of "My Fair Lady" dazzle, was about to dance figuratively, at the embassy ball, astonishing her inadvertent Professor Henry Higgins: her husband, George, who stood at her side.

Diverted by and focused on gearing up his second campaign for president of the United States, Governor George was handing Lurleen the gubernatorial control reins, confident that as Alabama governor, the wife he thought he knew would do what he told her to do.

As her puppeteer, he reckoned he could continue running Alabama by proxy while also running for president of the United States. He congratulated himself for so cleverly circumventing his one-term constitutional limitation as governor by running his wife as a candidate.

He figured he had made out like a bandit, achieving the un-achievable: keeping his cake while eating it, too.

Self-obsessed and consistently apart from Lurleen and their children for extended periods, campaigning for higher and higher state political offices during the 24 years since their marriage, George's image of his wife was frozen in time.

His mind never installed updates or hit the refresh button on their withered relationship.

George continued viewing Lurleen through his personal prism, as still the eternally 16-year-old deferential, star-struck girl he had met and impressed at Kress's with his quick patter.

But prisms refract—bend—light as the light moves from one medium to another, deceptively revealing only colors of the visible spectrum. Colors of the invisible spectrum remain hidden.

It never entered his distracted mind that Lurleen's long-time, no-choice, forced self-reliance could metastasize, forging in her an inner core of iron-willed, independent personal strength equaling or exceeding his.

George had not factored into his smug, confident expectation of Lurleen's unquestioning obeisance that at 40 she was a matured woman—a grown-savvy survivor of his emotional and financial deprivations, who, through stark necessity, had, years ago, learned to live without him.

Perhaps George did not remember, if he ever knew, that Lurleen Burroughs Burns at 14 was one of two females in her Tuscaloosa County high school shop class, shattering cultural molds for fe-males in 1941.

When Lurleen and a female classmate proved themselves inept in a sewing class, at the suggestion of their I-give-up sewing teach-er, the girls disregarded convention, boldly joining a male-bastion

14

shop class, preferring to make bookcases and magazine racks with the boys.

Small clues of her independent inner core, some obvious, some hidden and discrete, were always there like signposts, should George ever have cared to ponder their significance for him.

George "was not someone who pondered big philosophical thoughts," one of his political colleagues noted dryly.

CHAPTER FOUR
NOW EVITA! NOW!
(AHORA EVITA! AHORA!)

On a continent and in a culture 5,000 miles away from Alabama, in what was said to be the largest public display of support in history for a female political figure, two million boisterous people shouted *"Ahora, Evita! Ahora! (Now Evita! Now!)"* over and over, louder and louder until their hypnotic, unrelenting chant vibrated like thunder, rolling along wide tree-shaded streets lined with Argentina flags, toward Casa Rosada, the government house blocks away.

Photos document palm trees and lamp posts hung full of admirers dangling precariously for a better view of what was billed as a rally for Juan Perón's run for a second term as President of Argentina.

Almost no one had come to see Juan.

Posters championing a Perón y Perón ticket, adding Evita as a vice presidente candidate, were plastered on buildings and sign-posts all over Buenos Aires.

Stunt planes flew overhead writing Evita Perón's name and Juan Perón's name across the clear, blue sky above.

The prior day, August 21, 1951, thousands arrived along the Avenida 9 de Julio, the world's broadest street. They camped

16

overnight to ensure getting a glimpse of *her*.

"*Evita, Vice Presidente!*" the crowd shouted repeatedly in unison even before Evita, 32, and her husband, Argentina's President Juan Perón, 55, stepped in front of four-story high portraits of themselves, hung as bookends above a huge scaffold constructed for the August 22, 1951, union-organized rally in Buenos Aires.

If she *were* vice president, the classically beautiful Eva, known by the affectionate name Evita, would, by law, automatically become president in the event of the death of her husband, President Juan Perón.

No woman had been vice president or president in Argentine history or in South American history.

Although Juan moved to the dais about 5 p.m., Evita was not with him. When a union official tried to speak, *los milliones* drowned him out with their cries demanding Evita.

They had eyes only for her. *Santa Evita. (*Saint Evita.)

Leaving the stage momentarily, Juan Peron returned with Evita. Her blond hair was pulled back into what had become her trademark braided chignon. She wore a dark business suit with jeweled earrings and lapel pin, looking every bit as a French bourgeoisie.

Her husband Juan, a military officer 24 years her senior, stepped beside her on a high platform to evince his visual support for a husband-wife Perón y Peron candidacy.

The audience's joyous enthusiasm and the theatrical scene almost defy conversion into words. The wide-angle black and white photographs of the millions looking like small dots on the urban landscape, and Evita and Juan as finials atop the high podium, give an idea of the spine-tingling reality as Evita began speaking.

Her voice and cadence bespoke her theatrical training.

"My General, here today as they were yesterday, your vanguard *descamisados* (the shirtless ones). The oligarchy, the mediocrity, the traitors of the country have not been overthrown yet. From their lairs they are plotting against the people and the nation," she told her audience, raising both hands high, palms open above shoulder level toward her face in a characteristic gesture that had become part of her persona.

In a dramatic, emotional call-and-response dialogue interrupting her speech, her devotees demanded that Evita declare, then and there, her candidacy for vice president of Argentina. First lady Evita Perón asked her supporters for more time to decide whether she would be a candidate for vice president, teaming with Juan.

Juan, running in 1951 for a second term as president, tried to speak next, but the 250,000 continually interrupted him, drowning his voice in chanting waves alternating across the crowd demanding: *Evita! Evita!*

Waving shirts and long banners snaking aloft on poles, they affectionately ignored her equivocations, demanding that she say yes immediately. *"Ahora Evita! Ahora!"* they repeated rhythmically as if in one voice.

As dusk fell, the determined crowd rolled newspapers into torches for light.

They waited. *Esperamos por ti.* We are waiting for you.

It did not escape Juan's attention that they weren't waiting for him. He had become secondary. A prop for his wife, Evita.

Finally, Evita, whose high profile was built on her persona as a radio actress and program hostess, told the two million florid admirers that she would announce her decision on the radio in a few days.

Peacefully, the crowd left Buenos Aires the next day, which was declared a national holiday.

. . . .

Juan may have felt a disquietude, a self-reprimand about his languished powers of observation. Affection and respect of the masses was the cornerstone of his power. While he wasn't paying attention, was his political moon slowly being eclipsed by his wife Evita's much brighter sparkly sun?

Originally, Evita amassed the votes for him. But it would be so easy for Evita to redirect the votes for her.

On paper, Evita wasn't the president or the vice president of Argentina…yet.

CHAPTER FIVE
EMPYREAL WINGS

At 3:14 p.m. Eastern Time on Monday January 16, 1967, the dime-store clerk, married at 16, a mother at 18, who raised four children almost alone in virtual penury while working outside the home and may not have graduated from high school, took the oath of office as the third woman elected governor of a state in America's history.

Lurleen Wallace was also the first woman governor of Alabama. She was elected with the largest vote ever given any gubernatorial candidate, carrying 65 of 67 counties. Her extraordinary feat, proportionate to population, has never been equaled.

At that time, she was the only female governor in America.

Lurleen's weather was blue-sky perfect, unlike the unseasonable bitter, blustery cold at George's swearing-in as governor four years earlier.

By Alabama tradition, Lurleen took her oath of office on the white marble west portico of the state capitol building in Montgomery at the same spot, marked by a small bronze star, where West Point graduate Jefferson Davis stood in 1861 when he was sworn in as president of the Confederacy.

In an ironic historical paralleling, Lurleen faced a potential inheritance of the similar turbulent historical period Davis was poised to inherit 106 years earlier when he raised his right hand standing where she stood.

Davis' 1861 legacy was roiled by the same national culture-

shattering divisive social issues as Lurleen inherited in 1967—
issues that, with the War in Vietnam, would go nuclear in 1968,
America's electrifying volatile turning point year of revolution in
the streets, when the fabric of American society was shredded,
seemingly beyond mending.

From where she stood becoming Alabama's new governor, she
had a clear view of buildings remindful of the genesis of factions in
the century-old struggle about race and society.

To her left she could see the White House of the Confederacy,
where President Jefferson Davis and his wife lived from February
to May 1861 when Montgomery was the capitol of the Confederacy.
In the senate chamber behind her, representatives of southern states
voted in 1861 to secede from the United States of America.

Straight ahead, Lurleen could see along downward sloping
Dexter Avenue to King Memorial Baptist Church where Dr. Martin
Luther King, Jr. served as pastor from 1954-60. From there he di-
rected the blacks' boycott of Montgomery buses—triggered when
Rosa Parks, a black woman, refused to surrender her seat
to a white man after the bus driver ordered her to do so in 1955.

On the lawn a few feet away was a monument to 122,000 Alabama
Confederate soldiers who fought in America's 1860s civil war.

All around her were vestiges of America's history of which she
would, as an elected official, become a part.

· · · · · · · ·

An athletic woman of about 100 pounds, "Leen," as close
friends called her affectionately, wore a black cashmere fitted suit
and matching pillbox hat designed and sewn by her home economics

teacher friend Mary Jo Ventress. They ordered the special fabric from Carmichael's, a Montgomery store.

As always, Lurleen's sparse makeup included her trademark lipstick shade: Fire & Ice.

She wore her favorite perfume: Estee Lauder sachet.

Although she could not know it then, a large building on her right across Bainbridge Street would be named in her honor: Lurleen B. Wallace writ large over the top of two doors.

Decades later, a painting of Governor Lurleen would be the first sight visitors would see upon opening the Alabama Capitol's west door.

CHAPTER SIX
LOVE & OTHER QUID PRO QUOS
(AMOR Y OTRA COSAS POR COSAS)

Evita Perón HATED men, television commentator Mike Wallace declares emphatically in a 1963 biographical video. He verbally emphasizes the word "hated," force-fully exhaling the "h" as if to enhance the credibility of his opinion aired as unabashed fact.

Wallace implies that Evita's alleged "hatred" of men results from her biological father's refusal to marry Evita's mother, thus marking Evita as illegitimate, a major Argentine social stigma in that era.

Hate men? Au contraire. Eva kept her eyes too much on the ultimate prize to waste valuable time stressing about a birth category she could not change. For women, the identical tough path to career success loomed for the legitimate and the illegitimate. Being female was more of an impediment than illegitimacy.

In fact, she and Perón had illegitimacy in common. For him, being born out of wedlock was never an obstacle to anything.

• • • • • • •

In Argentine culture of the time, sexual promiscuity and prowess were admirable—for men. It was said during Evita's era that if a male had only a wife, but no mistresses, he was suspected of being homosexual. For men, multiple sexual partners outside marriage confirmed masculinity and conferred bragging rights to leadership ability.

However, when Eva chose male lovers whose business and social connections could smooth her way to top billing on Argentine radio shows and develop her movie career, then she was labeled a prostitute, a whore—according to the double standard of that time.

Men who cultivated important males who could help them develop their careers were praised as enterprising go-getters, cited as obsequious examples to follow for the sons of men.

Beautiful, politically ambitious women of humble birth who starred in popular nationwide radio shows and movies—as Eva did—were rare. Such anomalous female conduct had to be attributed to something other than what it was: clever ambition and talent equal to male ambition and talent.

Hatred of men, whore—as the analysis of what motivated successful women like Eva Duarte Perón, these words provided a glib explanation for Mike Wallace and many other Evita critics. That Wallace's statement was untrue or gender disparate didn't matter. It was attention-getting.

· · · · · · · ·

Eva liked men very much indeed. They possessed what she aspired to.

Eva was pragmatic.

Because men were the gatekeepers of social and political power in 1940s and 1950s Argentina, friendship with men was her ticket to board the career success train. Women could achieve success only as derivative from men. Women got as much power as they could convince or cajole men to allocate to them. It was a hard, cold fact.

Given that unavoidable reality, Eva Duarte chose her lovers well, like an aspiring executive moving up a company ladder by cozying up to company executives who already possess power and clout. As a beautiful woman, she attracted a large group from which to choose. She had unerring instincts for selecting men who could assist her in furthering her career goals. Why waste time with nobodies and underachievers?

With regard to Juan, the quid pro quo was simple.

She understood Colonel Juan Perón's career dynamic because it matched her own. Her first words to Juan January 22, when she took the empty seat beside him, focused even then on under-standing and supporting his need to ensure his longevity in office.

In order to get what she wanted, she had to provide Juan with what he wanted. She had a plan mapped out to achieve both their objectives to their mutual satisfaction.

Just as Lurleen and Evita married men with astonishingly simi-lar backgrounds—both grew up in small, rural areas and had college careers as boxers—the two women chose mates addicted to political power. Juan's top priority, the same as George Wallace's, was staying in political power indefinitely. In the 18 months

25

before they met, Argentina had had three presidents and forty ministers. As both war and labor secretary and vice president in 1944, Juan's tenancy at sufferance was twice as unstable, and he knew it.

A Cassius always waited in the corner with a "lean and hungry look."

· · · · · · · ·

Early on, Evita could justifiably denominate herself as Juan's good luck charm.

After he and Evita became lovers in January, Juan was appointed vice presidente on July 8, 1944, by Edelmiro Farrell, who, with Juan and other military types, had overthrown President Pedro Ramirez in a coup on February 25, 1944. Farrell was vice president when he and his colleague Juan ousted Ramirez. Farrell appointed himself president.

Ferrell gifting his friend Juan with the vice presidency moved Juan one step further up the power ladder. And, the VP appointment was a no-exertion freebie. Juan wouldn't have to expend time and money running for VP as stepping stone.

The team of Juan and Evita could immediately target the presidency.

Juan and Evita wasted no time, gearing up for the presidential election date of February 26, 1945. The winner would take office in June 1945, when Farrell's term as president ended. Farrell had decided not to seek the presidency again.

National office by musical chairs was how it went in Argentina.

Men with guns showed up one day in your office to convince you that signing a resignation letter they placed on the desk in front of you with a pen was your earnest desire all along.

Then, as scripted, you hurriedly departed the premises, most usually to catch the 30-minute boat ride across the Rio de la Plata river to refuge in Uruguay before the sun set.

If the actors weren't such dark personalities and the consequences so deadly, the scenario would have resembled a zany Gilbert & Sullivan operetta. Even the style of the military uniforms bespoke G&S.

. . . .

If Eva made herself politically indispensable to Colonel Perón by making sure he had the votes in perpetuity to be elected president and remain in power, he would stay with her. Eva possessed self-knowledge. As a realist, she knew her concomitant wants and needs, too.

Juan would interest her as a man only as long as he remained in power. Politically powerful men were the ladder rungs to success in any endeavor. If Juan faltered or lost his government position, Eva would have to look elsewhere for symbiosis.

Whether Colonel Perón would stay with Eva because he loved her, or she loved him, wasn't a factor in the equation.

Love was nice. Political power was nicer and usually lasted longer with more tangible benefits.

An assured voter base indebted to Evita would keep Juan Perón on top.

To stave off the fickle winds of Argentine politics, Juan needed blocks of votes he could count on as a virtual certainty. Eva knew where the vote pantry was and how to attract votes from it.

CHAPTER SEVEN
TOO DRUNK TO TYPE

"As life is passion and action, it is required of a person that she should share the passion and action of her time, at peril of being judged not to have lived."
—Oliver Wendell Holmes

To take the coveted gubernatorial prize, Lurleen Burns Wallace triumphed like a tank over nine male opponents in the May, 1966, Alabama Democratic primary, which included as opponent candidates two former governors, a U.S. congressman, and the Alabama attorney general.

Her victory at 39 years old was a jaw-dropping political masterpiece still unequaled, proportionate to population and number and status of competitors, by a man or a woman in all of America's political history on any jurisdictional level since.

She deftly avoided a primary runoff by winning a frog strangler with 480,841 votes: 54 percent, a clear majority.

·   ·   ·   ·   ·   ·   ·   ·

On the night Lurleen Burns Wallace won really, really big, Anita Smith, one of the first women reporters hired on the Birmingham News, had to type up the story on Lurleen's historic victory.

"I helped the two male political reporters get to it because they were too drunk to type and file the piece," Smith remembers with disdain.

Whether male journos were drunk because being drunk was routine for them or whether they became too intoxicated to do their job as their way of obliterating the thought of Lurleen as governor is left unsaid.

. . . .

As her adroit encore in the November 1966 general election, the woman whose father nicknamed her "Mutt" received 537,505 votes, 63 percent, mowing down Republican and Independent party candidates. The Republican candidate was a U.S. congressman: Jim Martin.

Lurleen's November, 1966, vote totals included a majority of the black vote—another jaw dropper, particularly since George made continued enforcement of racial segregation a fiery tenet of his early political rhetoric.

As governor, George's most infamous public goal was immortalized in his January, 1963 inaugural speech for his first term as Alabama governor: "Segregation now, segregation tomorrow, segregation forever."

His prevalent identity also included a June 11, 1963, heart-stopping moment, played and replayed on national television, when Governor George Wallace faced down Nicholas Katzenbach, U.S. Attorney General.

As six-foot-two Katzenbach stood with a white handkerchief moping rivers of sweat cascading down his brow in the ferocious heat, five-foot-seven George Wallace, unwilted, blocked an auditorium door at the University of Alabama where two black students sought, supported by a federal court order, to enter as students for the first time.

Nationally invisible then as George's wife, Lurleen escaped being painted with that opprobrious brush of racial prejudice.

"Lurleen was not connected with any of the racial business. She had no involvement in that directly. So it would be a little hard to throw stones at her," said Ed Ewing, one of her press aides.

CHAPTER EIGHT

WINNING A TRIFECTA OF VOTES
(GANANDO UN TRIO DE VOTOS)

Eva knew there were three significantly large, untapped vote larders in Argentina: women, who comprised about 50 percent of the population; the poor, who comprised a similar percentage, and unions. Eva's gender and her humble birth and background exemplified all the trifecta vote pantries.

The three groups would identify with her, and she with them. Even before meeting Juan, she had founded a union of radio workers. If she could attract that trifecta vote block for Juan, his election prospects for president would soar.

. . . .

In 1936 at 17 years old, Eva Duarte had toured the fartherest provinces with a theatre troupe. In small towns where theatrical entertainment was scarce, people were likely to remember a gorgeous actress they saw in person and heard on the radio.

They were accustomed to listening on the radio to what Eva Duarte had to say. And to help elect Juan, she would have a lot to say.

Radio was the 1940s and 1950s influence and power equivalent of the Internet in current times.

In her inaugural address, Governor Lurleen Wallace spoke with admiration of American women gaining voting rights in 1920 after a long, sometimes violent struggle literally fighting in America's streets.

But in 1945 Argentina, women were still prohibited by law from voting—until Evita.

And the poor—known as *descamisados*—the shirtless ones? Their votes did not have to await legislation the way voting rights for women did. No one ever considered the poor as a potential source of a significant percentage of votes. No one ever courted their votes in a major plan—until Evita.

A third group, unions, were nascent, but growing in power and more organized than women and the poor. Eva had earned credibility with unions.

Counter to the bromide that she was an airhead, when she was 23 years old, Eva had the foresight to organize a radio union: Argentine Radio Association. She served as its president before she even met Juan Perón.

Unions burgeoning in other labor fields took favorable notice of Eva's organizing skills and personal popularity.

Because Eva's voice was heard almost daily into the remotest corners of Argentina via her popular radio programs, she had an established platform, an audience who knew and liked her already.

Juan liked that about her too.

. . . .

Juan could do the vote cache math.

Forging a reliable trifecta alliance among women, the poor, and the unions to cement a voting juggernaut to elect and retain Perón in power would require Juan and Eva to blend their talents and work as a team.

Eva's contacts were invaluable to Juan. Juan's contacts were invaluable to Eva.

Eva was the numerator to Juan's denominator.

CHAPTER NINE
SNOWBALL IN HELL

Snickering print pundits and white males in the national and local press corps who had smugly predicted Lurleen's defeat even *as* Governor George Wallace's wife quickly developed post-election amnesia about their cloudy crystal balls, stashing them in the nearest bottom desk drawer with the proverbial empty Jack Daniels whiskey bottles.

Other analysts face-lifted their flawed prognostications by marginalizing her victory, saying snarkily that anyone ambulatory with a pulse who is Mrs. George Wallace would have won. Or that in voting for Lurleen, Alabamians felt they were voting for George. The coattails effect.

A few journalists and academics, less dismissive, allowed as how although Lurleen began as a timid, unpolished public speaker when hellfire-and-brimstone master orator George trotted her out on the campaign trail, she was a woman of innate poise and southern grace, a veteran of four years as First lady in Alabama --- a quick learner whose speaking style improved exponentially as her 1966 campaign for governor evolved.

Other wags, more generous toward historic achievement, commented: She may have started out as Mrs. George Wallace, but at the end of her campaign to be governor of Alabama, Lurleen Wallace won because SHE won.

One of George's biographers agreed that Lurleen alone, on her own merit, owned her stunning 1966 election victory.

"...she simply could not have run that powerfully without an attraction that went beyond her husband's popularity," he acknowledged unhesitatingly.

CHAPTER TEN

RISE UP WITH PRESENCE
(LEVANTESE CON PRESENCIA)

Resourceful Eva Duarte knew she was capable of scaling the mountain of increasing and stabilizing Juan's voter base for their mutual benefit. But as part of that attainable goal, she had to vault a hurdle that was, societally, more arduous and less attainable.

She had to convert her mistress role into wife status: marriage. Mistresses are passing fancies. Temporary.

To attain credibility in garnering votes for Juan, and to enhance keeping Juan after she worked to help him, she had to have the surface security that a marriage contract provided in that culture.

In that era, Argentine men rarely married a mistress.

Eva's project to marry Juan was somewhat less daunting because Juan was a childless widower. That made her goal slightly easier. No pesky spouse or ex-spouse and demanding children constituted a favorable factor.

She began by ousting the teenage girl with whom Perón was cohabitating. Eva wasted little time.

Shortly after she and Juan became lovers January 22, she

went over to Juan's apartment in Juan's absence and ordered the girl, whom Juan nicknamed La Pirana, out.

Then she moved Juan's belongings into the apartment next door to hers. When Juan returned and realized what had happened, he said nothing.

Eventually, Eva and Juan shared an apartment. Even that brought criticism. In addition to not marrying their mistresses, men did not actually live with their mistresses.

Unmarried Eva and Juan were about to flaunt another norm. They would begin traveling openly together in pre-campaign forays.

· · · · · · · ·

Juan, in his official capacity as secretary of labor and war, and later vice president, began what contemporary politicians call fact-finding trips—usually thinly disguised campaign junkets.

Juan teamed with Eva traveling to remote agricultural and crowded industrial centers, as well as bars and factories across Argentina. They hosted informational gatherings with the general public, inviting *la gente*, the people, to meet Juan and Eva in person and share their issues, complaints, and ideas with them.

La gente identified with Eva. Although they were respectful to Juan as vice president, Eva was whom they came to meet. Her plebeian background was the same as theirs. She was one of them and she had succeeded very, very well in life.

· · · · · · · ·

The Spanish language has two distinct "tracks," used in two distinct specific circumstances. The familiar form of the Spanish language is traditionally reserved for family and close friends. The formal form is to be used with strangers, or non-family-members or in very formal situations. Eva spoke with workers in the familiar form.

Her public breaches of linguistic etiquette dismayed Juan's military colleagues and ruffled feathers at the top levels of Argentine society.

Eva did not care. Votes were votes.

If she could get votes by using the familiar form *tu* instead of the formal form *usted* for the word "you," for instance—so be it.

After the fact-finding excursions, Juan, as labor secretary, signed directives that minimum wage should be paid to lower-level workers. Critics grumbled that Juan and Eva were buying votes. Business owners were not pleased with the extra expense, but were somewhat mollified because Argentina's economy was booming.

As an outgrowth of their countrywide meetings, Juan and others, with Evita's help, founded an umbrella organization of unions called CGT, which eventually boasted four million members.

CGT would be the spine of their future power.

Evita and Juan weren't just thinkers and sideliners. They got into the fray and seemed to enjoy doing so as a couple. A meat packers strike ended after Juan, with Evita at his side, walked near the picket lines. Everyone knew her.

CGT got an influx of new members.

Eva and Juan had built the foundation of the first two components of the trifecta alliance to retain Juan in office: labor votes and union votes.

Getting women the right to vote was next. That would take longer because it required legislative action plus a realignment of hundreds of years of cultural custom.

. . . .

Evita and Juan's apartment became the epicenter of political strategizing and camaraderie among Juan's colleagues, and it became Evita's school room. She was an apt student.

Instead of becoming invisible, serving docile in the kitchen during the frequent gatherings, Evita, 25 years old, avid, and animated, socialized and talked political maneuvering with the much older men. Juan treated her input respectfully, making sure she was included in discourse.

Evita absorbed it all, factoring how what she was learning could be put to use on Juan's behalf — which was the same as her behalf.

She also brought her resources forward.

Around June, 1944, she began mentioning Juan and his political ideas on her radio programs. One month later, his July, 1944, appointment to vice president perhaps illustrated that radio commercials really do work.

Only about six months after they met, they had begun consolidating the first components of a trifecta power base — the poor, unions and women.

And none too soon.

The men with guns were increasingly unhappy, not directly with Juan, but with Evita. They didn't like her around all the time.

They were unhappy with Juan because Juan was happy with Evita.

Evita was standing on their air hose: full unfettered access to and with Juan.

Eva kept her eye on Juan's trump card: the largest untapped voter cache in Argentina: women—50 percent of the entire population.

Juan knew Evita would be successful in attracting the votes of women. He wasn't about to kick Evita to the curb just because his male friends didn't like her.

CHAPTER ELEVEN
PROPORTIONAL GRACE

In her 24-minute, 10-page inaugural address, along with requisite thanks to voters and patriotic invocations of Alabama and American history, Lurleen chose to pay specific public homage to 1920, the year that American women were accorded voting rights —only six years before she was born.

Although George, the outgoing governor, stood beside her near the podium, he was present only physically in Alabama. His thoughts and most of his departure remarks—which were supposed to center on introducing his wife, Lurleen—were national, focusing on how quickly he could return to his all-consuming ambition to be elected president of the United States. Thus, Lurleen's inclusion of references to female political pioneer predecessors in her debut remarks as Alabama's first woman governor recorded no warning blips on his internal radar.

Lurleen spoke confidently, unhesitatingly; character traits that had begun surfacing as her pre-Facebook, pre-Twitter, pre-Internet, boots-on-the-ground 1966 campaign attracted larger and larger live audiences across Alabama.

"A woman has been elected governor of Texas, and a woman has been appointed governor in Wyoming. My election marks the second time in the history of the nation that a woman has been elected governor of a state* (see footnote). This is, indeed, evidence of adaptability and continuity in our institutions of self government— by which we have seen rapid development of a larger meaning of freedom," she told the quarter million fans who showed up in person.

42

In George's 1946, 1950, 1952, 1958, 1962, 1964, 1968, 1970, 1972, 1974, 1976, and 1982 campaigns seeking various state and federal public offices, he never came close in Alabama, to matching Lurleen's 1966 vote totals, proportionate to population and number of opponents.

After her inaugural ceremony, Lurleen's affable press aide, Ed Ewing, called a press conference to introduce Lurleen to the media, transitioning from her role as first lady to her role as governor. Even the London Times was there.

After a couple of softball pro forma questions for Lurleen, the press ignored her and zoomed into George, making him and his 1968 Presidential campaign the focus of their frenzy, "as if she weren't even present," Ewing recalled.

Lurleen walked out unnoticed.

George stayed, basking peacock-style in the national attention his presidential ambitions attracted.

"Lurleen sent for me after the media left," Ewing remembered.

"Next time you call a press conference for me Ed, don't invite George!" she snapped.

"Lurleen!" I exclaimed. "That was the only time I called her Lurleen after she was elected governor.

"I was shocked, because it was so uncharacteristic. I had never seen her like that," Ewing remembers incredulously.

George, who had remained at the press conference, was not present for Lurleen's foreshadowing retort that got Ewing's attention a few hours after her swearing in.

"Later that day, she looked me up and hugged my neck."

"I'm sorry, Ed. I know you couldn't help what they ask," Lurleen said.

Governor Lurleen's researchers erred. Her election was the third time in America that a woman was elected governor of a state.

CHAPTER TWELVE
AS YOU WISH
(ASI TU QUIERES)

Eva Duarte, born in 1919 in rural agricultural Los Toldos, Argentina, was one of five illegitimate children of Juana Ibarguren, the mistress of a local *estancia* (ranch) owner Juan Duarte, who was legally married to, and fathered children with, another woman who lived with him not far away from Juana.

Both women knew of the share-a-man arrangement and accepted it because that was the prevalent cultural norm.

Like that of Alabama First lady Lurleen Wallace, Eva's formal education was limited, falling short of high school graduation. Growing up, Eva's interests centered around acting in school plays and attending the cinema.

As in the lives of many children who later become high-achievers, there were early indications of Eva's independent spirit.

To and from school as a pre-teen, Eva passed a music and record store broadcasting tunes into the street. As a sales gimmick, passers-by were invited to come inside to use the sound system to sing or speak over the microphone, airing their music and commentary outside the store.

Eva often stopped to seize that opportunity, reading poetry she had memorized and practicing bits of drama over the public microphone.

She also begged to take the dish-drying job of one of her sisters, so she could earn money to purchase movie magazines she enjoyed reading.

In about six years, her dreams and wishes would become realities. Eva would be featured prominently in those same magazines and succeed in other ways beyond her imaginings.

(In 1939 Sintonia, a movie magazine she collected as a child, featured her on the cover. In 1940 she made the cover of Guion, and in 1941 the cover of Cine Argentine).

As with Lurleen, age 15 was a pivotal point for Eva, who was working as a cook. In 1934, her biological father abandoned her mother and Eva's siblings, leaving them in financial straits. Then he was killed in a vehicle accident. Juana supported herself and her children by taking sewing jobs until she found another man.

Eva Duarte realized that neither a theatrical career nor a prince charming on a white horse was ever going to materialize for her in remote Junin.

The exciting, glamorous life Eva dreamed of and read about in the movie magazines was not going to seek her in Junin and entice her away, as happened with Lurleen in Tuscaloosa when George drove up in a truck. Eva would have to go hunt for what she wanted.

A photograph of the time, taken by her brother Juan, shows her with her sisters. Eva, who appears to be maybe 13 or so, stands at the right. Her body posture—hands hanging limply at her side while her sister Elisa's arm embraces her warmly— indicates Eva's total physical and psychological disengagement from her siblings and from the photographer.

Her facial expression is sullen, unsmiling, almost hostile. Her eyes stare straight ahead. Although she is standing within the group, everything about the photo bespeaks Eva's internal mental separateness.

In the photo, although Eva is physically under the shade trees on the banks of the Gomez lagoon near Junin, in her mind she is on her way to Buenos Aires.

Elegant and urbane, in the late 1930s, Buenos Aires (BA) was becoming known as the Paris of South America.

CHAPTER THIRTEEN
TOMBOY

Lurleen Burns was 8 years old in 1934 when Eva Duarte was leaving rural obscurity for the bright lights of cosmopolitan Buenos Aires.

In eight more years, Lurleen would leave rural obscurity for what she anticipated would be love and bright lights, too.

Born in tiny Fosters, Alabama, Lurleen moved with her family to Northport when she was about a year old, then later moved to Knoxville, Alabama. Neither Evita nor Lurleen had an indoor toilet where she grew up.

Lurleen's farmer father Henry, who built one of their modest houses himself, was a bargeman on the Black Warrior river, later working in the Mobile shipyards as a crane operator. Mr. Henry, as he was called, enjoyed talking politics, but never with his daughter, whom he nicknamed Mutt because she devotedly followed him everywhere with starry eyes.

Lurleen's mother, Estelle, a housewife, was the daughter of three generations of farmers who had occupied the rich Alabama land for about 150 years. In the south, longevity on the land is an important, admired virtue.

At that time, Lurleen and her older brother, Cecil, lived the classic rural childhood experiences that Lurleen's daughter Bobbie Wallace Parsons remembers from her own childhood visits to her maternal grandparents' farm in tiny Knoxville, Alabama.

"When we spent time with our grandparents in Knoxville, we

would go to the Warrior River with all the cooking utensils. You would fish all day and then that night you would set up on the river-bank, build a fire, and put the pot on with the oil to cook the fish."

From childhood, Lureen's father taught her to fish.
"Fishing is my first memory of mother," Bobbie said.

"My mother was known as a tomboy in high school," her only son, George Jr., remembers. She loved hunting, fishing, and athletics.
"She could scale a fish, gut it, and clean it faster than you could turn around. We'd fry it up, and pick all the little bones out for Lee, who was three or four," Peggy remembered.
"Mother had such beautiful hands, and long painted finger-nails," Peggy added.

Cooking and sewing were Lurleen's desultory interests. But as an adult, she became minimally skilled in both as the social con-ventions of the era required for females.
Eva had similar disdain for cooking. She was known to open cans of food for guests in their presence, avoiding even a pretense of cooking.

CHAPTER FOURTEEN
NO PLACE LIKE HOME
(*NO HAY LUGAR COMO SU CASA*)

Although historical texts habitually describe Eva Duarte's birthplace, tiny, rural Los Toldos, as bleak and poverty-stricken, photos of the home and village that depict solid brick business buildings seem to contradict the degree of dire poverty claimed.

As one example, a famous photo shows Eva, age two, with her brothers and sisters dressed in elaborate costumes and hairstyles lined across a stage, with stage lighting, posing for a carnival celebration. The level of expense for the attire, shoes and hairdos, and the theatrical setting seem at visual variance with the claimed "grinding poverty" of Evita's childhood.

The mere fact that Juana and her children had money for a camera, film and developing, or money to pay a photographer for that photo, seems to cast doubt on later claims of financial destitution.

In another photo, Juana is depicted with other smartly dressed women at a formal luncheon honoring their certificates of completion at a seamstress school.

Eva's parents, Juan and Juana, in formal dress, appear in "studio" portraits, hardly the venue for the very poor.

An oft-told anecdote recounts how they were so poor Eva's mother bought Eva the doll Eva wanted, but a doll heavily discounted in price because it had a broken leg.

Juana told her daughter that the broken leg was the result of the doll falling off a camel of one of the three Wise Men who journeyed to visit the baby Jesus. Juana explained that the Wise Men wanted Eva to care for the doll.

The anecdote may be apocryphal.

. . . .

The family moved to Junin, a bit larger town nearby, in 1930. Historical accounts portray their lives in reduced circumstances, including living in "an adobe shack."

In what would seem another contradiction, Eva poses in Junin in front of their home, which has an almost elegant look. The building appears to be made of smooth white blocks resembling marble, entered by a beautiful door arch with carved finial. The front windows are covered with elaborate wrought iron decorative filigree, and the street in front of the home is brick paved.

Another Junin photo shows Eva as an unsmiling pre-teen wearing a fashionable dress with ruffles and pleats, on a street of neighborhood homes that would be middle class in any culture —not even close to "dire poverty" or "grinding poverty."

There are three main versions of how and with whom Eva left Junin at 15 years old for Buenos Aires. One is that she left with a tango singer she sexually enticed after he played a Junin gig.

A second version is that her mother Juana accompanied Eva to Buenos Aires, chaperoning Eva's cold calls to radio stations and theaters to try to get work as an actress.

A third version is that Eva, at 15 (or sometimes stated as 13) left on the train to Buenos Aires holding a cardboard suitcase, totally alone.

· · · · · · · ·

At 16, the age when Lurleen married George Wallace, Eva, an aspiring actress, began finding beginner's success in Buenos Aires, playing small roles in low-budget movies in 1943. Her long dark hair enhanced her already alluring beauty.

Her skin was described in superlatives as "the color and texture of magnolias."

In Buenos Aires, she hoped the anonymity of a metropolis would minimize Argentina's cultural stigma of illegitimacy. Her goal was to be a dramatic actress.

CHAPTER FIFTEEN
AMAZING GRACE

For the first time in Alabama history, racially integrated bands marched in Lurleen's 1967 inaugural parade, as did Vietnam veterans, at her invitation.

Lurleen made history again by declining to hold the traditional inaugural ball gala that evening. She explained that it did not seem appropriate to be merry making while men were dying and being wounded in America's faraway Southeast Asia war.

She carefully put away the long, cream-colored ball gown with ermine collar, pausing to remember how she and Mary Jo happily worked together for weeks designing it, chatting about how the gown was a physical representation of how far they each had journeyed since their lonely years keeping each other's spirits up as young wives in Clayton.

She and Mary Jo had ordered the small semicircle of ermine fur from a Birmingham furrier. They were so excited when it arrived. Mary Jo stitched it onto the neckline of the gown that would now not be worn for its elegant intended purpose.

George had blithely deprived her of an only-once-in-a-lifetime opportunity to be Cinderella at the ball—if only for an hour or two.

Lurleen said stoically that she would save her beautiful chiffon velvet inaugural gown and the matching elbow-length gloves for other occasions.

Such jubilant celebratory social occasions never arose again for "Mutt."

· · · · · · · ·

George's detractors contended that military events in Vietnam had nothing to do with the cancellation of the traditional elegant gala event to honor a new governor. George cancelled his wife's festive inaugural ball because he could not bear the thought of Lurleen getting more attention at it than he, they said.

The night of what would have been Lurleen's inaugural ball, the pinnacle of affirmation—where Lurleen, the dime-store girl from Northport would have shined as the glittering princess, George met with his presidential campaign workers at a Montgomery country club to strategize with political operatives from four southern states.

George's aides sold his Wallace for President paraphernalia at Lurleen's inauguration ceremony.

CHAPTER SIXTEEN
BLONDES HAVE MORE FUN
(LAS RUBIAS SE DIVERTEN MAS)

Although Eva was a brunette when she first met Juan January 22, 1944, she became a blond in May 1944 and never looked back.

She bleached her hair for a 1945 movie called Circus Cavalcade, whose plot about a nineteenth century touring circus group was redolent of her real gypsy theatrical life. At 17 years old, Eva toured small towns as part of a theatrical ensemble cast.

Eva deemed the lighter color so becoming—as did others—that she decided to leave it blond ever after. Blond hair became one of her trademarks.

In an historical coincidence, 1945 was also the year American Norma Jean Baker bleaching her hair blond would catapult her into mega stardom. Norma Jean walked into a Los Angeles hair salon at 6513 Hollywood Boulevard, emerging as Marilyn Monroe, and never looked back, according to a pop culture writer.

It was during filming of Circus Cavalcade that Libertad Lamarque, who had top billing in the movie's poster publicity, took her revenge for Eva taking Lamarque's chair—and Juan—at the gala a year earlier. Observers say that after an argument about Eva's alleged tardiness, or perhaps after Evita sat in Liberdad's personal chair on the set, Libertad Lamarque slapped Evita hard across the face in front of witnesses during a break in the filming.

If the fracas was about a chair, Libertad had no difficulty recalling that the last time Eva sat in Libertad's chair, Eva stole the man Libertad coveted.

Lamarque denied that she slapped Eva. However, she complained that Eva was not professional and not on time for the shoot. Eva never publicly responded, but Lamarque's records were never played in Argentina after that. Years later. when Lamarque confronted Eva, asking Evita if she was involved in the embargo on her work, Evita denied involvement. Lamarque moved to Mexico, where she was already an established artist.

Accounts of Evita's personal behavior on movie sets contrast and conflict. Some accounts list Evita as haughty and uncooperative. Other accounts describe her conduct as professional: timely, cooperative with other actors, and knowing her lines.

Her manner when she worked with Radio Agentina in 1942 was described in superlatives by the head of production as "well-behaved, nicely mannered, and serious. She arrived at rehearsal an hour early, left immediately after the broadcast, and never talked to anyone, " he said.

Her final movie, "The Prodigal" in 1944, was one she said she liked. The plot involved an affair between an older woman, who helped the poor, and a young engineer.

There would be no more movies for Eva after 1944. Although her political life with Juan took center stage over her film career— her work on radio would continue unabated as one of the strong pillars of her identity and success.

Eva Duarte's real life journey would be more than an adequate replacement for any movie role.

At the age of 18, Eva had performed in 26 soap operas, five movies and 20 plays since 1935.

CHAPTER SEVENTEEN
EVITA FOLLOWED ME LIKE A SHADOW
(ELLA ME SIGUIO COMO UNA SOMBRA)

In addition to the fact-finding trips around Argentina in the January 1944-October 1945 period when Evita and Juan developed their personal and political relationship and their get-out-the-vote strategy, Evita was elected president of a union of radio workers.

On August 14, 1944, seven months after George and Lurleen first met a continent away, Eva implemented Step 1 to corral for Juan the votes of unions and the poor.

She began a 30-minute afternoon radio show called "Toward a Better Future," which aired to all parts of Argentina after her morning soap operas. The "Toward a Better Future" text publicized social issues like statistics on disease, malnutrition, and illiteracy. Who could resolve these difficult issues? Juan Perón.

Evita's subtext was lionizing Juan Perón as the people's savior in a classic pre election get–out-the-vote drive.

In this same time period, Lurleen, pregnant with her first child Bobbie, as well as working outside the Clayton home part-time as a clerk, was beginning years of "grunt work" to help George get elected to a series of state offices: addressing envelopes and making phone calls or brief appearances on his behalf.

Unlike Evita and Juan's situation, George wasn't with her. He was out somewhere speechifying and shaking hands. She worked evenings after her day job, and after the children were in bed. At first, she enjoyed it because it gave her something constructive to fill the emptiness.

At first.

. . . .

Juan and Evita were laying political ground work too.

In the evenings, they held political strategy sessions in their apartment with a multitude of advisors and fans from the trifecta groups whose votes they sought.

Neither of Juan nor Evita drank liquor. Juan smoked heavily.

Evita occasionally smoked fashionable French cigarettes with red dyed tips. The dye, called carmine, is created from the ground-up body scales of cacti -attacking insects.

A photo shows Evita in a floor-length skirt at the apartment grand piano, smiling over her right shoulder, as if playing for the politicos. A framed photo of Juan and a huge bouquet of fresh flowers decorate the piano top.

In his memoir discussing mentoring Evita during that period, Juan comes off as a Renaissance man way ahead of his time, for admiring the aspirations and abilities of a woman. "She followed me like a shadow, listened to me attentively, assimilated my ideas and worked them out in her extremely quick mind," Perón wrote of Evita.

As with Lurleen and George, the structure of the facial features of Juan and Evita was remarkably similar. Psychologists posit that, because we admire our own visage, evaluating ourselves as attractive, we unconsciously seek out and gravitate to people whose facial features resemble our own.

CHAPTER EIGHTEEN
RIDIN' IN GEORGE'S VOTE ROUNDUP

Sometime in high school Lurleen began her heavy smoking habit that continued unabated through her life: Benson and Hedges cigarettes one after the other: stubbing one out, then lighting the next.

She also loved hot dogs, lots of coffee, and being on or near the water and in the sun as much as possible.

Such an unhealthy lifestyle is recognized now as a lethal cocktail inviting an early death.

Neither Lurleen nor George drank liquor. They banned the serving of alcoholic beverages at mansion functions.

. . . .

Lurleen bore her first child, daughter Bobbie Jo, in 1944 when she was 18. Peggy Sue came along in 1950, followed by George Jr. in 1951. Daughter Lee, the last child, was born in 1961.

During the early years of their marriage, George was serving (from October 20, 1942) as a sergeant in the U.S. Army Air Corps, hopscotching to military bases all over the United States, sometimes followed by Lurleen, toting infant Bobbie.

Within a few months of marrying George, Lurleen was back working as a dime-store clerk—this time outside a military base in Amarillo, Texas where scorching hot drier-than-dry winds blow dust across the pancake-flat, treeless earth in the furnace summers, and merciless snow blasts in the freezing winters. Her salary was $12 a week.

George was assigned to desolate Amarillo in 1943 after requesting to leave the Army Air Cadet program because of what he considered its too-strict discipline protocols.

George said he couldn't tolerate being told what to do.

His surly departure ended his chances of becoming a pilot.

Returning so quickly after marriage to the type of dime-store clerk job she so recently left—with highest hopes for a brighter future with lawyer George—were backward steps she had not anticipated.

George's character began to reveal itself further to her. The revelations were not reassuring.

When Lurleen arrived at an Alamogordo, New Mexico Air Force base to spend some time with George, he had made no housing arrangements. The three of them made do in a converted chicken coop.

After George mustered out of the military on December 8, 1945, he and Lurleen settled in Clayton, population 2,000.

"Clayton, Alabama, then was right out of the novel To Kill a Mockingbird. The people, the houses, the culture was just like Harper Lee described," George Jr. remembered.

If Lurleen retained any illusions about George as her knight in shining armor, whisking her off on his white horse to a quiet domestic life of constant familial togetherness, those romantic images had become seriously frayed at the edges, given George's often thoughtless disregard of her since their marriage.

. . . .

Via political connections he cultivated assiduously when he was a teenage state senate page in 1935, George got an attorney job with the Alabama attorney general's office at a salary of $175 per month. The low-paying attorney work was, as was everything, only a pausing prelude to his ultimate goal: elective office.

As far back as 1942, when he met Lurleen, George planned to begin his political climb to the top by running for the Alabama state legislature. He took a leave of absence from the attorney general, after a relatively short employment, to gear up his 1945 campaign.

Lurleen was about to be schooled as his campaign drudge, sucked into his political vortex with an inexorable gravitational pull.

If she wanted to exist in George's orbit, she had to help him campaign and win votes. She had to ride in his rodeo. He had demonstrated, unequivocally, he wasn't going to be a stay-at-home with her or with his children.

His truck motor was always running

CHAPTER NINETEEN
AFTERNOON OF THE COLONELS
(LA TARDE DE LOS COLONES)

Fate, in the form of Argentina's volatile government by musical chairs, would unwittingly award Evita exactly what she aspired to —marriage to Juan—and Juan's critics would humiliate themselves in the process.

Via Evita's shrewd magic, his enemies would all fall on their own swords, victims of their own jealousy and miscalculations of Evita's intelligence and reach.

In Argentina's 1945 macho culture, a man who did what a woman advised was suspect as a man. As World War II ended, the military junta of which Juan was a part became increasingly angry about what its members considered to be Evita's power over Juan Perón and her 24/7 presence with him.

It was too embarrassing to have a military dictatorship run sub rosa by a female. What kind of military dictatorship is run by a woman? they asked Juan. Cartoons spoofing the situation began appearing in local newspapers.

What particularly irritated Juan's junta friends-now-enemies was that Perón allowed Eva to stand beside him (rather than behind him) at official appearances and at their apartment.

And, at political schmooze fests at their apartment almost nightly, Juan allowed Evita to listen to and absorb all the political strategizing and gossip. In the Argentine culture of the time, politics was the sole province of males, as was voting.

Encouraging Evita to be, in effect, one of the guys was Juan's unconventional behavior his colleagues were less and less able to tolerate. In candid terms, they had an aversion to Perón's girlfriend, Eva Duarte.

It wasn't that Eva "didn't know her place." She knew her "place," but, buttressed by Juan's support, she stepped out of her "place."

The men around Juan agreed they had to do something, and do something fast, about Evita. But what?

To do something about Eva, they had to do something about Juan.

Moving against General Juan was something else entirely.

· · · · · · · ·

A tall masculine man with a deep voice, in a culture that prized masculinity, Juan, like George Wallace, liked to comb his hair slicked back, plastered down with oil in the male greasy pompadour fashion of the time.

Compared to other darker menacing personalities in the parade of military juntas, Juan had an easygoing disposition. He read widely and could speak several languages well including passable English.

He had a red, blotchy condition of the skin that was a kind of rosacea for which he kept much of his face and chin covered with a flesh-colored pomade that was the subject of much uncomplimentary private comment and gossip questioning whether the pomade was actually makeup.

Perón's paternal grandfather, like George's, was a physician. Born in 1895, schooled in military institutions, and part of the Argentinean bourgeois, Juan ranked several social classes above Eva, as did George compared with Lurleen.

People liked Juan because he could talk easily with anyone in any social class, from chatting with the macho gauchos in baggy trousers who ate slabs of bleeding beef speared on the tip of a very sharp knife, to swapping stories with factory workers over a beer, or holding his own with discourse within Evita's milieu of artists, actors and musicians.

Like George Wallace, Juan was an amateur-level boxer. He was also a fencing champion.

Juan's first wife, Aurelia Tizon, whom he married in 1929, died of uterine cancer in 1937 at age 29. They had no children.

CHAPTER TWENTY
POKER FACE

"The more a man can achieve, the more he may be certain that the devil will inhabit a part of his creation."
—Norman Mailer

The 1947-1951 period when George campaigned for, and three consecutive times won, a seat in the Alabama state legislature was an increasingly unhappy one for Lurleen Wallace as she matured into her 30s. In modern psychoanalytic parlance, she struggled to process the realities of George's character that she could no longer ignore. Nothing was or ever would be as important to him as seeking political office.

In the 1946-1950 period, nonstop campaigning for a state legislative seat, a first rung on the political career ladder, meant George neglected his desultory solo legal practice in Clayton, barely eking out a living while campaigning. Actually practicing law had never really interested him anyway.

Lurleen, forced by circumstance to continue being the family breadwinner, worked at the Clayton branch office of the Alabama Department of Agriculture as a clerk and also as a courthouse clerk. The inadequacy of her meager salary made her despair for their impecunious personal finances.

George, who earned almost no money to support his family, borrowed money for his political needs from whomever he could collar. For George, financing his quests for public office superceded supporting his wife and children.

Lurleen Wallace's once-treasured girlhood memories of meeting the dashing young lawyer George faded, obliterated by the harsh quotidian grind of juggling the time-immemorial responsibilities of women: working at a job out of financial necessity, while at the same time taking care of children and home, with no help from an absent spouse who evinces no inclination toward sharing family responsibilities.

For a time, they lived in a rented third floor attic space filled with coal dust from a heat stove, where she set traps nightly for rats.

George campaigned daily for the 1947 legislative seat, driving around Barbour County, Alabama, in a car borrowed from his physician grandfather, stranding Lurleen and toddler Bobbie Jo without transportation to perform basic needs.

Instead of spending any available free time with Lurleen and their first child, Bobbie Jo, George often played poker or socialized with good ol' boy political pals at Billy Watson's Store in Clayton.

Decades later, as an adult, Bobbie Jo said she forgave George. But forgiving is not forgetting.

Bobbie Jo did not forget her father's disengagement from her and from Lurleen and his disinterest in providing them even minimal financial support. For all practical purposes, George abandoned them to their own devices.

Old sins cast very long shadows.

CHAPTER TWENTY ONE
I'M DOWN TO MY LAST BROKEN HEART

One day, like a story in a country western song, Lurleen reached the end of her patience with George's chronic failures to share any of his time with her and their first child Bobbie Jo. Borrowing a car, she drove to a farm where she knew George was playing poker with his buddies. (Some accounts say it was a farm, some say it was under a big ol' shade tree, some say the game was in the back room of a store.)

With toddler Bobbie Jo in arms, she stormed into the farmhouse, thrusting his daughter at George, screaming that he had left her with a baby and no car. "OK, you look after her!" Lurleen shouted. "Maybe you'll come home pretty quick."

George was impervious, unfazed.

He did not apologize.

After she slammed the door and left, George continued playing poker as if what had just happened had not happened. Since Lurleen supported George financially with her meager earnings as a clerk, presumably he was using her money to gamble at cards. His desultory in-name-only law practice provided almost no income.

Not wanting to be distracted by his toddler child from maximizing his poker hands, he gave money to a male hanging around the game as payment for taking Bobbie Jo on a tour of the farm to see the animals.

A few hours later as night fell, when George had not returned, and worried about what had happened to her toddler daughter, Lurleen borrowed another car and drove again out to the farm on dark roads.

George was still there, playing poker unperturbed.

This time, in an even more anguished state, Lurleen pleaded with George to come home, having to humiliate herself by begging in front of his good ol' boy buddies and her daughter, around a poker table.

"You've played enough poker for today. The baby is tired and wants to go to bed," she entreated.

Finally, he left the poker game.

Utilizing the Internet, iPhone technology era of ensuing decades, one of the poker group might have videoed George's loutish disregard of his wife and child. Unflattering video images quickly would have made their way to You Tube, then the nightly news and Twitter retweets within an hour, perhaps ending his political career.

But boys-will-be-boys was the jocular cultural reaction of the era. Although there were many male witnesses to the louche incident, there were no public repercussions.

Reflection on that in-your-face public rejection, degrading for her and for her daughter, was not the first time Lurleen agonized through all the classic stages of grief: denial, bargaining, anger.

Acceptance, the final stage, was more difficult to attain. Admitting, a mere three years after the marriage ceremony, that the relationship with George wasn't working necessitated a tacit admission on her part that at 16 she may have erred in her choice of husband.

Her mother Estelle had always warned Lurleen that all that glitters is not necessarily gold.

Parental "I told you so" observations are unwelcome to offspring ears.

.

CHAPTER TWENTY TWO

PASS ME BY IF YOU'RE ONLY PASSIN' THROUGH

In their Clayton-Montgomery sojourns for three legislative sessions in 1947, 1949, and 1951, George habitually left Lurleen alone to cope— in a $25 a month garage apartment, and other spartan living accommodations they occupied in those years.

Some of the rentals were so small you couldn't cuss a cat without getting fur in your mouth.

She had sole responsibility for two additional children, Peggy, born in 1950, and George III, born in 1951.

"George's interest in his children was little more than perfunctory," a biographer wrote.

George's $20 per diem that he earned only during the two months every other year the Alabama legislature was in session was insufficient to support them, but might finance getting his foot on the next rung of his political ladder.

There was no surprise which of the two options George chose.

To support them monetarily, through his political connections, George got Lurleen a part-time job while they were in Montgomery, as an enrollment clerk in the Alabama House of Representatives for the 1947 and 1949 sessions.

They had to keep Lurleen's employment as a House enrollment clerk under the radar because Alabama's applicable nepotism laws forbade employing relatives and spouses, George confessed to a biographer years later.

Being constantly on guard to avoiding a potentially embarrassing nepotism violation with a subrosa job added to Lurleen's distress.

The uncomfortable, gnawing reality popped again on Lurleen's mental screen: that perhaps when she chose George as a life partner at age 16, she had not yet acquired the maturity to choose either wisely or as well as she thought in 1942.

The idea of legally extracting herself from what barely qualified as "marriage" with George began intruding more and more into her daily thoughts.

In Cinderella terms, the golden coach had turned back into a pumpkin, and the glass slipper was badly chipped.

CHAPTER TWENTY THREE
THE KINDNESS OF STRANGERS

"It was a lonely life, yes, except the life we made for ourselves".
—Mary Jo Ventress

During Lurleen's 1947-51 stressful years shifting residences and her part time clerk jobs back and forth between Clayton and Montgomery, she was befriended in Clayton by Mary Jo Ventress, a quintessential, genteel, formally educated, mannered lady of the south for whom time never eroded the mutual comfort of their life-long bond.

Women of all cultures have a mantra among themselves, an unspoken pact: Men come and men go in and out of your life: Jes' passin' through. But friendship bonds among women are forever.

"We were both wives of men in the military service. We married just a week apart in 1943. She married in Tuscaloosa, and I married in Birmingham at my home.

"After my husband Tom got out of military service, we moved to Clayton, which was Tom's home. A few years later, in 1945 when George was discharged from military service, he and Lurleen moved to Clayton because that was the county seat and he was a lawyer," Mary Jo Ventress remembers. George's home ground was Clio.

"We were both there as young wives. Lurleen was three years younger than I. She and George lived in an apartment. Lurleen would walk up and down the street with Bobbie, who was just a little tyke at the time. Lurleen was so petite herself. They looked so cute.

"I was teaching home economics to the ninth through twelfth grades at Lewisville high school. Lurleen was working in Clayton as a secretary for a branch office of the Department of Education.

"I think we actually met for the first time at the City Café. Tom and I and George and Lurleen would sometimes go there for supper at night. Tom and George knew each other from high school events.

"I thought Lurleen was cute as a button and a lot of fun, always laughing and telling a good joke. I mean a nice joke. She was really a private person. But she had such a sweet personality, and we just liked each other and liked doing the same things," Mary Jo recalls.

"Lurleen loved to fish more than anything else. But I never did have a chance to go fishing," Mary Jo said wistfully.

By several accounts, George never went fishing with Lurleen either during their two decades together.

Mary Jo, who taught public school classes in sewing, home decoration, flower arranging, prenatal care, personality, and hairdo, coached Lurleen on cooking, which everyone who knew her well said she disdained.

"We made a little chart of recipes, planning meals she could do, what she could have for a week: maybe hamburger steak, macaroni and cheese and a salad. Cooking is something you have to do. So you might as well just do it. We did learn to knit. Something simple, the knit and purl stitch.

"George was absent all the time campaigning. She never knew really when he was going to be there. She took the responsibility of the household and raising the children."

· · · · · · · ·

Did Lurleen lead a lonely life?

"I would say that she did," Mary Jo said. "Except what we made for ourselves."

"My husband Tom was not gone out of town. But he was working all the time. So I was by myself, and she was by herself. So we just stayed together.

"In the summer time recess from my teaching, we would go to Montgomery to shop and look around. We'd have the best time walking up and down the street. We'd eat lunch at Kreske's dime store.

"Right as you went out the front door, Kreske's had heated nuts. We'd usually buy the cashews. Our idea was to take cashews home to her children. We put the nuts on the car seat between us, and it was hardly half a sack when we got home!"

In those simple pleasures, did they find a communion to sustain them both?

"Absolutely."

Years later, when Lurleen went to Montgomery in 1962 as first lady, Mary Jo went along to a job in the state department of education.

And when Lurleen herself was elected governor, Mary Jo was there, too. She designed and sewed Lurleen's inaugural attire.

CHAPTER TWENTY FOUR
EVITA'S MARVELOUS DAY
(DIA MARVELOSA DE EVITA)

February 24, 1944, a month after Eva became Perón's mistress, his friend Edelmiro Farrell appointed Perón vice president. Farrell promoted himself from colonel to general and became president of Argentina.

Perón continued as labor secretary and war secretary. At that time, Perón held three top positions simultaneously—but within the instability of South American political musical chairs.

On October 9, 1944, what passed for the Farrell-Perón alliance apparently cooled, because Juan Perón was coerced into signing a resignation letter. Evita was with him when he was arrested and carted off to an island prison not far from El Tigre river islands, where he and Eva became lovers about 17 months earlier.

Accounts indicate that Perón was terrified of being killed by the naval men who arrested him, physically trembling and begging for mercy. He was Army.

. . . .

Evita, however, declined to cower. She screamed obscenities and spit on the arresting naval officers. In acting, such an outburst is called scenery chewing.

...y had been ordered to arrest Evita, too. But because they ...dn't know how to cope with an shrieking, obstreperous 25 year old female, they decided to let her go.

"That was an error of judgment (on the part of the arresting naval officers) that was to change the course of Argentine history," wrote one historian.

That analysis wasn't hyperbole.

Evita's years of polishing her acting skills came in handy, discombobulating the naval officers with her histrionics. Now she was free to circulate among her contacts and Juan's, soliciting their assistance in freeing Juan—instead of being held incommunicado in a prison with him.

Her months as a sponge, learning the political ropes as an acolyte at their apartment gatherings paid off, too. As the apt student of Juan's mentoring largesse, she knew whom to contact and how best to present Juan's case for release.

"I flung myself into the streets searching for those friends who might still be of help to Juan," Evita wrote in her autobiography.

· · · · · · ·

Juan was arrested because he and Evita had been too successful. As labor minister, Perón, with Evita as coordinator, had system-atically courted *descamisados* (manual laborers and working poor) to such a degree that Perón's opponents worried that Perón's burgeoning popularity might adumbrate Farrell's image and power.

Their assessment of Juan's profile was correct.

Juan's growing power was a threat to their grip on power. Lagniappe for the junta was that throwing Juan under the bus would probably also rid them of the annoying female pest Evita. Where Juan was, Evita was, Perón's opponents reasoned. If he's in prison, she's in prison. In ousting Juan they would simultaneously oust Evita, they thought.

The junta's crossed signals proved catastrophic for them.

Juan and Evita together could flex political muscles Farrell and friends never dreamed the couple had stockpiled.

• • • • • • • •

Eight days after Juan's arrest—on October 17, 1945—a sea of humanity, estimated at between 250,000 and 350,000 people, began surrounding government house, called Casa Rosada, demanding Juan Perón's release.

The size of the rapidly arriving crowd got the alarmed attention of his captors, who hurriedly changed their strategy to accommodate the reality of Perón supporters assembling around the building they themselves occupied.

The crowd chanted "Pay-roan, Pay -roan," sang songs, and waved placards with Juan's photo. The vocalizing grew louder with each hour.

As aides kept him informed of the masses congregating and restive outside their door, Eduardo Avalos, one of the generals, got on the phone immediately to Perón, in what must have been one of the most awkward and embarrassing political calls ever made.

Perhaps that is why General Avalos, rather than President Farrell, made the call.

Remember when we arrested you, Juan? Well, that was all a big, big mistake. Actually my friend, you were never under arrest. We took you to the prison for your own safety, General Avalos must have explained disingenuously as the crowds demanding Juan's release began banging on the Casa Rosada doors with the generals inside.

He and President Farrell probably hoped that Perón could not hear the outside commotion over the phone connection.

They began thinking that maybe they could tolerate Evita just a bit longer after all.

Was getting rid of her influence really worth all this?

Falling on your own sword is not only painful; it is humiliating as well.

Later, people ask you about the circumstances of the wound.

· · · · · · · ·

Evita had been visiting Juan at Martin Garcia island prison. Unannounced, a boat plucked him and Evita from there, when his captors finally realized, as crowds increased in size, that perhaps arresting Juan was not the best idea they ever had.

Events escalating outside their windows—crowds holding placards peering in and screaming Juan's name—did not seem to be trending in their favor.

They began checking the boat schedules from Buenos Aires across the Rio de la Plata to Uruguay's metaphorical Club for Those Who Left Argentina in a Hurry.

Historians credit unions with organizing the massive public protest that freed Juan. Evita worked behind the scenes for seven days, mining all her contacts, in unions and otherwise, to lobby for Perón's release.

She never forgave an attorney who declined her desperate entreaties that he file a Writ of Habeas Corpus on Juan's behalf, to attempt to free him from prison.

Nevertheless, some academics and others refused to accord Evita even any tiny share of tribute for organizing the assemblage that freed Juan, derisively labeling her as only an vapid actress with no political clout.

Evita was the elected president of a union of broadcast performers she formed in 1944. Further enhancing her credibility as a Juan Perón supporter, she launched and hosted a daily radio soap opera extolling Juan's accomplishments and virtues.

. . . .

Arriving directly from the island prison, Perón appeared on a Casa Rosada balcony in operatic high drama, thanking the crowd for influencing his release.

"Perón for president!" They chanted back.

That, for Juan and Evita, was the plan all along. October 17 was really Juan's first campaign event to move up from vice president to president.

Reflecting on the events later, Juan parsed out exactly who had helped save his derrière from the slammer: Eva Duarte, 25, actress.

Juan well understood that in the world of bare-knuckled politics in any country: Loyalty is way, way more valuable and infinitely rarer than love.

CHAPTER TWENTY FIVE
THE GIFT OF MARRIAGE
(REGALO DE MATRIMONIO)

From what Juan experienced as his mistress's unwavering fidelity and undaunted courage in adversity helping organize the public rally that freed him, Juan understood that Evita deserved the highest accolade that he could give her—his public validation: marriage.

In Argentine society at that time, males rarely married their mistresses.

But Juan's marriage proposal to Evita was not entirely gratitude based. There was pressure to marry Evita—and not from Evita.

For months his military peers and fellow politicos had hectored him that although mistresses were socially acceptable in their culture, mistresses who so openly and publicly shared the daily public life of their benefactors, as Eva did, were not.

An hypocrisy, but also a fact.

They advised Juan of what he already knew: that his prospects for promotion would certainly be adversely affected if he did not marry his mistress, Eva. Even in the socially duplicitous culture, personal life scandal awaited to savage his ascent to president, they warned.

Juan Perón, like canny George Wallace, understood that in hard-edged political triage, practicality and reality are priority one. Romance is a side consideration at best.

. . . .

Juan Perón and Maria Eva Duarte were married in a civil ceremony in her home town on October 18, 1945, and in a church wedding December 9, 1945.

The alluring actress with limited formal education and "obscure antecedents" (the Argentine code word for illegitimate), who began life with no money and no family backing, who left a small town at age 15 had, a mere ten years later, married the man who would soon become president of Argentina.

. . . .

On December 15,1945, Juan, vice president of Argentina, formally announced his candidacy for president of Argentina.

"I join the ranks of the *descamisados*," he told the crowd of about 150,000.

A mere eight weeks earlier, he had been in prison.

For those who would later aver that Evita was, literally, a saint, the events of October 17, 1945, could qualify with the Vatican as her first miracle.

Getting Juan to marry her could be her second miracle.

The Vatican requires three.

CHAPTER TWENTY SIX

TOO YOUNG TO VOTE

"(The South) is still a place where you must have either been born or have 'people' there to feel it is your native ground."
—Tim Jacobson, Heritage of the South

Lurleen, age 18 with one child, was too young to vote for George in 1946. Legal voting age was 21 in Alabama.

George joked that he hoped he wouldn't lose by one vote.

"A man should have a wife old enough to vote for him," George added with a thumbs-in-suspenders smirk.

Despite George's wink-wink-nudge-nudge attempt at humor, Lurleen, as a dutiful young wife, was willing to do whatever she could in 1946 to help George, 26, plant his foot firmly on the first rung of the political ladder: election to a seat in the Alabama House of Representatives.

Across the southern United States, particularly in a legislative district of small towns and close-knit insular communities, personal contact in asking for votes is everything, then and still.

Very, very important.

On the campaign trail, as well as in non campaign interactions, Who are your people? Or: Who are her people? are common questions sometimes asked outright, but usually voluntarily answered immediately—on the assumption that the questions will be asked.

In Los Angeles culture, that would translate to asking: Who do you know? Translation: Who are your backers? Who are your friends?

In NYC, the equivalent question would be: In what geographical location in the city do you live? Upper East Side? Brooklyn?

In southern states, the proper response to the inevitable inquiry is you have to "call kin": verbally share who your friends and relatives are or were, where you and they were born, to whom they are related or whom they might know in common with whom you know.

The custom is also called "kin-ection" (connection).

All y'all's y'alls.
An early version of LinkedIn.

If you can't do it, you will still be treated very politely. But you probably won't get the vote of the person asking you the question.

. . . .

Lurleen worked as a clerk in the Clayton office of the state department of agriculture (probably beginning about 1945) during the day, providing their only real, reliable income for the family.

Sometimes she served as a substitute teacher, as did other parents, even though she did not have college training.

She spent evenings in their one-room rental, usually alone, except for toddler Bobbie Jo, hand writing letters to everyone she knew, asking for their vote for George, who was continually absent from her life.

At that time, Lurleen rarely joined George in campaign appearances because she was the sole breadwinner and responsible for a toddler daughter.

On the rare occasions George was home, Lurleen added to her long, physically exhausting day the task of preparing George's evening meal, after which he often immediately abandoned her and their daughter Bobbie Jo, choosing to spend his available time gabbing with Clayton's ol' boys at Billy Watson's store.

It mattered little that Lurleen never developed enthusiasm for cooking. She told a friend George covered everything he ate with ketchup—except, sometimes, ice cream.

Her friendship with Home Ec teacher Mary Jo Ventress and Clayton newspaper editor Bertie Gammell anchored her while she acclimated to living alone in George's major absences.

In the May, 1946 primary, George won the Democratic nomination for the state House seat from Barbour County with 56 percent of the votes, tantamount to election because there was no Republican nominee in the fall.

At 37, he was Alabama's youngest state legislator.

The state legislature was home ground George could hit running, having served as a state Senate page in 1935. He already knew where some of the "bodies were buried."

•   •   •   •   •   •   •   •

Because George devoted his time to perpetual campaigning rather than earning money, they teetered at the brink of poverty level, rescued only by Lurleen's periodic employment. They shuttled from small rented space to small rented space as George was elected twice more to the state legislature in 1949 and 1951.

George said that while serving as a state representative, he hitchhiked to Montgomery because he couldn't afford a car.

His brother Jack Wallace got out of law school and joined George's solo law practice, or better said, began a law practice. George had done virtually nothing or very little to develop a business. His law practice was, for all practical purposes, in name only.

At one point, they moved to the boarding house room with a single bare light bulb dangling on a wire from the ceiling, where George had taken her on their wedding night three years earlier. The other boarders still included transient male railroad employees.

For Lurleen, a return, after three years, to the low-rent literal wedding night locale, must have been disappointing—even disheartening.

Where you are is who you are.

And Lurleen felt she was nowhere.

Her relationship with George was not progressing in the positive directions she had envisioned.

It had become a dirge. A forced march, with few rations and no rest stops.

CHAPTER TWENTY SEVEN
STEP ONE: GET WOMEN THE VOTE
(PRIMERO, VOTAS POR MUJERES)

Encouraged by his sensational October 17, 1945, release from prison, Vice President Juan Perón began campaigning as a candidate for President of Argentina.

With union and *descamisado* support so publicly added to his gravitas with Evita's help, Juan had his foot on the bottom rungs of the political ladder. He was ready for the climb to the top.

All that stood between him and the presidency was attracting more votes than any opponents.

One half of Argentina's adult population in 1945 did not have the legal right to vote for him or for anyone. Juan's new bride, Evita, was part of that bulging, untapped storehouse of votes: women.

She saw this disenfranchisement of women as an opportunity to gain votes for her husband.

Like Lurleen, to sustain her marital relationship, she had to make Juan's campaign for votes her campaign for votes; his ambition, her ambition.

The ambition part was easy. Evita could match Juan in the ambition category from the day she came out of the womb.

Although Evita was masterful at public speaking, campaign public speaking and presence asking for votes were different scripts and different roles. Learning to campaign for votes could be done only by traveling around Argentina actually campaigning.

The courage to step out with a smile.

Recover quickly from missteps. Conserve your time and energy diligently.

In 1945, Evita began making radio addresses supporting women's suffrage. She published articles in the *Democracia* newspaper urging males to support granting Argentine women the right to vote.

A bill granting women the right to vote was introduced in 1945. In February 1946, while the bill still pended, Juan was elected president of Argentina without women having been granted voting rights.

He would be sworn in as president on June 4, 1946.

At 27 years old, a mere 13 years after she came to Buenos Aires at age 15 with no money and not knowing anyone there, Eva Duarte Perón was first lady of Argentina: the president's wife.

Lurleen, at age 37, became first lady of Alabama in 1962.

Both women, with humble backgrounds and limited education, would transcend fast and by far the powerful, charismatic men whose light they would outshine as female pioneers.

· · · · · · · ·

In Argentina, Evita had to pry open a bolted and locked door that America had already opened for women. Evita had to persuade an all male legislative body to vote to give women the vote.

Juan and Evita intensified their work behind the scenes to convince legislators that women's voting time had come.

No one gives up power for the mere asking of it.

The bill granting women the right to vote stagnated, gathering dust in congressional committees of men who were unenthusiastic about unleashing the power of women to vote them in or out of public office.

Shortly after returning from her barnstorming tour of Europe, Evita strode into Congress and told the delegates she would remain there until they voted to give women the right to vote.

Always cognizant of the power of publicity, Evita made sure the visitor galleries were packed with women. Thousands more women literally surrounded the building. That got the men's attention.

Former President Farrell grumbled that some of the right-to-vote demonstrators were lead by "persons of the opposite sex" (women).

Two days after Evita's sit- down, on September 9, 1947, Congress voted to accord voting rights to Argentina's women.

Juan made a great flourish by signing the culture-shifting legislation in a public ceremony. Then he gallantly handed the bill to First lady Evita, a gesture signifying the nationwide accomplishment as hers.

A photo immortalizes Evita holding her arms aloft over a sea of appreciative women.

Four years later in the presidential election of 1951, when women could vote, Juan gained a second term in office, with his tally swelling to 63 percent of the total for his re-election.

It was the women's big Thank You to Juan, reciprocated with Juan's Thank You to the women.

. . . .

As her follow up, with Juan's help, Evita created the Female Perónist Party to harness the politically crucial cache of new voters.

The Party originated on July 26, 1949, when Juan spoke to 6,000 Perónists in Luna Stadium, where five years earlier, he first met Eva Duarte.

While Juan grew up in the culture that denied women political power, he could cast those prejudices aside and acclimate to new thinking when Evita reminded him that the vote of women could put him in public office and keep him there.

Explained that way, it was an irrefutable reality Juan could cozy up to.

As planned, on July 26, 1949, after Juan's rousing remarks, 1,500 women left the group and met in the Cervantes Theater to hear First lady Evita outline goals of the new party. With her actress background, Eva felt at home in the Cervantes, urging the newly franchised female voters forward, not only to vote, but to seek political office as candidates.

An archival theater photo reveals the rapt attention of their faces as Evita speaks to them.

"Because I have seen that women have never had material or spiritual opportunities—only poetry took them into account—and because I have known that women were a moral and spiritual resource in the world, I have placed myself at the side of all women of my country to struggle resolutely with them. Not only for the vindication of ourselves, but also of our homes, our children, and our husbands," Evita told her audience.

The Perónista Feminist Party, with Evita as its first president, was born that day.

As a tribute to Evita's organizational skills and hard work, in 1951 Argentina's first large female political party boasted 3,600 headquarters across Argentina and half a million members.

Biographers credit Eva, like Lurleen, as an early torch bearer, inspiring women to venture beyond just voting for candidates; to run as candidates for public office themselves.

Neither woman had any female role models in politics to guide or mentor her. Both were alone.

They were the political role models: the first to step up to the plate.

Courage is stepping out there with a smile.

CHAPTER TWENTY EIGHT
"WOMEN ARE ALL WE GOT"

In her marooned and abandoned Clayton years, Lurleen began a friendship with the woman editor of Clayton's weekly newspaper — a media contact with a stalwart dynasty of female editors that would serve both her and George well over many years as campaigners and office holders.

Small town weeklies are powerful voices.

As editor in chief of the Clayton Record weekly newspaper from 1954 to 1960, Pearle Gammell would not let anybody run the printing presses except her.

Miz Pearle alone fed the paper into the press. No exceptions.

She said she just felt like she could do it better than anybody else," said her granddaughter and 1998 editor successor Rebecca Beasley.

"Grandma Gammell was trained as a musician. She said the press had a kind of rhythm—like music—as the pages went through. She'd get in the rhythm of hearing those presses, and she thought if you didn't hear that rhythm, you shouldn't print," Rebecca remembered.

Pearle Gammell was also one of Lurleen's close friends and female role models during the same bleak years Mary Jo befriended Lurleen in Clayton. They all shared a mutual interest in music.

Grandma Pearle Gammell (1892-1960) served as editor from 1954-1960. When she died at home of a heart attack, Pearle's daughter Bertie Gammell Parish (1915-1998) (Rebecca's mother) took the editor in chief helm from 1960-1998.

Bertie, who became close to Lurleen and championed Lurleen's candidacy, also died of a heart attack at home.

"My mother Bertie graduated in music from University of Alabama. She had not been very involved with the Clayton Record. But she was the only surviving sibling.

"So, she went to work'.

"I'm going to get out a newspaper. It's like having a baby. I've got me a baby now. I have to take care of it," Bertie told everyone.

. . . .

Rebecca, the third woman editor in chief of the Clayton Record, grew up in the newspaper business, starting as a young child. "I just hung around. I always liked to get in the middle of everything."

A sure sign of journalistic bones.

"When I was about eight years old, they put me in a chair. The papers were folded mechanically and spewed out a chute. I would sit in the chair and catch the papers as they came out of the folder."

Her two brothers would label the papers, then stamp subscriber names on them with a stamping machine.

"I went off to college after mother died. I didn't think I would ever come back to the Clayton Record. I got my masters degree in communications from the University of Alabama. Then my husband and I started a family, and I returned to the newspaper and to Clayton in 1998," Rebecca said.

She does some of the writing too. In a small paper, everyone does everything.

. . . .

Rebecca, born in 1949, remembers meeting Lurleen when Rebecca was four or five years old and played with Lurleen's daughter Peggy. "Clayton's a small town. Everybody knows everybody here."

Bertie is the source, not President Lyndon Johnson as George liked to claim, who suggested that Lurleen should present herself as a candidate for governor when George couldn't run..

"Mother said: 'Lurleen, if we can have a Ma and Pa Ferguson governors in Texas, we can have a Ma and Pa Wallace in Alabama. Go for it!'

"Bertie had a lady in Clayton make one of those old fashioned hats, kind of like a bonnet with a tie. She handed it to Lurleen and said: 'Throw your hat into the ring,' " Rebecca remembers.

" 'Just step in and do it!' Mother told Lurleen."

Later, her mother, Bertie, played the organ at Bobbie Jo's wedding and Lurleen's 1967 inaugural festivities. "She had me sit next to her and turn the pages as if she needed me.

"When George won for governor, Mother thought she was in heaven, because George was from our home town. But when Lurleen won, mother really thought she was in heaven," Rebecca said.

" 'There's nothing like knowing the governor personally,' Mother said."

The family was received often at the governor's mansion in both the George and Lurleen administrations. "We went to the mansion anytime we wanted to," Rebecca said.

· · · · · · · ·

"As governor, Lurleen Wallace was an independent woman.

95

I'm sure she took George's advice. But she was her own person. She gained more confidence serving in public office.

"I wish we had more people like Lurleen Wallace in politics, for the right reasons of service, not for their own personal gain.

"The character and image Lurleen was for Alabama, just extraordinary. She made a mark in Alabama history, not only as the first woman governor, but one with such integrity," Rebecca said.

Rebecca's grandfather, Tom Parish, came from the Dothan, Alabama, Eagle newspaper to purchase the Clayton Record in 1915 when he married Pearle. Then it was called The Clayton Banner, founded in 1871, and owned by Grandma Pearle's family.

Women have edited the small town weekly newspaper for 143 years.

"Women editors. That's all we got," Rebecca said brightly.

CHAPTER TWENTY NINE
LEARNING TO CAMPAIGN
(APPREDIENDO A CAMPANA)

The life paths of the two men, George Wallace, and Juan Perón, and their wives, Lurleen and Evita, which had patterned toward each other for more than two decades on different continents, tracked on virtually contiguous rails in 1945, as each man sought political office—dipping their toes in the treacherous, physically exhausting rip tides of personal campaigning in a pre-Internet age.

Spouses of political candidates, reluctant or enthusiastic, prepared or ingenue, cannot float uninvolved on the often roiling surface of public life. Political spouses are enticed to either tiptoe from the shoreline into the public eye, or be thrown into the high profile life's unforgiving ebb and flow. They must to learn to swim sturdy very, very quickly, lest they drown.

Fortunately for Evita, because of her radio and theatrical careers, being in the public eye was her milieu—her world—at the time she met Juan.

In fact, Evita thrived on public attention. She understood the benefits and the pitfalls and was skilled at navigating both, as was Juan.

. . . .

Buoyed by his crowd-sourced 1945 release from prison, Juan Perón, 50, set his political sights on moving up to the summit via the 1946 election, from vice president to *El Presidente* of Argentina.

At the same time, George, 27, was making his first run for the 1946 Alabama state legislative seat.

Because Juan had been appointed vice president, his quest to move up to president was his first political campaign via election.

Replicating the support she rallied for her husband in his October 17, 1945 jail release, Evita, defying the conventions of the time, became Juan's full high visibility partner in campaigning.

Evita began by joining Juan on a campaign train, the then-popular mode for candidates to travel the interior of the vast nation. Ironically, the train stopped in Junin, the small rural village that she left about 11 years earlier at age 13 or age 15 (both are cited) to seek her fortune in Buenos Aires.

Photos from the campaign train show an engine festooned with palm fronds and a drawing of Juan. At a stop in Tucamen, Perón spoke to workers about improved working conditions, angering the landowners and sugar magnates in the region, notes one photo caption.

Other campaign train photos show Juan and Evita dining on white tablecloths in an elegant car. In photos of Evita distributing political flyers and buttons from a train window, her face seems to register caution at the many eager, outstretched hands, a sort of surprised hesitation on her part in seeing her radio audiences in person.

In similar photos years later of her with crowds, she is more poised and self-assured.

CHAPTER THIRTY
LURLEEN AUTHORS JUDGING FOR DUMMIES

After three four-year House terms in the Alabama state leg-islature, George set his sights on the next rung: a judicial circuit judgeship based in Clayton that paid $600 a month. He had added two children to his family, Peggy Sue in 1950, and George Jr. in 1951.

He got advance notice in 1952 that Judge J.S. Williams in the 10th Judicial Circuit, Barbour County, would be retiring and would not seek reelection to the six year term beginning in 1953. George's Grandfather, a physician, had been a probate judge.

His judicial opponent in the Democratic primary was patrician Senator Preston Clayton, a 16-year state senator and legislative col-league of George's from a distinguished Alabama family of accom-plishment.

•   •   •   •   •   •   •   •   •

Lurleen now mothered three children, in addition to working as a clerk at the Clayton courthouse, while George continually disap-peared plying the political speaking circuit. She spent evenings in a tiny garage apartment hand writing thank-you notes to voters George glad-handed at campaign events, this time for a judicial rather than a legislative post.

As Preston Clayton's competitive political adversary, George evinced short memory for Clayton's past inestimable cosponsor assistance helping George pass a bill giving free college tuition to widows and orphans of Alabamians killed or disabled in World

War II, for which George basked in widespread public acclaim.

In that judicial campaign, No-holds-barred George played to his base, casting Senator Clayton as an aristocratic, detached dilettante and himself as a po' boy one-of-the-people—a comparison the chivalrous Clayton, gallantly adherent to the Marques of Queensbury rules, was unable to counter effectively against a no-rules, kick 'em in the groin street fighter like George.

After a raucous race, he bested Preston Clayton, with approximately 6,700 votes to Clayton's approximately 2,400 votes. At 33, he was the youngest circuit judge in Alabama.

Ironically, in the politics-makes-strange-bedfellows conundrum, years later, Clayton later represented George as George's attorney in a fierce public fight over a federal court-ordered peek into Barbour County election records held by George.

•   •   •   •   •   •   •   •

Assuming George would win the judgeship, Lurleen gifted him with hours she spent preparing judicial resource materials he could utilize to look good on the bench.

According to George's biographers, Lurleen, a non lawyer, with no college education, volunteered to analyze reams of legal materials. She spent weeks summarizing civil and criminal legal precepts and case law, which would have been challenging even for a college graduate.

She inscribed the complex material on flash cards, which she organized into an index George could reference daily and quickly while on the bench, particularly when trying cases.

Hers was a thaumaturgical feat.

100

Privately, George Wallace felt "professionally uncomfortable" in his new incarnation as a courtroom judge, justifiably wary of inadvertently unmasking himself as a legal arriviste. His concerns were realistic. He had never spent much time as a practicing lawyer, and little or no time in courtroom trial law.

He was the chasing dog who finally caught the car, then realized he didn't know what to do next.

Fortunately, Lurleen knew.

The Dime Store Girl stepped in big time to save his posterior by authoring the equivalent of Judging for Dummies.

George began the six-year term judgeship on February 2, 1953, relying daily on legal materials prepared by Lurleen, whose formal education was seven years less than his. The exceptional, quick mastery Lurleen evinced in preparing the equivalent of a Judging for Dummies Cliff notes for George, while caring for three young children and working outside the home, apparently escaped his self-obsessed notice.

His friend Judge Walter B. Jones of Montgomery also assisted as coach, providing George with templates and case law for the most frequently recurring legal issues.

By all accounts, although his family boasted two judges, his uncle and his grandfather, George had no genuine interest in the judiciary. The judgeship was another mere expediency, a lucrative pause.

He wanted the local prestige of the bench as platform—with steady, albeit modest, income of $600 per month—for his planned 1957-58 run for governor of Alabama. And he saw judges' prerogative of tailoring their own work schedules, as opportunity to campaign for the governor slot while on the judicial bench.

Reports from blacks and whites about his racial even-handedness as a judge abound.

A biographer cites a comment from J.L. Chestnut, Jr. the only black attorney in Selma Alabama in 1958, who praised George Wallace as "the first judge to call me Mister in a courtroom."

But during George's judicial term in Clayton, a black woman in 1955 Montgomery, Alabama, refused to surrender her bus seat to a white man, as local custom and law required. Rosa Parks's act triggered social reverberations like a tsunami across America, a turbulence that would roil and ripple for decades, upending American culture for many of the same reasons as the Civil War 100 years earlier *(See Footnote)*.

George, as a state level circuit judge, continued to be involved in controversial public skirmishes with federal authorities, usually over issues of race or related subjects. His judicial contumaciousness, coupled with the mindset of his days as a college boxer, cemented a public image consistent with his nickname: the lil' fightin' judge.

George served one six-year term as judge 1953-1959, during which he continued rodomontade speaking and visiting, spending, as usual, little time with his family. As his judicial term neared its end, he implemented his plan to keep his judge seat warm while he positioned himself for his Mount Everest climb toward the governorship.

He'd run his brother Jack for judge. Keep the paid work in the family.

Jack campaigned successfully to fill the judicial seat George was vacating. The Wallace brothers campaigned in the same election cycle for different offices. George had carefully crafted the legal-judicial-legislative resume requisite for higher public office. The House seat had been just a pause, a place to refuel before his planned full speed gallop into a 1958 candidacy for Alabama governor, to take office in 1959.

On January 20, 1958, George Corley Wallace announced his candidacy for governor of Alabama.

Since American Evita is about Lurleen, and because there are multiple books detailing George Wallace's clashes with authority during this time period, those historical controversies will not be revisited here.

CHAPTER THIRTY ONE
HELPING JUAN WIN
(*JUNTARSE CON JUAN PARA GANAR*)

Until Evita stepped forward to help Juan campaign, no female in Argentina had appeared so publicly, so visibly supporting her husband's quest for political office.

A husband-wife or mistress-sponsor team was nonexistent.

But Evita recognized that as a historical first, she must begin slowly. She could not begin by upstaging or seeming to upstage her husband, Juan.

Lurleen followed much the same pattern as Evita, laying low initially, then, after George became ill, taking the speaker's helm on short notice and knockin' 'em dead.

Evita literally stood beside Juan as he made himself hoarse with the same stump speech in town after town from December 1945 through February 1946—the same time George was stumping with his igneous rhetoric in Barbour County, Alabama.

Historic photos of Evita on Juan's campaign train, particularly a photo of her twisting slightly into a side view, indicate she was overweight. Her waist and hips are thick and significantly large — the "before" version of the svelte, fashionable figure she became.

Initially, Evita handled some of the behind-the-scenes campaign detail work—as Lurleen began—working in the background on behalf of her husband.

Voice, nuance, the dramatic ingredients of speech making were expertises Evita, a veteran radio actress, could share with Juan, who was an accomplished public speaker himself.

Like Lurleen and George campaigning with the raucous C&W band, Evita also had a fine-tuned understanding how the razzle-dazzle show biz component of political campaigns trumps voter interest in issues and ideas.

Evita understood what George Wallace understood: that in seeking elective office anywhere, personal popularity with the audience is the only attribute that counts. Attracting entertainment-level ratings with music and hoopla—and attracting political votes—equate when measuring success in both arenas.

Although Evita often stood beside Juan and was an experienced dramatic actress, she made no campaign speeches at first. Like Lurleen did with George, initially Evita remained quiet and on the sidelines studying how the land lay in each locale where the train chugged to a loud halt.

Perón, product of a military education from childhood, well knew that to win respect, leaders have to project a powerful image using authoritative rhetoric. He could match, in verbal bombast, any politician. In a nationally broadcast speech in his campaign's finish line, he attacked his opponent as a communist.

Evita chose a seat in the back car of Juan's campaign train named Descamisado (a linguistic reference to the poor as the shirtless ones). She would lean out the window to touch people who had come to meet the woman attached to the voice they knew well from listening to her on their radios.

Black and white archival photos show the adulation with which she was greeted.

They scrambled to touch her, as if by that touch they might acquire some vicarious stardust from this extraordinarily beautiful woman with long blond hair, a Cinderella born into twin stigmas of illegitimacy and rural poverty that might have defeated an ordinary person, but had not defeated La Senora Evita. To them, Evita represented a fantasy Cinderella who met her prince charming and was living a fairy tale existence with him.

If they couldn't share her life in reality, they could share it vicariously.

While Evita held court in the back of the campaign train, Juan, physically exhausted, acquired a lookalike railway employee to sit in a train window waving.

·   ·   ·   ·   ·   ·   ·   ·

On Feb 25, 1946, Juan Perón won the presidency of Argentina with 52 percent of the vote. Candidates he favored won all but one provincial governorship.

Eleven years after arriving in Buenos Aires as a 15-year-old with zero contacts, Eva Duarte Perón was First lady of Argentina, the wife of President Juan Perón.

At that time, Argentina was one of the world's richest countries.

CHAPTER THIRTY TWO
SHE LIKES ELEGANT AND ORDINARY CLOTHES
(ELLA LE GUSTA ROPA ELEGANTE Y ORDINARIA)

As an adult extension of her childhood enthusiasm for the cinema, Evita loved fashion. Fashion was one of the reasons Evita scoured the movie magazines as a pre-teen.

Like Lurleen, Evita enjoyed dichotomous clothes choices, both high couture fashion, and casual, almost tomboy outfits.

Evita also loved jewelry—major, serious jewelry: diamonds, rubies, emeralds.

Her major supplier of jewelry was Alberto Dodero "a very rich shipping magnate" of Italian ancestry who immigrated to Uraguay, then moved his business to Buenos Aires. Dodero's company was the largest in South America. He gave Aristotle Onassis his start in the shipping business, people said.

A news article states that in the 1944 WWII years, his cargo ships alone earned for him a profit of about $100 million.

Historical records feature Van Cleef & Arpels sketches of a small portion of the magnificent pieces of jewelry Dodero gave Evita as gifts along with Rolls Royce vehicles.

Most Argentine government shipping contracts were awarded to Dodero, whose three decades younger wife Betty, was a social friend of Evita.

In the lapels of his suit, Dodero wore gold profiles of Evita and Juan, who loaned him money to purchase more vessels.

Love died however, in 1949 when the Argentine government took over Dodero's companies by reminding Dodero, just in case Dodero had forgotten, how eager he had always been to sell to the government at a price the government quoted.

. . . .

Evita would appear in her private box at the gilded Teatro Colon Opera House in dazzling Paris gowns, but sometimes appear before friends in Juan's rolled-up pajamas.

One of the Christian Dior full-skirted gowns plus a kind of cape, depicted in many photographs, consists of rows and rows of ribbon-like fabric that cascade in the skirt, like a waterfall in various hues of blue.

For her dress at Juan's inauguration as president of Argentina, she chose elegant gray silk with one bared shoulder. When Evita's uncovered shoulder was photographed at an angle appearing to be under the nose of a Roman Catholic cardinal seated next to her at the pre-inaugural banquet, her public was not amused.

The cardinal made no public comment.

Later, at a popular Buenos Aires vaudeville-type theatre, a comedienne appeared in a comedy spoof wearing a gray silk gown with one bare shoulder to which a small, stuffed cardinal bird was affixed.

Illustrative of Evita's eclectic haute glamour vs. more plebeian sartorial tastes, was a clothing quick change she executed during a post-inaugural familiarization tour she, Juan and friends took of Unzue Palace, the 283 room presidential residence, in the middle of a park.

Juan and a friend slid down the banister of the grand staircase.

In the bedroom after the tour, Evita unwound her braids, changed into Juan's pajamas, then sat on a bed deshabille, eating an orange as she greeted her surprised friends, wrote one biographer.

As First lady, Evita welcomed an opportunity for personal reinvention. "She found herself made new," a biographer observed.

Evita's elocution style was tailored to her radio and theatre stage careers, which usually involved speaking a written script. As part of her metamorphosis into first lady, Evita overcame an initial shyness about public speaking extemporaneously, without a written script.

Freed from the constraint of reading someone else's words, Evita, using her dramatic training, forged herself into a mesmerizing public speaker, earning immediate adulation.

. . . .

Evita acquired a woman companion—a personal assistant in contemporary parlance—Liliane Guardo. Like Lurleen's mentors Mary Jo Ventress and Bertie Gammell, Liliane was born and educated in a social class above Evita's.

Liliane, mother of four and wife of Richardo, majority leader in congress, acted as a sort of social graces tutor for Evita.

Every morning, Evita's car arrived at Liliane's home to chauffer her to Evita's office. Sometimes Liliane's duties included riding with Evita in a truck to distribute clothing and food to the poor. Or a day could include visits to factories or diplomatic functions or the Colon Opera House in the evening.

At Evita's request, Liliane sat near Evita daily, as a personal consultant when Evita, as First lady, met with union leaders and other "business" visitors in Evita's Labor Department office.

On the social calendar, Lilian tutored Evita on the very subtle, nuanced conformities of manners and clothing socially accept-able at beau monde events—what females born into certain social and economic strata in all cultures absorb from childhood as unwritten rules.

Liliane helped Evita sort through the many gifts those seek-ing favors left for Juan, including jewelry and fine china. Liliane taught Evita to distinguish the valuable high-end gifts from the merely modest.

Liliane tried to curb Evita's enthusiasm for "dressing like a film star" in spike heels, large hats and bold jewelry, pointing her to-ward the more tailored, classic, conservative look of a politician or business executive.

Her biographers quote Evita as sometimes contradicting Liliane's conservative sartorial suggestions in favor of more flash-and-dash outfits.

"Poor people want to see me beautiful. They all have their dreams about me, and I don't want to let them down."

CHAPTER THIRTY THREE

EVITA BUYS FACEBOOK, TWITTER: DEMOCRACIA
(*EVITA COMPRA FACEBOOK, TWITTER: DEMOCRACIA*)

In early 1947, about seven months after Juan was elected president of Argentina, and before she went on a European tour, Evita, with borrowed money, purchased a stagnant tabloid newspaper called Democracia.

Later she also purchased the newspaper El Mundo.

She had controlling interest or owned four Buenos Aires radio stations. She also "exercised influence" over 33 radio stations throughout Argentina, according to historical accounts.

As a veteran of radio herself, and founder of a radio union, Evita was savvy to the muscled influence of media. Or, as one American editor in the 1960s described the kingly power of print and paper in that era: Nobody beats a 30 Merganthaler press.

In the decades before computers democratized media access by making the equivalent of a 30 Merganthaler press available to everyone via Facebook, Twitter and their siblings, freedom of the press, in reality, belonged to those who owned a press, a fleet of trucks, and distribution lists.

Around the world in the George Wallace-Juan Perón eras, the juggernaut of media domination was concentrated in the judgments of a few white males. The meek and lowly, with no access to a 30 Merganthaler or any press, had only the concept of freedom of the press...and maybe a mimeograph machine.

Purchase of a newspaper in Argentina or anywhere was purchase of power. Radio was, as it is still, an equally powerful opinion creator.

Perhaps Evita was wiser than her detractors thought.

Owning a newspaper in 1947 was the modern day equivalent of opening a Facebook and Twitter account with few or no other Facebook or Twitter account competitors.

She was 26 years old and so smart.

When photos of Evita began appearing, which they did daily, Democracia's circulation jumped from 6,000 to 40,000 daily. That was the entire idea.

Democracia became the amanuensis of the Perón regime, printing Juan's speeches and Evita's advice to housewives. Photos of the alluring Evita in glittery haute couture splendor at upscale social events; in chic outfits at the track chatting with handsome champion race car driver Maunuel Fangio; in glam Parisian couture gowns by Christian Dior at Colon Opera House, appeared regularly. Democracia was sold out of copies early the next day

Special issue runs of Democracia numbered 400,000 copies when Evita photos were featured, which was often.

A biographer quoted an editor: "There was a vast identification with her. People who bought the newspaper wished they were her."

In Facebook terms, she attracted a lot of "likes."

Her "followers" were in the millions.

CHAPTER THIRTY FOUR
EVITA'S JUNIOR YEAR ABROAD
(VIAJES DE EVITA EN EUROPA)

In the years 1947-1952 Evita Perón reached her Mount Everest of respect and acclaim way beyond Argentina's boundaries.

Evita glided at the zenith of her glamour arc. It was her time to live in the moment. Carpe Diem. Seize the day she did. The months and years, too. Her prescience was prescient.

Upper-class Argentinians considered annual visits to Paris a rite of their class. All things Parisian were considered the high water mark of excellence, even though Hispanic cultures were their heritage.

Evita had never been to Paris. She had never traveled outside Argentina. She had never even flown on a plane.

President Francisco Franco of Spain, who desperately needed financial help and wheat from Argentina, sent word to Argentina in April 1947 that he would be conferring the Grand Cross of the Order of Isabel the Catholic Medal on First lady Evita.

Although Franco suggested he would send Evita the Cross, one of Spain's highest honors, Evita said she would come to Spain and pick it up herself.

After Spain, France would of course, be on Evita's itinerary. Why not? As long as they were going, Evita added Italy and Switzerland, too.

Male biographers, used to tossing a suit, tux, and three ties into a suitcase 30 minutes before departure, note with obvious shock and cluck-clucking disapproval that her luggage included "64 complete outfits, fur coats and a magnificent selection of jewelry."

Female writers, if there had been any, would wonder if that wardrobe was sufficient for a trip of eight weeks. Maybe 64 outfits weren't sufficient.

On an official trip representing a country, even with the minimal two outfit changes per day, with coordinating jewelry, 64 outfits would be enough clothes for only a month. And what about shoes, hats, hose, and handbags?

. . . .

In June 1947, the middle of the Argentine winter, Evita left on her first plane ride and her first trip to Europe. To wish her bien viaje, 150,000 Argentinians showed up at the airport.

"I go as a representative of the working people," she told them.

Juan decided not to accompany his wife, when his advisors counseled that visual public reminders of his World War II support of Generalissimo Franco's fascist regime in Spain might not resonate well in the post-World War II world.

It was Juan's wise choice, because nobody would have noticed him.

Juan would have found himself second fiddle to a glamorous wife who stole the show, as President John F. Kennedy famously did during a May 1961 visit to France with America's first lady.

114

At a June 2, 1961 conference in Paris, referring to his pushed-to-the-background role, President Kennedy told his audience: "I do not think it altogether inappropriate to introduce myself to this audience. I am the man who accompanied Jacqueline Kennedy to Paris. And, I have enjoyed it."

Shipping colossus Dodero also accompanied Evita on portions of her tour, as part of her entourage. He made several of his European homes and estates, and his yachts, available to Evita for rest and relaxation at her several European stops.

· · · · · · · ·

Evita went to Europe as a sort of good will ambassador. With his wife and daughter, Generalissimo Franco himself met her at the airport. As they drove through Madrid, balconies groaning with Madrileños shouted her name affectionately.

In every country she attended several formal social functions daily, and, sure enough, her attire was the favorite subject of press, who relished describing the several different outfits she wore during a single day

Evita was a smash hit. Boffo box office.

In Spain, fireworks, dancing, and displays greeted her almost everywhere she traveled. A handsome Spanish bullfighter grumbled one afternoon, pouting that everyone had come to see Evita, not him.

There is an unintentionally hilarious video of when, on a balcony in front of hundreds of thousands, Franco tried to place the Grand Cross of Isabel the Catholic around Evita's neck.

Her usual fashion advisor Liliane Guardo must have been off duty that day, because Evita chose a hat with an enormous feather decoration in the rounded shape of a very fluffy horse's tail more than a foot long, hanging down one side.

Generalissimo Franco, not known for his sense of humor or his height, makes several comical attempts to get the Grand Cross over Evita's hat and over the feathers. He finally succeeds, perhaps by praying that he would. Fighting the civil war in Spain must have seemed easy by comparison.

She is reported to have looked at the thousands assembled in the square, and whispered to Franco: "Next time you want a big crowd, contact me."

. . . .

In Rome, at the Argentine embassy, a crowd gathered outside chanting her name.

Just like home.

In Paris, Evita was driven in a vehicle that had belonged to President Charles deGaulle and had been used by British Prime Minister Winston Churchill.

Fashion never took a back seat. For future long distance purchases from Argentina, she left her measurements at the preeminent Paris fashion houses of the era.

Biographers relate her dazzling appearance in film star mode at an elegant reception for the Latin America diplomatic corps. She wore "a gold dress, skintight and décolleté, with a long fish-tail train, a gold veil over her blond hair, an enormous jeweled necklace, and gold sandals with jeweled heels."

Photos of this event bear witness to Evita's great beauty.

Evita had journeyed a light year's distance from her job as a 15-year-old cook in rural Junin, Argentina.

. . . .

Biographers nominate the years 1947-1950 as those when Evita began to be visibly powerful. Her power derived from her work with the poor, unions and women—through whom she amassed her own political coterie.

She knew that.

Evita's efforts as first lady were, in Argentine culture, tantamount to Lurleen's as Alabama first lady: opening the Alabama governor's mansion to the public, touring schools and hospitals, and accepting frequent speaking engagements at public receptions. On the side, each woman built her own power base.

Evita and Lurleen were careful not to challenge their husbands directly. They began by establishing their own political personalities within the context of what their husbands were accomplishing.

But each woman, intentionally or unintentionally, was also establishing a political base personal to her, based on her personal contacts, that was not derived from a spouse.

It was also the period within which Juan as president of Argentina coasted on updraft political winds, increasing his own power—as did George—serving de rigueur time in the Alabama state legislature as groundwork for his intended run for governor.

CHAPTER THIRTY FIVE
DID EUROPE INCLUDE COSMETIC SURGERY?
(SE INCLUIA EUROPA CIRUGIA COSMETICA?)

In Paris, Evita spent several days secluding herself in her suite at the Hotel Ritz, receiving few if any visitors. She blamed her uncharacteristic languor on the heat wave sweeping Europe that 1947 summer.

"She stayed at the Hotel Ritz but rarely left her suite. Her intense schedule and the extreme summer heat had exhausted her," explained one male biographer.

Historical records indicate that the press made no—even surface—inquires into this schedule detour.

The first discordant note in that explanation for her "hiding" from public view for several days in one of the most beautiful cities in the world was that she was born and raised in a country that is very hot for many months a year.

Surely functioning in intense heat would not be a new or enconquerable challenge for Evita Duarte Perón.

Secondly, in Argentina she had built a reputation for working extremely long hours, rising at 5 a.m. to go to her office for her work with the poor and needy. With the exception of a long lunch with Juan, she customarily did not return to Unzue Palace, the president's official residence, until very late in the evening— after

118

more intense hours in social welfare work, plus receiving official guests. In fact, Juan had complained about her long hours.

That strict regimen apparently never exhausted her.

But Spain and Paris did?

Unlikely.

Could she have, during her Paris time, been recuperating from facial cosmetic surgery? Paris would, of course, have some of the best plastic surgeons in the world.

· · · · · · · ·

Women generally keep plastic surgery quiet.

If she had cosmetic surgery in Argentina, the details would leak out in days. But in a foreign country, it would be easier to keep the damper on.

Two American facial plastic surgeons examined photos of Evita before her European trip, during, and after. Changes in her facial appearance seem to begin in the Paris photos, they indicated.

The possibilities include rhinoplasty, commonly known as a "nose job," they said. A bump at the top bridge of her nose appears the same before and after Paris. So perhaps any surgery was a partial "nose job," they suggest.

But the plastic surgeons noted other facial changes reflected in photos.

Their observations of possible rhinoplasty were based in part on a "notch"-like depression near each of Evita's nostrils, which is absent in photos before Paris. The notch narrows the appearance of the nose along the sides. In standard rhinoplasty in 1947, the nose cartiledge was actually cut to change the nose shape, they explained. Cosmetic surgeons discontinued the "notch" procedure after about 1970, the surgeons said.

By examining the photos, they also suggested that perhaps she had had some cosmetic surgical procedure done on her chin. Perhaps chin augmentation, or perhaps work to highlight or minimize a cleft in her chin.

Another possibility they suggested from examining photos, is surgery to change her jawline and cheek area. Reporter Fleur Cowles, one of the few females writing for American audiences about Evita, is quoted by another reporter as noting that after her European tour, Evita's face had a mask-like appearance. Cowles attributes this to illness.

But plastic surgery can also create a mask-like look.

The surgeons looked for tell-tale face lift scars along Evita's facial hairline, but found none visible in the photos—suggesting she did not have a facelift. But such scars are often not visible in photos and disappear into the hairline—which is the goal of a plastic surgeon, they explained.

Recuperation from rhinoplasty is relative short—two or three days, they added. But the bruising and splint are visible during that time. That analysis would match the time of Evita's self-imposed seclusion at the Ritz Hotel.

•　•　•　•　•　•　•　•

First lady Evita Perón "received the most tumultuous welcome back ever staged for any woman in the Americas," wrote one journalist describing Evita's August 23, 1947, return to Argentina after her knockout triumphal European tour. She had met the pope, and presidents had kissed her hand.

Her trip was an incontrovertible success. Her harshest critics could summon no reason to say otherwise.

A crowd of 250,000 greeted her with a chant: "Uno, dos, tres! Evita otra vez! (One, two three, Evita again!)"

A widely circulated photo of Evita in a mink coat at the bridge railing of her arriving ship shows her clutching a huge white scarf over her nose and a middle portion of her face. It is several times the size of an ordinary handkerchief. More like a towel.

The biographer attributes this very unusual pose for publicity-savvy Evita to her emotional tears on arriving home.

However, the cloth over face is a disconnect for an Evita who loved publicity. She loved having her photo taken. She understood what photographers wanted and accommodated them.

That she would chose to cover most of her face with a large cloth at the exact moment she well knew photographers would be snapping dozens of photos of her arriving is extraordinary.

Was that her attempt to conceal rhinoplasty or other recent cosmetic procedures that she feared photographs would reveal?

Apparently the cosmetic differences have always gone unnoticed until now.

Evita did believe in cosmetic procedures to improve appearance.

Juan suffered from dental issues, particularly pyorrhea, an unsightly disease of the gums often called bleeding gums. Evita reportedly suggested more than once that he have his teeth capped for a better appearance. It is unclear whether she had her teeth capped, although actresses and actors customarily do not shrink from cosmetic enhancements.

In the theatrical community where she got her start, actors and actresses were always trying to up their game face.

Some weeks after Evita's return from Europe, Liliane Guardo, Evita's long time attire and manners mentor and everyday companion, came to the mansion to replay some money she owed Evita. Mounting a stairway, Liliane was stopped by a guard.

Her husband had been expelled from Perón's inner circle. The two women, once inseparable in Evita's days as a freshman first lady, never saw each other again, writes a biographer who does not offer an explanation for the falling out.

Perhaps Liliane knew too much.

CHAPTER THIRTY SIX
BUILDING EVITA'S FOUNDATION
(CONSTRUYENDO LA FOUNDACION de EVITA)

*"She was not a woman's woman. Not a man's woman either.
But a woman politico. A woman too fabled, too capable, too sexless,
too overbearing, slick, sly, diamond-decked, revengeful, ambitious
and far, far too underrated for far too long by our world"*
—*Fleur Cowles, Journalist*

Evita herself had intimate, personal childhood experience
with poverty. Rural poverty is what she grew up in. So Evita's 1946
tours of factories and other working class venues, and her new
position of authority as Argentina's first lady, gave her an opportunity for personal expression related to her past life experiences
—just as similar personal visits gave Lurleen impetus for legislation assisting mental facilities.

"Still of them and with them," wrote one journalist describing
Evita's allure for the poor.

· · · · · · · ·

Now that she was First lady, Evita wanted to formally organize
countrywide social service assistance as a legal entity, funded
with private donations to help the poor.

On July 8, 1948, about a year after she returned from Europe
on August 23, 1947, Evita established the Maria Eva Duarte de
Perón Foundation, whose general charitable purpose was to help
the poor. The first donation was hers: 10,000 pesos.

Within a couple of years, the foundation tallied assets of about $200 million, with 14,000 workers. In addition to building 12 hospitals and a neighborhood of 600 basic houses, the foundation distributed shoes, sewing machines, cooking pots, and more.

"The Foundation coincided with the fat years of Perónism," wrote a biographer.

On a personal level, Evita made herself available each day to supplicants seeking personal requests such as jobs, food, dentures. One writer called it a tableau with Evita as a chess grand master playing multiple games simultaneously at high speed.

She spoke to each person personally.

Even her enemies praised the diplomacy, patience and kindness she displayed, untiringly, toward each supplicant. At times when the peso notes she kept handy to distribute to finance the poor's journey back to their villages in remote parts of Argentina dwindled, she would call out down the hallways to union and other officials waiting to see her, asking them to dig in their pockets to refill the depleted peso note jar.

Evita worked such long hours with her foundation that Juan complained he had lost his wife in the years 1950 and 1951. Eva would work all night for many nights and come back at dawn, passing Juan as he left for work at government house.

. . . .

In one of the most evocative of the thousands of photos taken of Evita Perón, she sits in darkness as a passenger waving from the lighted back seat of a uniformed chauffer-driven vehicle

124

with perfectly polished chrome and scrupulously clean white wall tires.

A huge outdoor clock, like London's Big Ben, is illuminated above her registering 4:45.

Because the viewer does not know, in the darkness, if it is 4:45 a.m. or 4:45 p.m. it is ambiguous whether Evita is going to her charitable work with the poor or returning home after a long day of charitable work with the poor.

Her severest critics conceded that she refused to leave her office until she had seen every petitioner waiting.

Her young, beautiful 28-year-old face is almost perfectly half lit in the photo, with the left side in shadow, and the right side illuminated from the car's interior light. The inadvertent divide seems to bespeak the two women she was: the Eva Duarte born in the darkness of illegitimacy and poverty, and the French couture fashion first lady Evita Perón who earned her way into the great glamorous star light of furs, jewels, mansions, and power of world-wide recognition.

She has what appears to be a genuine smile of genuine happiness. Whatever she is going to or coming from delights her soul.

She is wearing a stiff, round straw hat with a wide black band, tipped rakishly to one side, to which a clump of artificial flowers is affixed.

· · · · · · ·

The foundation work completely changed Evita.

Her biographers write that her passion for her foundation work helping the poor attained the devotional level of a mission.

Her Parisian haute couture frocks and high-end flashy jewelry were replaced by black suits, cut like a uniform, described as "now the costume of seriousness and dedication."

Elegant dress hats, stored in a special room in the presidential residence—her visual identity trademark—were an exception. Evita continued wearing the beautiful hats from time to time.

Evita created controversy when she routinely allowed the poor to kiss or touch her, and she would kiss them in return.

"She could touch the most terrible things with a Christian attitude," wrote a poet.

Biographers note that Evita kissed a young girl whose "lip was eaten away by syphilis." She allowed lepers to kiss her.

Historical records indicate contradictorily both that she did not know then that she was dying of uterine cancer and the opposite: that she did know of her cancer and her impending death. Also, there are ambiguous statements that her cancer diagnosis was generally known to the public, and other writing that the diagnosis was known only by Juan and a very few confidantes who in 1950, when her cancer was first diagnosed, did not tell her.

Her casual disregard for her personal hygienic safety in these encounters with the sick and diseased could indicate that she well knew her days of remaining life were winding down quickly. Perhaps she reasoned that in her imperiled health situation, there was nothing to lose by touching others near death.

Whom she touched or allowed to touch her mattered little if her death were imminent anyway.

"Time is my greatest enemy," Evita told a journalist during this time period.

CHAPTER THIRTY SEVEN
WHEN A MAN SEEKS THE PRIZE OF HIS LIFE

"When a man seeks the prize of his life, he does not stop to count the horses" is a Native American aphorism describing a suitor's all-consuming, unhesitating ardor toward possessing his desired lover. Brides were sometimes attained by the "payment" of large numbers of horses.

For George, being elected to the governorship of Alabama, was, at that time, the political prize he had worked and planned toward all of his life. His "bride" he was courting, so to speak.

However many "horses" were the necessary "price" to be paid for consummating his passion, he planned to herd them right up pronto without quibbling the count.

George Wallace woke each morning thinking about votes and went to bed each night thinking about votes, a biographer noted. No price was too high, no avenue too long, too narrow, too bumpy, too daunting.

His judicial term would end in 1959. He officially launched his governor's campaign on January 20, 1958. But he had been laying the political groundwork for decades. He was 38 years old.

The escalating strain on their distanced marital relationship was somewhat eased by George's purchasing for Lurleen a three-bedroom house in Clayton, with a yard and front porch across from a Baptist church.

Lurleen, 30, was relieved to move with their three children out of rented rooms.

But a home at last was to be another home alone, a small consolation for Lurleen. George's habitual neglect of her and their children was about to ratchet through the roof.

· · · · · · · ·

He had 12 opponents (some sources say 14) in the Democratic primary, the only primary that really mattered because Republicans were without power in Alabama at that time.

Although Lurleen rarely spoke publicly at campaign events she attended, she worked tirelessly behind the scenes in the non-Internet era, addressing, stamping, and mailing campaign materials after working part time at the courthouse and mothering—alone — three children ages 14, 8, and 2.

She made hundreds of phone calls on George's behalf at a time when each number could not be punched in quickly, but each number had to be dialed, waiting for the metal circle to slowly reset after each digit.

Occasionally, mainly on weekends, George featured George Jr., 6 years old, with him on the campaign stage, beckoning the child forward to repeat "With God's help, my Daddy will make you a good governor."

Photos show George Jr. in suit and tie, standing on a folding chair near a podium, with George holding onto his son's trouser leg, presumably in an attempt to keep him from falling.

But despite George's foot-to-the-floor strenuous campaigning, he lost to Attorney General John Patterson, a sympathetic young figure statewide whose father, Albert, a 1954 candidate for Attorney General, was gunned down by mobsters 17 days after he won the statewide post. Albert's campaign rhetoric had focused on investigating gambling figures in Phenix City, a border town with Georgia, and a military base.

·   ·   ·   ·   ·   ·   ·   ·

Patterson, who endorsed continuing racial segregation more strongly than Wallace and had Ku Klux Klan support, would be, by law, governor only four years. Like all Alabama governors, Patterson was limited to one four-year term by the state constitution.

In another truth-is-stranger-than-fiction twist, years later Patterson and Preston Clayton, George's former political opponents for the governorship, represented George as co-counsel in a skirmish over a court order that George allow inspection of Barbour County voting records. Eventually, after a long hide-and-seek, nya-nya-nya game with the feds, George allowed limited inspection.

·   ·   ·   ·   ·   ·   ·   ·

The day after his 1958 defeat, George, by all accounts, was despondent, disconsolate.

But his recovery was quick.

Seeing daylight and opportunity in the term limit that would automatically eject Patterson four years hence, George began campaigning for the 1962 governorship within days of his loss of the 1958 battle.

Starting in Montgomery, he began shaking hands with everyone he met, thanking them for the vote he received. Whether they had actually voted for him mattered little.

For George, the past campaign was mere prologue.

Lurleen was not amused.

Their wobbly marital relationship, eviscerated by consecutive years of campaigning, financial hardship for her and their children, his near-constant absence, and the expense of the statewide governor's race just run, would reach critical mass.

Meltdown.

CHAPTER THIRTY EIGHT
A LONELY AND PAINFUL TIME

Despite years of adversity in her marital relationship with George, friends universally describe Lurleen as, in her interactions with them, upbeat with a well developed sense of humor.

"Lurleen was very private. George was gone all the time and she never knew when he was going to be there. She had all the responsibility of the household and raising the children," her friend Mary Jo said.

"My husband was working two jobs, so Lurleen and I spent a lot of time together in Clayton from 1946, and after I moved to Montgomery when she was elected governor.

"I taught home economics at the school, which was two houses away from their house. The back of their house was situated so she could go out her backdoor and cross over to the backdoor of the Home Economics building. At 10 a.m. when the children had recess, she would come out her door, and come in the back door of the Home Ec building. We called it 'Turn the pot on.' I'd come in the kitchen and we'd sit there and drink coffee during recess."

Lurleen continued chain smoking Benson & Hedges cigarettes.

Did Lurleen ever mention to Mary Jo or discuss her troubles with George because he was an absent husband and father?

"Yes."

"And did Lurleen say that she and George discussed divorce?"

"Oh, yes. And I had problems with my husband. We had a lot of similar experiences to talk about and cry about, and laugh about.

She was frustrated, and she always knew I was frustrated of things happening I couldn't do anything about.

"We shared secrets we'd never tell anybody. We don't tell the secrets."

Mary Jo's tone implies she does not intend to divulge those secrets even now.

"Lurleen would get so mad at George she could pop. That would be when he had promised to be home, like to go to the children's recital or something at the school, and then he wouldn't make it. That made her mad with him. He didn't put the family first.

"When we first moved to Clayton, my husband had a big back-yard garden. He sold vegetables to the grocery stores. I came in from teaching school and did the bookwork for the grocery store. Then we ran the picture show. He was manager of the picture show, and I sold tickets. My husband started in the bank (in Clayton) as a teller. Finally we bought the majority of the stock, and he became president of the bank."

CHAPTER THIRTY NINE
THE BROKEN ROAD

"A few miles out of town, the grass blows long. Out here, the present leaves you. Nearby, the farm, your grandfather's—is empty and the sun still shines through curtains in a room you liked to sleep in when you came here, shines on fields he showed you—miles of summer days."
At the Cemetery Near Mendon—for John Anonymous

Peggy Wallace Kennedy, even in her 60s, remains a beautiful woman. Candidly describing herself as "boy crazy" in her teens, petite Peggy projects earnest grace and unvarnished honesty about her childhood as George and Lurleen's second daughter, born in 1950.

Hers is not candor that engenders unease or pity in the listener. Rather, it evokes admiration for the frank, non-spin perspective she has forged as an offspring of historical, very politically famous parents.

Peggy lives near Montgomery, married to retired State Court Judge Mark Kennedy, with whom she has two adult sons. Peggy holds a 1973 bachelor degree in special education from Troy State University, Troy, Alabama. She has taught in Birmingham.

Peggy's first memory of her mother is first grade, when Lurleen came to her school as a substitute teacher. Parents were sometimes called in as substitute teachers, even though they did not have college educations, she explained

Peggy was about six years old.

"Since my mother was the teacher, I thought I could do anything. I was very mischievous. That didn't work out so well.

"I went up in front of the class and said about 50 times 'I want

133

to go to the bathroom.' Finally she said: 'Sit down! You can't go to the bathroom again!'

"But I remember well that I was very proud that she was in the room, and that she was the teacher that day.

"We were all close to her, because (George) was gone a lot. That really was the way it was at home. Politics is the family business, like a shoe salesman or a meat man. We were glad to see him when he came home. But she kept the home fires burning."

Without rancor, Peggy describes Lurleen as a disciplinarian, who meted out physical punishment when punishment was deserved.

"If we did bad, she would tell us to go outside alone and find a switch from a tree or bush. She gave us the option of selecting the size of the switch. You didn't want to select a too small switch, because then she might have you go back to select a larger one. And you didn't want to choose a too big switch, because, if she used that selection, it could really hurt.

"So we all chose a medium sized switch. And Mother wasn't shy about using it," Peggy remembered. She relates the anecdote with affection and a smile.

Physical punishment for childhood transgressions was not unusual. It was the widely accepted custom and fashion of the time in America.

CHAPTER FORTY
YOU'LL DRIVE AWAY

"You'll drive away as if to school and winter, leave behind the house, the
filled barn, supper, all you have—knowing again you leave,
and never leave"
At the Cemetery Near Mendon-for John Anonymous

Achieving a perspective on the 1957-1962 year period of her parents' disintegrating marriage, after George lost a first race for governor in 1957-1958, then immediately began campaigning again for the 1962 governorship, has been difficult goal for Peggy Wallace Kennedy as an adult.

Those were the blighted years when Lurleen's vexations with George's chronic absences and inability or unwillingness to earn a living for them reached a nuclear meltdown.

George Jr. described it as "a sad and lonely time."

During the rare moments George was home, he and Lurleen argued nearly constantly and violently. Through the walls, the children could hear their parents screaming at each other.

George Jr. writes in his book about his father that when they heard the violent screaming, the children "heard things hit the wall."

That is an attention-getting sentence.

What "things" hit the wall? Why did anything "hit the wall"?

One conclusion is that the "things hitting the wall" were a human being hitting the wall. A further conclusion is that in domestic violence, the male is usually the aggressor and does the hitting.

Therefore, a conclusion, from his son's writing, could be that

George was physically abusing Lurleen—that he was hitting, kicking, or punching or pushing his wife against the wall, or causing her to lose her balance so that she fell against the wall.

He was a trained boxer who knew how to punch leaving a mark, and how to punch without leaving a mark.

. . . .

Lurleen and the three children bolted for a time, to Lurleen's parents home in Knoxville, Alabama.

Whatever of George's misdeeds impelled Lurleen to finally, actually physically flee the house must have exceeded the usual financial and emotional deprivations George meted out.

Hitting her could fall into that category.

How long did they all stay in Knoxville?

"Long enough for me to go to school there." Peggy said.

Reliable sources confirm the accuracy of previously printed stories of George's sexual dalliances outside marriage during this time and other times. Lurleen complained to friends about it. He was unfaithful to Lurleen with many women, these sources confirm.

George always denied it.

It was a bitter time, a chaotic, negative atmosphere that did not escape the children's notice.

As an adult, with her husband and adult son Barnes, Peggy returned to visit Knoxville, the small town where Lurleen's parents lived, and where Lurleen and the children fled from George.

The rural house she knew and experienced happiness in as a child with her maternal grandparents had deteriorated drastically.

Grass and weeds had grown up very high in the inexorable steathful embrace of time passing. Peggy remembers watching as her young son Barnes ran through the accumulated brush, joyously picking wildflowers for her.

The symbolism of the beauty of flowers growing out of the same ground that constituted the childhood refuge of her memory, presented to her in a bouquet of affection and innocence by her son, evoked Peggy's mixed memory of past and present indistinguishable in those moments of time collapsed.

"MaMaw and Mr. Henry's house had fallen in. I was very upset. That was my safe place." Peggy cries openly, still experiencing, as if it were present moment—not five decades later—the frightening marital discord between Lurleen and George that sent them fleeing to this safe house in the Alabama farm country.

Now the safe house was gone, as were Lurleen and George. There was no more safe house. Even now that there was no longer Peggy's need for a safe house, Peggy still experienced the fear and what the need for that place of safety had felt like. What if the need returned, now that the safe house and MaMaw and Mr. Henry all were gone too?

· · · · · · · ·

"There were a lot of problems between my Mom and my Dad. They had really loud arguments behind closed doors. So when the problems came, Mom would just take us and drive to Knoxville to our grandparents. (Lurleen) had had it with (George)."

So longstanding rumors that Lurleen intended to divorce George are true?

"Oh, yes." Peggy responded unhesitatingly.

Lurleen always sidestepped the divorce question by quickly changing the subject.

"When we would drive the road to Knoxville, going into the country, there was another road up to the side where the asphalt came up. We called it the broken road.

"Then we knew the road to turn to go down to MaMaw and Mr. Henry's road was very close. We would be so happy because when we saw the broken road, we knew we were close to safety and happiness."

It was that unhappy with your mother and (George)?

"Yes. He just couldn't give (politics and campaigning) up. He was driven. That's just the way he was. But we loved him very much.

"They moved several times. When he was elected judge, that meant more money. That made mother happier. She thought that money would maybe bring some sort of stability to the family, which it didn't. It just drove him more," Peggy said.

Lurleen never confided their desperate financial straits to the children, except—Peggy said—maybe with Bobbie, the oldest.

CHAPTER FORTY ONE
UNQUIET LIVES

Photos are worth 1,000 words.

"I've seen lots and lots of photos of her (Lurleen) way back then when we lived in Clayton. And the pictures of mother are of loneliness, and of...let's see if I can find the word," Peggy said.

Abandoned?

"That's it!"

Resignation?

"Yes: This is it. I'm never going to get out."

Trapped?

"Trapped."

How old was she then?

"24."

So Lurleen is 24 years old, with three young children and no money, and George is always absent?

"Yes. No money."

That could be very depressing.

"Yes."

"My grandparents did not like (George). They wanted us to stay, and live with them."

"She was their daughter. They did not like the way (George) was treating her.

"(George) came there (to Knoxville) once...or, maybe a few times. But he always bragged about how he put running water and a bathroom in my grandparents' house.

"They had an outdoor toilet, which I thought was fun," Peggy said with an tonal edge of defiance toward her father's gift of the bathroom.

. . . .

Children's recollections match and vary, depending on or reflecting the phase of their parent's relationship into which they were born and their observational skills.

Daughter Bobbie Wallace, the firstborn in 1944, remembers the bleak 1946-61 years in Clayton when George was running for the four-year state legislative terms beginning in 1947 and 1951, then for the 1953 judgeship, the 1958 governor's race, which he lost, followed by George's grim, raw aftermath 1958 gubernatorial rerun for a term beginning in 1962.

Both Bobbie and George Jr. particularly recall the 1946 -1961 financial hard times when Lurleen's low level clerk jobs in Clayton provided almost their sole income. Sometimes her meager earnings were insufficient for even bare basics of life: food.

"She would have to borrow money for food," George Jr. remembers.

"I think there was some embarrassment there too, because mother would send *me* to the grocery to charge food," Bobbie said.

One historian quotes a family friend describing George's parsimonious disengagement: "He'd dole out about $5 a week and expect Lurleen to buy groceries and keep herself and the children clothed with that. When she'd complain, he'd tell her how much money she was wasting."

CHAPTER FORTY TWO

DIVORCING GEORGE WAY MORE THAN RUMOR

Both George Jr. and Bobbie Jo remember that George and Lurleen separated formally with a formal separation agreement. They estimate it was in the mid- to late 1950s.

Other sources indicate Lurleen left George about 1959-61 during the time he was running a desperate, nail-biting second time for Alabama governor. The children estimate the formal separation lasted about two months, but continuous marital discord caused shorter separations many prior times.

"We moved to her parents' tiny two-bedroom home in Knoxville. George and Lurleen separated formally. Mother was serious. She had had it," Bobbie said.

"It was similar to the time when I was a toddler, that mother took me to where dad was playing poker. Her message to George was: Let me get your attention. I'm serious about this.

"I remember being very glad to go (to her grandparents) because it would be quieter.

"Mother and dad argued a lot. Through the walls (as a child) you hear things. Just voices. You didn't know what they were saying," Bobbie said.

"Dad was ambitious and focused like a laser," George Jr. said. "Everything else around him was just…"

"Superfluous" Bobbie jumped in quickly to complete her brother's sentence.

• • • • • • • •

"Yes, there was a formal, legal separation agreement," Bobbie Jo revealed.

Did Bobbie herself see an actual document?

"Yes!" Bobbie responded quickly and emphatically.

"After the separation, mother got the deep freezer. Literally. It was mentioned in the formal separation agreement. Can you imagine something like a freezer being such an important thing at that time?" Bobbie said.

"That freezer was never moved out of the house in Clayton," Bobbie added, perhaps implying that even then there were cracks in Lurleen's resolve to take the next legal step: to obtain an actual divorce.

"Mother talked to me about the formal separation."

What did she say?

"That (George) was gone so much. And no money. And that wasn't the life she wanted. But she loved him deeply. She wanted one thing. He wanted something else," Bobbie said.

"I was mother's (ally), right or wrong. I was mother's confidante. She really didn't have anybody she could talk to. Just Mary Jo Ventress and me," Bobbie explained.

Psychiatrists call children in Bobbie's ally role the "Hero Child."

"Their two ambitions collided. Mother wanted a home, family and tranquility. He wanted to be governor of Alabama. It's very difficult to stay home and become a governor," George Jr. added, asking Bobbie about a photo he remembered from the time Lurleen left George.

"Is that the picture when (George) would come to MaMaw's? I am holding his left leg. He's got a suit on. You and mother looked tense standing beside him," George Jr. continued.

"Yes. That picture's in my office," Bobbie Jo responded quickly in flat tones.

George Jr. recounts in his 2011 book about his father that Bobbie Jo and their father George were estranged for many, many years. "In her young life, she and my father would have heated arguments as Bobbie took mother's side," George Jr. wrote.

Bobbie's confrontations with her father, in her mother's defense, are psychiatric textbook "Hero Child" patterns.

Bobbie and her father reconciled in her father's final years, George Jr. writes.

In interviews, Bobbie did not say this. She remains silent at George Jr's comment about reconciliation.

. . . .

Lurleen always used humor to deflect questions about whether she considered divorcing George in the 1952 period. She even laughed when reporter Anita Smith and others asked her point-blank or wrote about the divorce rumors.

"I do wish that writer had identified the friends who saved me from divorcing George. I need to look them up and thank them," Lurleen told Smith blithely.

It was a nuanced lawyer-like response. Not a confirmation, not a denial. Masterful.

No one asked about a separation agreement.

CHAPTER FORTY THREE
WAS EVITA TOLD ABOUT HER CANCER?
(FUE EVITA INFORMADA SOBIA SU CANCER?)

In January 1950, Evita fainted at a ribbon cutting and was taken to a hospital where, the newspapers said, she had her appendix removed.

She may or may not have had an appendectomy. But the overriding diagnosis was much darker and foreboding.

Although it was not publicly aired in 1950, as part of medical procedures, a doctor performed tests whose results he apparently disclosed privately to Juan only, and not to Evita, indicating that Evita was suffering from uterine cancer.

At that stage of discovery, apparently her cancer could have been treated, although the treatments were not yet sophisticated.

What happened then, and what happened next is clouded by varied and contradictory historical accounts that are difficult to reconcile .

Some biographers suggest that although her physicians knew in 1950 that she had cancer, they told Juan, but did not tell Evita.

Juan decided not to tell his wife that she had cancer, according to some accounts. To some degree, keeping alarming medical news from patients, particularly female patients, was an accepted culture of the time.

Also, Juan may have been wary of how that revelation about First lady Evita might impact his political fortunes.

According to other scholars, a physician did inform Evita in person in 1950 that she had uterine cancer and recommended that she have her uterus removed, a hysterectomy. Those versions have Evita angrily refusing the hysterectomy that physicians may have suggested.

Other accounts indicate that although Juan did not tell Evita what the physicians told him, she found out in some manner before the cancer recurred approximately a year later.

Exactly what transpired regarding Evita's initial uterine cancer diagnosis is cloudy. Whether Evita was offered treatment but declined, or like Lurleen, was not offered an opportunity to make that personal decision, is inconclusive. But the fact that Evita, like Lurleen, had no medical treatment to stop the spread, after an initial medical indications, is clearer.

For Juan, Evita's cancer diagnosis at 31 years old must have been overwhelming déjà vu. His first wife Aurelia Tizon died of uterine cancer at age 29.

Although he apparently knew, from conversations with her physicians, that Evita had cancer, he continued referring to her condition, publicly and privately, as anemia.

Whether this was his political subterfuge because his political fortunes so closely depended on maintaining her glamorous full-of-life profile, or his personal "in denial" stage, or Evita's request to

Juan for personal privacy, is unknown.

Perhaps, if Juan was hiding the cancer report from Evita, calling it anemia was his way of concomitantly concealing the seriousness of her illness from the Argentine public as well as from her.

. . . .

In the days following her 1950 cancer diagnosis, Evita worked even harder meeting the poor and distributing assistance from her foundation—which might suggest that she did know of her cancer and was in a race-against-time mode.

Evita's focus on the poor had begun just after Juan's 1946 inauguration when she joined him, as first lady, in visiting factories. Then she began visiting factories alone, as well as stopping at other venues of the poor. Even though Evita had come from a humble backgound, she had not fully grasped the extent of the needs of the working poor.

Evita's physicians insisted that she rest on weekends at San Vicente quinta ranch. She and Juan had spent time there in the first halcyon days of their marriage.

When Juan had the phone wires cut to keep her off the phone while at the ranch, she had the lines reconnected so she could work with her foundation by phone.

Descriptions of the few companionable days she and Juan spent at San Vicente read like romantic scenes from the films "Dr. Zhivago" or "The Way We Were." "She cooked a little, rode horses with Perón and wore his lieutenant's tunic..........."

Evita and Lurleen, both products of childhoods on a farm, were accomplished horsewomen. Evita kept a horse or two at the Estancia ranch she and Juan used on weekends. Lurleen kept a horse for many years at her brother-in-law Gerald's farm where she traveled regularly to ride.

These years just before her death were, for Evita, both the height of her ascendant power and her descent from life itself.

As with Lurleen, a continent away and 16 years later, Evita's applause and requiem shared the same time slot in her Cinderella life.

CHAPTER FORTY FOUR
A RACE AGAINST TIME: RENUNCIATION
(UNA CARRERA CONTRA RELOJ: RENUNCIA)

Nine days after the dramatic August 22, 1951 Cabildo Abierto crowds of two million fans shouted their love and fervent support, imploring her to run for vice president, Evita announced in an August 31, 1951, evening radio broadcast that she would not run for the office.

The day became known as her "day of renunciation."

Few if any of the millions who heard her statement on the radio, her sentences interspersed with moments of her silence, knew what intense machinations among the ruling military junta had preceded her emotional announcement.

All that would come to light later.

As they huddled around their radios, listening intently to her familiar voice resounding on the airwaves across the grassy pampas and the crowded impoverished urban miserias listening intently, Eva began:

"It is my irrevocable decision to refuse the honor which the workers and the people of my country wished to confer on me at the open forum of August 22, 1951.

"I declare that this decision was born in my innermost consciousness and is therefore perfectly free and has all the force of my final will.

"I have passed the best years of my life at the side of General Perón, my master. I have no higher goal in life than to continue to serve him and the people of Argentina.

"I am not resigning my work, just the honors. I will continue as a humble collaborator of Perón.

"I only want history to say of me: There was a woman alongside General Perón. A woman who took to him the hopes and needs of the people. Her name was Evita," Evita concluded.

. . . .

Among the people, Evita's declination of running for vice president took on an aura of selfless sacrifice.

Scholars and pundits have multiple theories of what transpired behind the scenes, none of which involved self-sacrifice.

One conjecture is that Perón did not want his wife to run. She could not go against his decision, according to biographers. This theory lacks a rationale of why Juan would not have wanted her to run. He was her champion, and nothing appeared to have changed his support.

One of the weakest presentments was that because "only" 250,000 supporters turned out for the August 22, 1951 Perón y Perón rally, Evita did not have sufficient popular support.

However, no one could remember any political figure who had attracted 250,000 fans for anything.

Speculation that First lady Evita could not run because the Constitution required candidates to be at least 30 years old was dashed when the "too young" rumormongers were reminded that Evita may have shaved two years off her date of birth by arranging to have the page with her year of birth torn out of the registrar's book in Junin, then having her date of birth altered from 1919 (the real date) to 1921. So in actuality, Evita did meet the 30 years of age requirement for vice president.

Another premise was that the men in the ruling junta pressured Juan into dissuading Evita because if Perón died or was assassinated, Evita would become not only president, but commander-in-chief of the armed forces. That, the military men could not countenance. A female telling them what to do and how and when to do it? No way, no how, they told Perón.

Women were not allowed to serve in the armed forces, never mind being commander-in-chief therof.

Junta members told him that if he allowed Evita to run for vice president, they would move against him in a way that would not be fun for him. He would lose his job as president. He could even lose his life they implied.

To see archival photos of some of them is to understand what Juan understood: These humorless men with small narrow moustaches and cold eyes were no longer to be trifled with.

To echo American actor Marlon Brando's character in the unforgettable "Godfather" movie screenplay, the junta operatives made Juan Perón "an offer he could not refuse."

· · · · · · ·

150

But the 1951 reality on which Evita's decision was predicated might have been irrefutable medical facts, residual from 1950, which could not be changed by any human threats or human political maneuvering.

In a few weeks, it became apparent that Evita's health, at age 30, had sharply declined. She was pale, thinner, with dark shadows around her eyes. Her legs were permanently swollen.

To those who loved and appreciated her, the August 31 to November 6 downward slide in her physical appearance—in which she always took such great pride—was ominous.

· · · · · · · ·

On Nov 6, 1951 Evita had a second gynecological surgery, a hysterectomy. The true diagnosis and surgery were made public this time.

Historical accounts have scant information as to what cancer treatments, other than surgery, Evita may or may not have had in this time period. Radiation? Chemotherapy? The archival record is largely blank.

On November 11, a ballot box was taken to her bedside so she could vote. Presumably she was one of four million Argentine women, voting for the very first time, who voted for Perón.

For Evita, there must have been overwhelming satisfaction because she got to vote for Juan for the very first time, and she got to vote for women candidates who were running for the first time.

But bittersweet because she must have known that she

151

would not live to observe how the female candidates fared through time and experience.

As officials left Unzue palace carrying the ballot box into which the extremely ill Evita had just thrust her ballot, Argentinians kneeling on the pavement to pray for her, reverently asked to touch the box that Evita had touched, accounts record.

Argentina's women, in their first opportunity to have a say in who represented them, elected six women senators and 23 women deputies. Women were also elected to office in municipalities and other smaller governmental entities.

From her death bed, Evita must have been as proud as a parent to see her years of leadership in getting women the right to vote yield such political bounty. If she couldn't make it to the top, maybe some of those first-time-elected women would someday — even if she were not alive to see it happen.

· · · · · · · ·

Although her appearance was shrunken and she had some difficulty walking, she attended Juan's June 4, 1952 swearing in for a second term as president of Argentina.

On that June 4 occasion, Juan publicly bestowed on her the title "Spiritual Leader of the Nation." It was an honor she would have fleeting time to savor.

She appeared then for the final time, in a public motorcade after Juan's June 4 swearing in, riding with Juan in an open vehicle down the Avenia de Mayo, waving to the adoring crowd. Her wave was more than the usual acknowledgement of her fans.

Her gesture was a true wave Goodbye: *Adios mis descamisados, amores de mi vida. Adios.*

She wore the spectacular Collar of the Order of St. Martin, which rivaled some of the Bristish crown jewels.

Visible in historic photos of Evita and Juan in the June 4 parade, its center is a diamond and emerald rosette containing an image of St. Martin, Argentina's Liberator, against a background of 16 gold and platinum rays. The jewelry piece features 758 diamonds, plus emeralds and rubies, "bridged by 3,800 platinum and gold elements."

Concealed under her full length mink coat was a wood structure designed to support Evita beside Juan in the vehicle's back seat, because she was too weak to stand on her own. She wore huge round diamond earrings and a small white silk off-the-face hat embroidered with black leafy branches and a tiny black veil overlay.

Haute couture hats were her identifying "trademark."

On July 9, when she and Juan failed to appear for traditional Flag Day activities, her *descamisados* and others began organizing prayer masses for her all across Argentina. There were indications Evita was being treated with powerful pain-killing drugs.

A congresswoman, newly elected when women could vote

for the first time, fainted in the legislature while on her knees in the aisle beseeching God to save Evita.

All over Argentina people sobbed and prayed, overcome with profound sorrow they could not contain.

On July 21, in a desperate gesture, Juan summoned two German cancer specialists who arrived on July 24. But it was too late, historical accounts note.

. . . .

On the afternoon of July 26, 1952, she lapsed into extremis. Like Lurleen, she weighed 80 pounds or less.

About 8:25 p.m. with Juan at her bedside in the Unzue Palce, Evita Duarte Perón died in her room with a window overlooking the river Plata.

Her mother Juana and her priest, the Jesuit, tall, young Hernan Benetiz, were there too. In Evita's now lifeless hand, she held the gold rosary given to her by Pope Pius XII during her 1947 Vatican library audience with him on her European tour.

Thirty days of official morning were announced.

At Juan's request, Spanish pathologist Dr. Pedro Arias began the process of embalming Evita's body, which had to be accomplished almost immediately to be effective in preserving her remains undefiled. He assured Perón that when he finished, Evita's body would never decompose.

Evita's death was the same month and day that Lurleen met George in Tuscaloosa Kress' for the first time exactly 10 years earlier.

CHAPTER FORTY FIVE
MOURNING EVITA: FAREWELL OUR LADY
(LAGRIMOS POR EVITA: ADIOS NUESTRA SENORA)

For several hours after the announcement of her death, an eerie stillness—an absence of sound—enveloped the bustling city of Buenos Aires, as if the significance of an event had hushed an entire country. Stores and cinemas closed or did not open. Traffic began disappearing from the usually clogged roadways.

Residents were psychologically processing the fact that Evita Duarte Perón, whom they thought larger than life, was dead at the age of 33 years.

A van took Evita's white mahogany coffin with silver trim from Unzue Palace to the Ministry of Labor, where she had spent so many days helping the poor, who came to her in the same gold domed room where her body was placed on a horseshoe-shaped bier of white and mauve orchids.

She was dressed in a flowing white garment, her head resting on a small white pillow.

As news of her death spread across the huge country, crowds began gathering, swarming around the ministry shouting: "We want to see her." Many knelt on the rain-soaked streets to pray in the cold Argentine winter.

Flowers piled up 20 feet high against the walls of the building and overflowed into the street.

Finally, police let crowds into the building.

As July 27, 1952 dawned, more than two million people began lining up, waiting in orderly rows of lines for more than 15 hours each—four abreast—just to glimpse Evita's corpse for 20 seconds. Sixteen persons were crushed to death in the crowd. Four thousand people were hospitalized.

All the anguish, praise and tumult was verified for history, captured on astonishing black and white photos.

As her August 9, 1952, memorial cortege, thirty five members of the Perónist Women's Party, which Evita founded, and the national labor federation, dressed in black trousers and white shirts, pulled her coffin on a carriage that the two million attendees showered with flowers along the route to the National Congress for the service.

Years after her death, memorial events in her honor continue to be held.

CHAPTER FORTY SIX
EVITA'S BODY HIDDEN IN ITALY
(*CUERPO DE EVITA ESCONDIDO IN ITALIA*)

From 1951-1955 Evita's embalmed body was displayed in her former office, while a monument and permanent tomb was being constructed in Buenos Aires.

But when Juan was ousted as president in a 1955 coup, and fled to exile in Spain, even possession of a photo of Juan or Evita was punishable by imprisonment. Unzue Palace, an architectural and historical national treasure, was leveled to the ground, its contents sacked and destroyed.

The new military government, in scenarios reminiscent of a James Bond movie, secretly removed Evita's body, transported her body to Italy, and buried it in a Milan grave under another name.

After Juan's 1974 death, his third wife, Isabel, who succeeded him as the first female president of Argentina, had Evita's body to Argentina where it was placed beside Juan's remains in the Olives presidential palace.

When yet another junta seized power in 1976 by ousting Isabel, Juan's body was re buried in the Perón family plot at La Chacorita Cemetery in Buenos Aires.

Evita's remains were relocated in 1976 to the Duarte family

vault in Buenos Aires' famous La Recoleta Cemetery, where officials say it remains today.

Largely because of the 1976 Broadway musical and 1996 film about her life, Evita's tomb is a major tourist attraction.

Upon entering La Recoleta Cemetery, helpful "guides" step forward offering, for a fee, to show tourists to Evita's last resting place. A left turn after the entrance, and down a tree-shaded walk a short way, is a structure resembling a small house, where, government authorities say, Evita's remains rest two stories underground through double trap doors for which only her family members retain keys.

Contemporary admirers leave fresh flowers at the site.

CHAPTER FORTY SEVEN
WHAT HAPPENED TO JUAN AFTER EVITA?
(QUE PASA A JUAN DESPUES DE EVITA?)

As a second-term president of Argentina, Juan was at his apogee of power at Evita's 1952 death.

But his second term, without "the woman alongside Perón" as Evita described herself, did not go well for Juan.

In the words of a classic Spanish song: *Sin ti, no podria vivir*: Without you, I cannot live.

The economy faltered because of a drought and a trade deficit.

Juan made the fatal mistake of attacking the Roman Catholic Church of which a majority of the population were adherents. "Evita never would have allowed Juan to do that," observed one journalist.

The church responded by excommunicating Juan.

Without Evita's guidance, Juan seemed rudderless, making a series of bad decisions.

On September 19, 1955, the Army and Navy joined as a junta to jettison Juan, who fled to Paraguay and then to an 18-year exile in Spain, from where he still was able to influence the vote of about 20 per cent of Argentinians, according to historical records.

Because he was banned from Argentina, Juan, then 78 years old, successfully ran a stand-in in the 1973 election. The stand-in promptly invited Juan to return home to Argentina.

At the Buenos Aires airport, 3.5 million people greeted him.

The stand-in resigned. Perón and a third wife, Isabel, were elected president and vice president a few months later, with 62 percent of the vote.

But Juan died in office of a heart attack on July 1, 1974. Isabel, by law, inherited Juan's presidency, but was deposed by a 1976 coup.

CHAPTER FORTY EIGHT
THY BROTHER'S KEEPER: GERALD

By most written accounts, George's two-years-younger brother Gerald, second born of three Wallace brother-lawyers, was a grown-rich influence peddler: a loud, heavy drinker like his father; an indiscreet, sometimes crude braggart, often married, lacking in even minimal social graces.

Whatever the accuracy of that portrait by many adult observers outside the family, Uncle Gerald was viewed favorably through childhood perspective of his nephew George Jr, who describes Uncle Gerald as "low key."

George Jr. remembers Uncle Gerald as a kindly father-substitute for George, the eternally absent father they rarely saw. George Jr. particularly, bristles at any even slightly unfavorable description of Uncle Gerald, whom he idolized.

George Jr. remains perhaps Gerald's sole admirer.

A 1972 IRS investigation of Gerald, an attorney, failed to reveal any improprieties. However, in a 1990 plea agreement, Gerald was sentenced to two years in prison, suspended, for income tax evasion. He was fined $100,000 and placed on five years' probation.

"I've heard you are the most powerful man in Alabama," the judge told him. Gerald died of cancer in 1993 at age 71.

According to Bobbie, Uncle Gerald was married "several times" and fathered two daughters.

·　·　·　·　·　·　·

"He taught me to tie my shoes" remembered George Jr.

Uncle Gerald lived with Lurleen and her children when Gerald was trying to recover from tuberculosis. George Jr. thinks the time period was 1955-56. But other indicators are that the time period may have been later, perhaps 1958-61.

"I was sitting in front of our brick heater in our living room, learning to put my socks and shoes on. I was getting them confused. I always got the socks on, but sometimes I'd get my shoe on the wrong foot. After he helped me master that, Uncle Gerald taught me how to tie my shoes," George Jr. remembered fondly.

Tuberculosis is a highly contagious disease of the lungs.

"Gerald had active tuberculosis when he lived with us. We all had to be tested for tuberculosis. Peggy tested positive once. I don't remember anything other than that Peggy was placed under observation. So maybe it was a false positive," Bobbie said.

"I remember seeing him every day drinking a concoction of raw eggs mixed with I-don't-know-what. I suppose it was to build strength," Bobbie recalled.

Gerald may have lived with Lurleen and the children when his TB was active and thus contagious, because the tuberculosis medical facilities in Alabama then were as deplorable as the mental health facilities.

"The conditions were horrible at the time I went into the county hospital. There were eight to ten patients crowded into each ward. The patients had to care for other patients. Many died while they were in the ward," Gerald is quoted by one of George's biographers.

Gerald seems to have played a role similar to that of Juan and Evita's patron Alberto Dodero.

163

Dodero is described as a "permanent house guest", keeping Juan and Evita company in the Buenos Aires Unzue mansion despite the fact that Dodero owned multiple lavish homes around the world.

Lurleen's brother in law Gerald apparently lived with Lurleen and the children periodically—like Dodero, a sort of permanent house guest in several time frames.

· · · · · · · ·

In the marriage meltdown years, which coincided roughly with George's second four-year long run, beginning in 1958, for the 1962 Alabama governorship, George "employed" Gerald as an emissary to try to convince the fed-up, I'm-Outta'-Here Lurleen that she should withdraw the formal separation agreement, remain as George's wife, and move back to Clayton.

Lurleen and the three children had left George and Clayton to move in with her parents in Knoxville, Alabama. Daughter Lee had not yet been born.

Because memories vary, particularly childhood memories for dates, there may have been some overlap within the time period Gerald served as George's emissary to Lurleen entreating her to drop the divorce idea and the time Gerald lived with Lurleen and her children.

Cynics say that George's frantic attempts at reconciliation with Lurleen in the early 1959-61 time frame had nothing to do with love and everything to do with George's interest in himself and his political fortunes.

George's Stel-la! Stel-la! pleas to Lurleen were coldly and dispassionately motivated by George's enveloping panic that Alabama voters would never, ever elect a governor whose wife had left him or divorced him.

On this analysis, his daughter Peggy agrees with the cynics. George was ruthless. He was focused, as always, on his own self-interest, not Lurleen's best interests.

"It wouldn't have looked good to the voting public had (George) been divorced, and the kids weren't with him. I mean my husband was a politician....," Peggy's voice trailed off at the obvious analysis.

"I mean I'm not stupid. I bet he (George) was not stupid either," Peggy said.

Everyone recognized Peggy's immutable cultural and political truth about the effect of divorce on electability in Alabama, including Lurleen. George's fears that Lurleen filing for divorce could damage his chances were justified.

"My mother wasn't stupid. She knew that, too," Peggy said. "She had to weigh that (George's insincerity) along with everything else."

Perhaps Lurleen perceived, after enduring all her lonely uphill years and financial hardship inflicted by George, that his 1958-61 push for the 1962 governorship was her last, best window of opportunity to gain sufficient leverage within their unequal relationship to possess and exert serious bargaining power over George: her chance to improve life for her children and herself.

And, Lurleen had added a fourth child to the equation: daughter Janie Lee, born in April, 1961. Called Lee, she was named after one of the South's most famous Confederates: General Robert E. Lee.

CHAPTER FORTY NINE
SHE'S GOTTEN GOOD AT GOODBYE

Not only did Uncle Gerald enjoy a long-term fatherly relationship with George's children, but by accounts of Bobbie, George Jr. and Peggy, Gerald and Lurleen were very close.

In fact, Uncle Gerald lived with the three children and his sister-in-law Lurleen for a time in the general 1959-61 period. Again, this exact time period is difficult to pin down because the adults involved are deceased and childrens' memories for dates and time are cloudy.

"Gerald and my mother had a relationship that was…I don't know how to explain it…that was special, because he lived with us for awhile, before the 1962 (second) race for governor," revealed Peggy Wallace Kennedy, Lurleen's second daughter.

Did Uncle Gerald and Lurleen have a relationship that went beyond friendship?

"It was a special relationship. It didn't have anything to do with that. I think Gerald was one person that mother could go to, that understood Daddy when nobody else did. Gerald was her person that she could talk to about George," Peggy explained.

During her loneliest years, Lurleen kept a horse boarded at Gerald's farm and would drive there to ride at every opportunity.

Peggy remembers the general time frame as 1959-1961, during George's do-or-die second campaign for governor. But the dates could have been a bit earlier. No person seems to recall specific dates when Gerald lived with them.

"Uncle Gerald had tuberculosis. He had a lung taken out. He lived with us for maybe a year. Mother took care of him. He was around us and we just loved him," Peggy remembers.

. . . .

Brother-in-law Gerald often traveled with Lurleen's campaign entourage across Alabama. He was one of the first to recognize and respect Lurleen's talents and effectiveness as a campaigner and speak out about it.

"In the beginning of her campaign, people were voting for George. But as the campaign progressed and more and more people saw Lurleen, they were voting for her," Gerald told his associates.

CHAPTER FIFTY

STEL-LA! STEL-LA! GEORGE UNRAVELS

George's ardent, increasingly feverish second quest to be elected Alabama's governor for the 1962 term was seriously imperiled by the existence of a paper document—the formal separation agreement.

The very real risk that that document, and George's egregious conduct, could go public, coupled with a possibility that Lurleen might make her move to her parents' home with the children permanent, George enlisted Gerald's help in convincing Lurleen to come back.

Peggy cries and reaches for a tissue when discussing their fleeing to Knoxville, Alabama—and the aftermath—as she remembers being in a time period when she was about 10 years old.

Peggy said that was not the first time she and her mother, with George Jr. and Bobbie, had fled to her maternal grandparents. She revealed similar escapes down country roads to Knoxville "many times" in the 1958-1962 period that one of George's biographers calls George's "desolation."

Lurleen's latest departure triggered George's panicked desperation. He may have felt that Lurleen had become an albatross around his neck, with the power to deny him, by filing for divorce, that gubernatorial prize to which he had devoted everything during this second try and, some say, sold his soul.

But whether she was albatross or inspiration, George had to do something about Lurleen, and quick.

For George, his nomadic life was unraveling at the most inauspicious time, spinning out of control in every aspect, just at the juncture when he most needed to sustain a public image of blissful domestic stability.

George's other brother Jack had the $600-per-month judgeship George gave up to campaign unsuccessfully for governor.

George had no job.

He disliked practicing law and made little or no effort to build a law practice or attract clients, preferring campaigning incessantly.

George was indiscreet and disloyal to Lurleen in other personal ways for many years, those who knew him confirm. George always denied that he was sexually unfaithful to Lurleen.

Men usually have sex or make love in the same pattern they behave in their everyday lives. As a slam-bam-thank-you-ma'am kind of guy in all aspects of his personality, George cannot have been a skilled lover.

But power is always a turn on.

With now four children, Lurleen had stopped working as a part-time clerk. She owed $414 dollars on groceries she had to charge because George provided no support money.

In those days, plastic credit cards were rare. Sole proprietors kept a running tab written by hand in a paper ledger.

Lurleen sent the children to the store for bare minimum food supplies.

CHAPTER FIFTY ONE
DOMESTIC VIOLENCE:
YOU'LL ALWAYS BE A FIRE I CAN'T PUT OUT

George understood that his younger brother Gerald, with whom Lurleen was close, was "the only one who could bring mother back," Peggy said.

Gerald was also the one who organized the state politically for George. He was masterful at that specialty, according to George Jr.

George sent Gerald as his emissary to sweet talk Lurleen into forgetting about the separation agreement as well as a divorce.

"I think mother thought about it for a long, long time, as to what she was going to do. I don't think she jumped to and said: 'OK, I'll go back.' Or, 'No, I won't go back.' She had no skills. She graduated from high school when she was 15 or 16. She was too young to go to nursing school, where she wanted to go. Then she married young.

"She had no skills whatsoever. What was mother going to do? So I think she weighed out everything as smart as she was, and she was. She turned out to be just the smartest woman I ever knew," Peggy continued.

"Mother knew the smartest thing she could do was to go back. And Gerald said to mother, 'I'm here to take you back.'

"I don't remember when Uncle Gerald came (to take us back to Clayton). I don't remember leaving. But things got better after that. A lot better."

In what way?

"Things were better at home. Just better all around."

Did her father spend more time at home?

"Yeah, I guess. Things seemed easier and calmer. There didn't seem to be any more fighting."

What does she think happened?

"I think that there were some promises made. I think Uncle Gerald had a lot to do with it. I think Gerald told Daddy: Changes have to be made on your part, or Lurleen is not coming back."

But after Lurleen did agree to return, didn't George almost immediately resume his campaign for the 1962 governor slot, so, he was still gone a good bit the same as always?

"Yeah," Peggy said softly.

· · · · · · · ·

Three decades later, American psychologist Leonore Walker would debut her 1979 best-selling book bringing to public attention for the first time what she outlined in detail as the Battered Wife Syndrome. In recent years, her pioneering theories have been renamed the Battered Spouse Syndrome.

Supplemented and refined later by other professionals, Walker's clinical theories gained widespread acceptance and respect even to the level of admittance as legal evidence in courtroom trials.

The basic domestic violence concept is not limited to actual physical violence. Equally potent psychological abuse is also defined as domestic violence.

The cyclic pattern of abuse Walker outlines involves the batterer's physical or psychological violence, the victim's learned helplessness, the victim's financial dependence on the batterer (which the batterer sometimes creates deliberately), the victim's belief in the superiority or omniscience of the batterer, and the victim's always futile hope that the batterer will stop or change the destructive behavior.

After weeks, months, or sometimes years repeating this cycle, a major crisis erupts, such as the victim's actually leaving the batterer, followed by the batterer's contrition and promises to change.

The batterer does not change.

Then, the cycle repeats.

Consequences vary.

·   ·   ·   ·   ·   ·   ·   ·

The fractious relationship of George and Lurleen Wallace during this time period ticks all boxes of Walker's theories characterizing domestic violence's classic patterns of psychological and physical abuse.

Lurleen was totally financially dependent on George, except for the intermittent low-paid clerical jobs he found for her. She was even dependent on him for arranging those jobs.

And, at a word from him, Lurleen could find herself out of a job.

Without Lurleen working, they would have had no income. They would really be incapacitated.

George created his wife's financial dependence deliberately so work wouldn't interfere with his full-time campaigning ceaselessly while she supported him and the family financially.

Because George was a college graduate and lawyer from a family of college graduates, lawyers, and a physician, and Lurleen did not graduate from high school, she believed that George was superior to her, smarter than she was: "better."

Batterers are not above reminding their victims of this disparity.

172

In confiding her marital anguish to women friends, Lurleen always expressed hope that George would change, just as Walker describes the patterning. Because Walker's theories had not yet been propounded in Lurleen's era, misguided, well-meaning friends often told Lurleen she had to remain with George or advised her to stay in hope George would change.

Walker's learned helplessness component is probably the least applicable to Lurleen, who was capable of feistiness.

Peggy indicates that although "things were better" from her childhood view after Gerald's negotiating Lurleen's return, actually nothing of George's behavior changed at all, she realized as an adult.

CHAPTER FIFTY TWO
THE BABY GRAND PIANO MYSTERY

"That sense of sanctuary which is the essence of love.
And in that sanctuary, there is even room for strangers."
Anonymous

George Jr.'s first clearest memory of his mother Lurleen is sitting beside her at a baby grand piano, perhaps when he was 9 or 10 years old.

That would have been in the 1959-61 general time frame when George enlisted his brother Gerald's help in persuading Lurleen to abandon her plans to divorce George, and at the same general time when Lurleen gave birth to her daughter Lee.

But weren't they as a family always struggling financially?

"Absolutely," Bobbie Jo responded.

Then how did Lurleen get a baby grand piano?

"I don't know.

"I remember waiting for the piano to be delivered. I don't remember it getting there. I just remember waiting outside the house for it to be delivered." Bobbie said. "I can't remember what year it was.

"What is really odd is that mother didn't, at that time, know how to play a piano," Bobbie added.

"Mother loved music," said George Jr. who, as a teenager, played in a sort of garage band and wrote some songs.

"I've always wished that I had asked mother why they got a baby grand piano at the time they did. Because they could not afford it. I just don't know," Bobbie said, puzzlement creeping into her voice even now.

"Bobbie and I took piano for a couple of years in Clayton from Jean Fenn. I think possibly mother was thinking about the children," George Jr. said.

"Mother took piano lessons from Jean, too," Bobbie added.

"He (George) made payments on it," George Jr. speculated.

· · · · · · · ·

Mary Jo Ventress, the Home Economics teacher who bonded with Lurleen in the lonely Clayton years they helped each other through, remembers Lurleen's piano well.

"They (Lurleen and George) were living in a house across the street from the Baptist Church. At night my husband Tom and I would usually take a little ride out to the end of the street, and go back that way to the end of the street.

"And so often she'd be at the piano playing," Mary Jo remembered.

"I'd look through the door that would be open, or the window, and see her there in the light at the piano."

Oh? Lurleen played the piano?

"Well, she wasn't a virtuoso, but she played a little. Lurleen could pick things out on the piano."

Lurleen and George were struggling financially. How did they afford a baby grand piano?

"I don't know whether George bargained for it. I just don't know. Lurleen had always wanted a piano," Mary Jo said.

"It was such a big thing. None of us had a baby grand piano. I had a little spinet light. But one of the other friends in Clayton had a piano, a grand piano," Mary Jo explained.

Was Lurleen's baby grand piano the only other grand piano in Clayton?

"Oh no. My aunt had a beautiful, old, gorgeous grand piano. And another cousin of mine had a grand piano.

For Lurleen, was the baby grand piano symbolic of something?

"Nothing other than a wish of hers," Mary Jo said.

· · · · · · · ·

As far as friends and acquaintances know, George was not in the habit of giving Lurleen any gifts during their bare bones bargain basement relationship, not even red roses, which were her favorite flower.

Although around 1945 while he was still in military service, George did a sort of reverse of the famous "Gift of the Magi" short story by O. Henry.

George pawned a wristwatch that Lurleen had given him as a gift on May 21, 1944, their first wedding anniversary.

Lurleen, on her $12 a week five-and-dime store clerk salary, saved for six months to pay for George's gift. He got $10 for the wristwatch at a pawn shop in Amarillo, Texas. George said he retrieved Lurleen's gift out of hock months later.

He never did reveal what he did with the $10.

Apparently, he gave her no anniversary gift.

· · · · · · · ·

George and his brothers, attorneys Gerald and Jack, grew up in a home with a piano on which their mother, Mozelle, gave lessons.

The baby grand piano arrived for Lurleen at the Clayton house around the general time frame Gerald lived, or had lived, with

176

Lurleen and her children there when he was recovering from tuberculosis. Or the piano arrival date could have coincided with the period when Gerald, at George's behest, was trying to woo Lurleen back to George.

It was well known that Lurleen loved music.

Perhaps the baby grand piano was a quid pro quo for Lurleen agreeing to return to George.

Perhaps it was a gift from Gerald in gratitude for Lurleen nursing him back into health.

· · · · · · · ·

One of Lurleen's favorite songs was the 1949 Hank Williams Sr. classic "I'm So Lonesome I Could Cry."

Perhaps, on her newly arrived baby grand piano, on quiet nights in the small town, after the children had been put to bed, when Mary Jo saw Lurleen's image framed through the lighted window, Lurleen, her left elbow resting on the piano cover, was slowly, carefully picking out on each key with her right hand the melody for some of the lyrics that described the lonely life George left her to cope with.

"I've never seen a night so long,
When time goes crawling by.
The Moon just went behind a cloud
To hide its face and cry.

The silence of a falling star
Lights up the purple sky.
And I wonder where you are?
I'm so lonesome I could cry."

177

"Mother also liked the song 'Carolina Moon.' I can still see her sitting at the piano playing that song," Bobbie said.

"Carolina Moon" was written in 1924 by Joe Burke and Benny Davis. But pop singer Connie Francis sent it to the top of the charts with her 1958 version.

"Carolina Moon keep shining,
Shining on the one who waits for me.
Carolina moon I'm pining,
Pining for the place I long to be.

I'm hoping tonight you'll go
Go to the right window
Scatter your light,
Say I'm all right, please do."

Lurleen was perpetually waiting for George. But who, as in the 'Carolina Moon' lyrics, was waiting for Lurleen? Who was Lurleen hoping would go "to the right window" as in Williams' song?

For what place was Lurleen longing to be?

George never waited for her or for anyone. So it couldn't be George.

For many years, Bobbie has kept Lurleen's piano in her Shelby County home.

CHAPTER FIFTY THREE
MY SISTER HAD THE SAME THING YOU HAD

After Lurleen's return to George and to Clayton, which probably saved the 1962 gubernatorial election for George, she began appearing with him at more and more campaign events running up to the November, 1961 voting.

Gerald was along too, running the organization and set up of the stops.

In April, 1961 she had just given birth to her fourth and last child, daughter Lee. She was still in recovery from Cesarean surgery, which in those years involved a painful, massive abdominal scar and months of careful recuperation and as much bed rest as possible.

Two people working as a campaign team can exponentially increase the candidate's visibility. Despite the fact that she was not fully recovered from the Cesarean surgery, George enlisted Lurleen's help.

On the campaign trail, Lurleen was initially stiff, timid and lacking in self confidence as a speaker. Her only prior public speaking experience was teaching Sunday school classes.

• • • • • • • •

Whatever is said of George's faults and shortcomings, even his detractors concede he was a vituoso orator, a stem-winder extraordinaire. Some political writers describe him as the most talented political orator of all time in America.

That would not be an exaggeration.

Thinking on his feet to respond to hecklers was his masterful specialty.

Nanoseconds after a verbal attack, he could deliver quick-witted, zingy retorts and clever put-downs for hecklers, journalists, and bureaucrats. He was hilariously funny with local anecdotes and mocking comebacks that did not cross the line into vituperation.

In sheer showmanship, George was a challenging act for anyone to precede or follow, let alone best.

· · · · · · · ·

But, late in 1961, after Lurleen had polished her speaking skills on the trail for several months behind the scenes in George's campaign, George became ill. Lurleen had to fly solo as a speaker for a few days, substituting for George.

She surprised even herself with how comfortably she fit in the driver's seat, and how well and easily she projected the campaign flash and dash without George around to give her directives.

As a speaker, she wasn't George. But then no one was.

The crowds warmed to her.

Gerald was not surprised.

He always knew. And he told her so.

· · · · · · · ·

Attorney Albert Preston Brewer was "kind of helping out" in George's second four-year gubernatorial campaign for the 1962 term. "I was in the legislature, running for my second term. I didn't have opposition."

He remembers spring, 1958, as about the time he first met Lurleen Wallace.

A skilled campaigner himself, Brewer watched her handle a campaign appearance alone, working for George's election.

She did extremely well without George he said.

Brewer, now a college professor, does not distribute high grades with alacrity.

. . . .

"Lurleen came through Decatur, Alabama, my home town, population about 20,000, to pay a visit to George's campaign head-quarters and to meet as many George supporters as we could get to come to headquarters.

.

"Oh, I remember it was hot as blazes. She was there probably an hour or so in early afternoon in a non-air-conditioned store front on Molten Street. She met with a group of people who came by to meet her.

What was she wearing to campaign?

"A broomstick skirt, a short sleeved or sleeveless blouse, and sandals. But most people in Decatur had on sandals that hot spring day. She was dressed for the weather.

"I was wearing a dress shirt and tie. I was the lawyer and working that day. My office was about a half block from where the reception was.

"Probably about 2 or 2:30, I suddenly realized that she hadn't had any lunch.

" 'No I haven't,' she told me.

" 'Come on! Let's go to lunch!' I suggested.

"We walked around the corner to a local popular restaurant. I do not recall whether anyone was with us. I recall there was a lady traveling with Lurleen. She also had a driver.

"That was sort of customary then with a candidate who was female or the wife of a candidate.

"Three or four of us at this restaurant spent a nice hour or so together on that occasion," Brewer said.

Where was George?

"He was off somewhere campaigning. He always spread out. Usually he split up because you can cover twice as much territory."

• • • • • • • •

What were Brewer's impressions of Lurleen's demeanor and social skills at that time?

"It was all new to her. I'm sure she helped with campaigning in Barbour County. But she had not been involved in a statewide campaign. I didn't think Lurleen felt very comfortable campaigning. But very few people, men or women, are comfortable the first time they start campaigning.

Brewer, a veteran campaigner, gave Lurleen high marks early on.

"Lurleen handled herself extremely well meeting people. That is, in shaking hands and making small talk. She was very good at that. She did not discuss politics or issues.

"She was purely social: Meet the people who came by. Also these people were for Wallace anyway. And here was a chance to meet his wife. She didn't make a formal speech. She asked for their vote for George of course," Brewer added.

"Then she got in a car with a driver and her female companion, and they left," Brewer said.

182

. . . .

Anita Halstead, known as Nita, accompanied Lurleen as her female escort on many campaign sorties Lurleen made to support George's run for the 1962 governorship. Lurleen's children are unable to provide any basic details about Nita's background or how Nita and Lurleen came to know each other.

At some time, perhaps in late 1961, or in 1962, a woman approached Lurleen from the crowd and said solicitously: "My sister had the same thing you had, and she's doing just fine now."

Lurleen paused to perfunctorily acknowledge the woman's kindness, then continued shaking hands with people in the line that had formed to meet her.

But Lurleen couldn't get the woman or what she said, out of her mind. Whatever else was on her plate, her attention kept clicking back to that remark.

Later, Lurleen asked Nita: What was that woman talking about? What did she mean: had what I have?"

"Oh, I don't know," Nita lied.

CHAPTER FIFTY FOUR
WALKIN' IN HIGH OL' COTTON

"Even though our dreams may vanish in the morning light, we loved once in splendor, how tender, how tender the night."
Lyrics by Sammy Fain and Paul Francis

After campaigning unceasingly for more than seven years in seeking the Alabama governorship for a second time, Wallace found himself in a spring, 1962, runoff with state senator Ryan deGraffenried, described as a handsome, articulate young man from an old money Alabama family.

In the first round of the primary, George received about 32.49 percent of the vote. DeGraffenried had received about 25.22 percent.

George easily won the runoff, winning 56 percent of the vote. DeGraffenried garnered 44 percent.

In the general election in November, Wallace won in a landslide with 303,987 votes, or 96 percent, against Independent Frank P. Walls. Republicans did not field a candidate.

· · · · · · · ·

In interviews with one of his biographers, George claims that on the reviewing stand during his January, 1963, inauguration day ceremony, Lurleen kissed him and declared that she now knew "it was worth it all."

George further claimed that in those moments, Lurleen experienced an epiphany wherein she "came to a complete understanding of what I had gone through."

Even his biographer does a verbal eye roll at George's self-serving statements, expressing dubiety at the wishful thinking reflected by George's claim of Lurleen's blanket exoneration of him, writing: "Wallace may have overstated reality…"

Those who knew Lurleen might have shared the biographer's smirk, countering to ask George if, on his inauguration day, did George come to a complete understanding of what *Lurleen* had gone through?

George would have qualified for at least Honorable Mention for a quadruple Pinocchio Award.

If Lurleen did make such *te absolvo* statements forgiving George, she must have considered an immediate retraction a few weeks later.

· · · · · · · ·

As they took occupancy of the elegant governor's mansion, peripatetic George began telling friends that he would be running for president of the United States beginning in 1964 while serving his mid-term as Alabama governor.

The engines of their moving truck from Clayton had barely cooled, leaking oil on the Governor's Mansion driveway.

· · · · · · · ·

After lean, lonely years traipsing in and out of downscale rentals, working in clerical jobs to support the family and support George, waiting for George to come home, fleeing often with the children to her parents, Lurleen had relished surcease in 1962.

At 36 years old, she moved into a beautiful neoclassical revival

19-room Montgomery abode: the antebellum two-story Governor's Mansion at 1142 North Perry Street amidst mature live oak trees and beautiful gardens. With its gleaming high gloss polished wood railing, the elegant double staircase leading right and left up from the entrance hall must have seemed to Lurleen as a stairway to heaven.

Built in 1907, the mansion was once the private home of the Lignon family.

A French crystal chandelier from New Orleans' famous Roosevelt Hotel hung over the staircase. French crystal sconces dotted the walls.

There was a sun porch with a cool red tile floor. Floor-to-ceiling 19th century gilt framed pier mirrors in the parlors to the left and right of the entrance reflected delicate marble fireplaces.

A mahogany table and chairs with petit point seat covers depicting symbols associated with Alabama history centered the dining room. The sideboard held sterling silver candelabra, punch cups, trays. and a tea set.
Oak and cherry wood floors featured mahogany banding.

Lurleen paid her $414 groceries-on-credit bill at a sole proprietor Cloverland Red & White store in Montgomery within days of George's ascent.
George's salary as governor was $25,000 per year, plus free lodging—a princely income in 1966.
Lurleen no longer had to send her daughter Bobbie Jo to charge grocery basics at Cloverland Red & White store.

To all appearances, they were walkin' in high ol' cotton.

In whatever time she could wrest from mothering four children including two teenagers, a pre-teen and a 2-year-old after arising daily at 7 a.m., Lurleen busied herself with what was then, and remains, a first lady traditional role, hosting and attending teas and receptions.

Decades later, another first lady, Hillary Clinton, referred indirectly to these social customs expected of first ladies who preceded her. Hillary's toss-off riposte created national headlines, television commentary and a firestorm of backlash against Mrs. Bill Clinton.

The controversy arose when a reporter asked Mrs. Clinton in 1992, during her husband's campaign, something about how she might combine or had combined her profession as an attorney with being Arkansas' and America's first lady.

Sensing in his question implied criticism of her interest in continuing in her lawyer career, Mrs. Clinton responded with tinged sarcasm: "I suppose I could have stayed home and baked cookies and had teas?"

How adult women were described publicly presented another contrast of historical eras.

Although Lurleen was 36 years old with four children, Ted Knapp of Scripps-Howard newspaper chain, in writing about her as first lady then, referred to her as a "girl," as did other print journalists routinely. There were very few women journalists covering politics, which, like sports coverage, was traditionally white male dominated.

It is difficult to imagine that the press corps in that 1962 era would refer to George Wallace at 36, or any 36-year-old white male, with or without four children, as a "boy."

CHAPTER FIFTY FIVE
STAY HOME AND BAKE COOKIES

Lurleen opened the mansion, on a regular basis, to the general public. As many as 1,500 attended the events, upping Lurleen's personal profile.

As always, because she was ignored by George and pigeon-holed as merely decorative by the press, no one noticed that via her social activities and her speaking engagements at Kiwanis, Rotary and store openings, Lurleen was actually doing what all politicians do: building a base of support by meeting VOTERS.

Thousands of voters over the four years were getting to meet a celebrity: "Miz" Lurleen. Meeting her in person would, in current times, be an experience sure to hit Twitter, prompting tweets and retweets. In that day, the voters took their treasured experience home with them, telling their friends and neighbors about this gracious woman, unpretentious, yet dignified and calm.

Of those thousands streaming into the mansion, most were females, who traditionally vote in a significantly higher percentage than males locally and nationally.

Wittingly or unwittingly, as first lady, Lurleen was, as expertly as any veteran politico, building a loyal reliable constituency

Even though she now had assistance from a domestic staff, she sometimes rinsed out punch cups with them after a social occasion. Her egalitarian gesture did not escape the attention of home folks, who held humility as an admirable value rarely observed in white males who dominated public offices then.

Lurleen continued her heavy cigarette smoking addiction.

Both she and George were teetotalers. They did not drink alcohol and made a public point of not serving alcohol at state functions.

. . . .

CHAPTER FIFTY SIX
LURLEEN, Juris Doctorate, TAKES FLIGHT

While first lady, Lurleen took flying lessons—an uncommon interest shared among very few women of that era. At the mansion, she hosted members of the Ninety-Nines, a women pilot club.

Her daughter Bobbie Jo attributes her mother's interest in aviation to Juanita Halstead, who was a pilot regularly competing in the Powder Puff derby, a flying competition for females.

"I think mother had hopes that she and Nita could compete together," Bobbie said.

Perhaps Lurleen wanted to explore flying in order to verbally share George's World War II airborne experiences as a B29 flight engineer.

Or, perhaps she wanted to physically, or at least metaphorically, break free into the sky from the 25 years of "surly bonds of earth" unpleasant experiences she had endured married to George.

In her April 16, 1967 commencement address at the all-women Judson College, Marion, Alabama, her remarks provided revealing insight not only into her motivation behind her two hobbies flying and fishing, but also her interior strategies as for coping with and surviving personal adversity.

"I enjoy flying and fishing as hobbies. I find both to be sources of many pleasures. As dissimilar as flying and fishing may seem, they do have a common element. Both are sources of fresh perspective," Lurleen explained.

The 129-year-old Baptist supported college conferred on her an honorary doctor of laws degree.

Lurleen Burroughs Burns Wallace, J.D.

At long last "Mutt" had attained, even though honorary, the college degree she had always wanted.

· · · · · · · ·

Although neither Lurleen nor George may have read the classic books, their new social "power couple" lifestyle as governor and first lady must have seemed in peripheral aspects to resemble the glamorous upscale lives detailed in the novels "Tender is the Night" by F. Scott Fitzgerald (1896-1946) and "Save Me the Waltz" written by his Montgomery-born and raised wife Zelda (1900-1948).

In the 1930s the literary Golden Couple lived in the house at 919 Felder Avenue, several blocks from what later became the governor's mansion.

CHAPTER FIFTY SEVEN
"THEY'S LOTSA THINGS FOLKS WANT, THAT THEY SHO' DON'T NEED"

Although George, as governor, claimed braggin' rights to the usual road improvements and other miscellaneous public works type projects standard for governors in many states, those projects would have occurred irrespective of who held the office.

Neither historians nor George cite any major innovative achievements or creative initiatives, beyond the basics, to improve the quality of Alabamians' lives that he could be credited with during his 1962-68 term as Alabama governor, except perhaps suggesting a system of junior colleges and trade schools. His term-of-office accomplishments were shallow or ordinary at best.

His spending ran up the state deficit.

Other than his internationally publicized attempts to thwart racial integration in Alabama, his 1963-1967 tenancy as governor was gossamer, a mostly blank screen except for his 1964 absenteeism as he attempted to ditch his governorship for his new love: trying to become president of the United States.

"George wasn't good at the doin'. He was good only at the campaignin'," said one long-time observer.

"Policy and details of actual governance bored him," said another.

"George's life was not as much about serving in public office as it was about campaigning," said Rebecca Beasley, Clayton Record newspaper editor and lifelong friend of George.

"George had little interest in grinding legislation in and out of committees and crafting policy," said a biographer.

George Wallace was like a celebrity who is famous for being famous. Governing by constant campaign, as one critic termed it.

Peripatetic George had no intention of "retiring" to a brick house on Farrar Street in Montgomery that Lurleen wanted him to buy—or anywhere else—except maybe the White House.

He had zero inclination to fulfill Lurleen's long-ago-disemboweled new bride dream of what their son defined: a husband who came home to dinner at 6 p.m. every night to interact with his family.

No Ma'm. Jes' ain't gonna' happen.

Ever.

· · · · · · · ·

CHAPTER FIFTY EIGHT
EXACTLY HOW POOR WERE YOU?

George's 1964 fortuitous showing as a presidential candidate proved that he was a contender. His successful showing fueled his ardor, strengthening his resolve to leave a national imprint way outside Alabama.

In a mere six weeks, in a last-minute shoe string campaign for president of the United States from April 1 to May 19, 1964, (his mid term as Alabama governor), George Wallace received 44 percent of the vote in Maryland, 35 percent in Wisconsin, and 30 percent in Indiana.

His vote-getting prowess against stand in candidates for incumbent President Lyndon B. Johnson shocked both the Republican and Democrat establishment movers and shakers. They were incredulous.

They now realized that George's little guy vs. big government message and in-your-face persona resonated well outside Alabama or outside southern states.

Wallace was not a flash in the pan.

Operatives awoke to the hard evidence of votes: that the identical populist themes which enraptured Alabama voters worked equally well outside Alabama.

National media began noticing George Corley Wallace.

. . . .

In other incredulities, Ted Pearson of The Birmingham News, routinely describing George as a "poor farm boy," was laughable, and very, very far from the facts—as was the appellation of George as the "son of a poor dirt farmer."

Another reporter described George as a "truck driver" who became governor.

Yes, George drove a truck—one summer after graduating from law school with a J.D. degree.

A photo of the "poor dirt farmer" Clio home George grew up in depicts a beautiful, stylish brick home, with fashionable canvas awnings tastefully shading the front windows and a landscaped yard—definitely upper middle class for that time period.

Had any reporter ever even really looked at the photo of George's family home or delved into any basic background, George's reverse-vainglorious self descriptions would have been exposed, evaporating in an embarrassing national poof.

The almost hilarious, factually inaccurate descriptions of George were classic herd journalism—writing whatever, because press corps peers wrote it.

No probing questions asked. The dirt farmer-to-president made more attention-getting copy.

．　．　．　．　．　．　．　．

As George sought higher and higher public offices, the poorer and poorer became the personal background he ascribed to himself.

Had he been elected president of the United States, by that time his self- described I-was-poorer-than-thou childhood would have had him proclaimed as having lived in a cardboard box by the side of a dirt road, picking berries for daily sustenance, barefoot, wearing only a loincloth.

Pearson wasn't the lone lazy reporter buying unquestioningly into George's carefully constructed marketing fiction designed make himself appear to have begun from a proletarian background more akin to the majority of voters whose support he sought.

Other journalists carelessly tapped out on their upright typewriters incorrect, conclusory information about George and about Lurleen without checking easily available basic facts. They never let facts get in the way of a good story.

George came from a family line of professionals with college degrees. His two brothers were attorneys. His mother, Mozelle Smith, was a pianist and teacher. George was the wily, college educated lawyer grandson of a prominent physician and judge, the nephew of a probate judge, and the brother of a circuit judge. His politically well-connected grandfather was entreated to Washington, D.C. to a personal meeting with President Franklin D. Roosevelt.

So much for the father George inveigled the press to continually describe disingenuously as a "poor dirt farmer."

In 1935 George served as a state senate page, a plum job customarily awarded to the sons of Alabama's wealthy, well born, and already influential.

Indeed, shortly before his death, George's father arranged for a friend to nominate George for one of the four positions as a senate page. At 16 years old, George's ambition was already in racing gear. George immediately canvassed the senators and got enough votes to win approval for the page position.

In that page role, George was a sponge—an A student in soaking up the lay of the land. Like a squirrel collecting acorns, the entrepreneurial 16-year-old became friends with many powerful men, storing the contacts away for future use.

The smart acquisitions included state senator Chauncey Sparks, who would later, as governor, help George get hired in the state attorney general's office, George's first job as an attorney.

· · · · · · · ·

In contrast to George's faux credentials, First lady Lurleen Wallace, initially marginalized by media except for brief print mentions on what were then called the Society Pages, was a genuine credentialed poor farm girl who actually accomplished what George claimed to have achieved: traveling only-in-America's fabled classic bottom-to-top Cinderella journey.

Lil' ol' Lurleen climbed a political mountaintop in a time frame when females were not valued equally in power wielding arenas traditionally dominated by white males, i.e. everything.

CHAPTER FIFTY NINE

HOW CAN WE MISS YOU
WHEN YOU WON'T GO AWAY?

Lurleen had hoped, in fleeting optimistic moments, that in the frenetic pinball machine that George's life replicated, when the lights flashed and the bell sounded, as the zig zagging ball racked up points, when he became governor he would find a personal peace.

But George was poised with another ever-present quarter, ready to slide it in the metal tray for another go at winning, his eager fingers firm on the flippers on each side of the addictive machine that dispersed the awards of political power.

George began thinking that maybe his impressive 1964 presidential primary showing in three states could be frog-jumped into a higher public arena. He analyzed his victories as more than a flirtation from voters, more than a fluttering infatuation generated by a glimpse of ankle.

Governor George Wallace thought maybe, just maybe, he really *could* be elected President of the United States. In successive tries, he would move breathtakingly close to that goal.

•   •   •   •   •   •   •   •   •

George, while still occupying the seat as Alabama's governor, withdrew as a candidate in the 1964 presidential race so as not to split any conservative vote for GOP presidential candidate Barry Goldwater. Then Senator Goldwater lost the presidency to Senator

Lyndon B. Johnson in a landslide, making George's sacrificial withdrawal look for naught.

Although George was exasperated that his backoff might have forfeited a genuine opportunity for him to be elected president of the United States, he was, on the other hand, very encouraged.

With his 1964 presidential primary vote totals as his national resume, George wanted to run again—for the 1968 presidential term. He would automatically be required to vacate the Alabama governor platform in 1966 because of term limitations, which he was unsuccessful in changing, legislatively.

What would George "do" from 1966-68? He wouldn't be holding any office. He would no longer have the $25,000 per year governor's salary to fund his presidential campaigns.

As a presidential aspirant, he had to retain a public platform redolent with some prestige, like governor of a state, to keep himself in the headlines and in the public eye.

Lurleen, who, at his insistence, had partnered with George a few times outside Alabama stumping for his 1964 presidential campaign, suddenly began waxing eloquent in 1965—as quoted by George, or quoted publicly—that she felt her experience joining George on the national hustings outside Alabama had boosted her interest in politics because she and George were together more in campaign mode than they were at home.

Beg pardon?

The radar of political sophisticates detected a "plant" quote that sounded more like George than Lurleen.

They knew that George, who fancied himself as a poker card shark, had at least a face card in his vest pocket. Maybe a straight. Anyone who knew Lurleen at that time saw her as a dutiful, but reluctant campaigner dragged into the spotlight when George saw her as useful to him.

Lurleen's interest in politics accelerating? Accelerating from zero? That dog won't hunt.

CHAPTER SIXTY

IN SICKNESS AND IN HEALTH: BETRAYAL

In November 1965, Lurleen's gynecologist discovered via biopsy that Lurleen had uterine cancer.

A week later, in remarks at Howard College, despite the devastating medical news for Lurleen, George, undeterred, hinted to the audience that Lurleen would run in 1966 as his proxy for the governor's term beginning in 1967.

In December 1965 as a follow up to her biopsy results, Lurleen endured painful gynecological radiation treatments.

In tandem with her medical news becoming more depressing and inconvenient for him, George continued, in the same time frame, to plant more and more public hints that his wife would run to replace him as governor.

His plans in view of her declining health seemed George's disconnect.

Lurleen's medical news continued to be bad.

On January 10, 1966, at Emory University Hospital in Atlanta, surgeons removed a malignant tumor from her uterus, performed a hysterectomy and appendectomy, and did a surgical exploration of her abdominal area. In that era, hysterectomies had recuperation and recommended rest periods of several weeks.

Before her January surgery, Lurleen told a reporter that she would run for governor as George's surrogate.

Had she been provided complete information about her medical condition, past as well as present, so she could carefully weigh reality, her decision to run might have been different.

Her cancer was not only an occurrence.
Her 1965 uterine cancer was a recurrence.
Cancer is generally considered cured if it does not recur within five years.

The 1965 discovery was four years and eight months since Lurleen's April 1961 medical lab tests had indicated cancer.

. . . .

For four years, unknown to Lurleen, George, in concert with Lurleen's women friends and others in whom Lurleen placed her closest, intimate trust, had engaged in an elaborate conspiracy, sometimes with many moving parts, to withhold from her vital information of her 1961 diagnosis of uterine cancer.

The truth was that the life-threatening disease was discovered in tissue samples collected during the April 1961 Caesarean birth of her daughter and fourth child, Lee.

Accounts of the dates or month Lurleen discovered the lies told to her and heart-shattering betrayals by her husband and closest friends, vary.

Some accounts indicate she learned the full truth well after she had decided to run for governor, and her 1966 campaign was well under way. Others indicate she learned the news just before or just after her December 1965 surgery when she may not yet have made up her mind whether to run.

But whatever the exact date, the way she found out, and from whom, was equally soul crushing. Conflicting discovery dates are cited by several sources. But there is general agreement that the divulgement probably came during her campaign.

CHAPTER SIXTY ONE
BETRAYAL, LIES, COVERUP

Lurleen stumbled on the revelation during a casual chat with a friend about her health.

Once, months before, a woman stranger had said something similar to Lurleen, but, distracted by a bustling campaign format, Lurleen had not asked the woman for details.

And Nita had played dumb when Lurleen inquired.

When another stranger again mentioned cancer to Lurleen, Lurleen asked the stranger, and later asked Nita, for more details.

"Well they thought you had cancer once before…" the friend told Lurleen, thinking and assuming that she already knew, according to reporter Anita Smith. The friend was the first to break the news to Lurleen about the results of Lurleen's 1961 medical lab reports: that some reports indicated she had cancer, other reports indicating that she did not.

This time, neither Juanita Halstead nor anyone else would put Lurleen off. Lurleen demanded answers. The answers would be soul-crushing.

She confronted George first.

He 'fessed up.

"I tried to pass it off when she talked to me about it. I remember saying to Lurleen: 'Now Honey, there was no point in you worrying about that,' " Anita Smith reported.

The news of undisclosed prior cancer, coupled with her discovery of the years-long George-lead deception to conceal the 1961 information from her, "drove Lurleen crazy."

Lurleen "freaked out," according to Smith.

Lurleen's friends told her they had "been asked" in 1961 not to tell Lurleen. Left unsaid is who asked them to conceal the information.

The suspect list had only one name on it.

Presumably George Wallace was the first and the only person to initially receive from her physicians the medical information about Lurleen four years earlier.

But George went way beyond just not telling Lurleen.

He participated with and encouraged others in elaborate schemes to keep hidden from her the true nature of her health.

· · · · · · · ·

The masquerade of actual concealment began in April 1961 shortly after Lee was born when George was told that some of his wife's lab results confirmed cancer.

Although her physicians told George, they did not tell Lurleen. George didn't tell Lurleen either.

The first portion of the continuing plan that Anita Smith labeled a conspiracy was put into motion when Nita Halstead and her husband invited Lurleen to travel with them to Atlanta. The trip was the underpinning of the subterfuge.

According to reporter Smith's account, "During the trip Nita Halstead, in consert with her husband and a physician, participated in a conspiracy to get Lurleen to be examined by a noted Atlanta cancer specialist whom the Halsteads knew personally, without Lurleen knowing why she was being examined."

As part of the trickery, a virtual script of treachery had been written, rehearsed and agreed to with specific lines to be spoken by the conspirators with George's consent and participation.

Deliberately within Lurleen's presence and hearing, Nita's husband suggested that Nita get a routine checkup while they were in Atlanta.

"I'm not going to get a checkup unless Lurleen wants one too," Nita said in a pre-agreed scenario of deception.

Innocent of how she was being manipulated by her most trusted friends, Lurleen agreed.

"The Atlanta doctor examined Lurleen as closely as he could without making her suspect he was actually looking for something. As far as he could tell, she was all right," Nita told reporter Smith.

Knowingly participating in such a cozenage to deceive a patient would be a shocking violation of medical ethics by the attending physician.

·　·　·　·　·　·　·　·

During George's campaign for the 1962 governor's seat, Nita Halstead was "continuously afraid someone on the campaign trail was going to tell Lurleen she'd possibly had cancer before," according to Anita Smith's reporting.

At least once, someone did. But Nita poo-pooed the red flags.

Many people in the state and some of George's campaign workers knew what Lurleen did not know, according to reporter Smith.

Nita, whom Lurleen later forgave, expressed amazement that Lurleen would be so upset about being hoodwinked by close friends about a life threatening illness for which early detection is essential and treatment available.

Lurleen's children are also dismissive of what George did.

While they do not agree with their father's conduct, they do not criticize or question it either.

They justify George's manipulations of Lurleen as consistent with the paternalistic culture of the era, which sanctioned withholding information from a patient about life-threatening medical issues on the grounds that the knowledge would upset the patient.

Her children discount analyses that George was motivated by concerns of how public revelation about his wife's health could affect his chances of being elected governor in his second, desperate four-year-long campaign for the 1962 term.

CHAPTER SIXTY TWO
NEVER CORNER SOMEONE MEANER THAN YOU

George was infamous for sending to the political graveyard anyone who blocked his agenda. His payback might take a short time, or a longer time. As an Old Testament eye-for-an-eye guy, he would punish. He was a devastating counter puncher, a bulldozer campaigner, his biographers note.

"Whoever is in his way gets pushed aside," wrote Tom Johnson, editor of the Montgomery Independent.

Politicians who opposed Lurleen's candidacy would be "run over," George threatened, discussing her candidacy on statewide television February 24,1966.

Usually he wasn't shy about leaving his fingerprints so the recipient of his revanche would know exactly who retaliated. But sometimes George moved undetected.

As one example of many, 10 of the 14 (some accounts say 17) state legislators who denied him, by inches, his attempt to remove gubernatorial term limitations from the Alabama constitution so he could seek a second term suddenly decided not to seek reelection. They did not need to find a severed horse's head in their bed, a la the 1972 "Godfather" movie, to predict how their attempt at re-election might go.

Toward the 14 men, Wallace began what reporters termed "the first stage of a campaign to ruin their political careers."

Sometimes his targets denied him the pleasure of retribution by falling on their own swords or politically doing themselves in.

Of the four remaining, all were defeated when they sought reelection.

George had a scorched earth policy.

"I am convinced that George Wallace would stop at nothing," legislator John Tyson said, describing the extreme but unsuccessful lengths George quarterbacked to try to get the Alabama constitution amended so he could succeed himself for a second term as governor.

· · · · · · · ·

In the 1966 primary season, as well as years later, fate assisted George in amazingly convenient ways.

Men who threatened to impede the way to Lurleen's election, or in later years, impede George's election, fell from the sky like flies —literally.

For George, the incidents were like the Biblical manna from heaven, providing George precisely whatever he wanted.

· · · · · · · ·

Handsome Ryan deGraffenreid was one of the 14 state legislators who backroom blocked George's attempt to change Alabama's constitution to allow successive governor terms. After that affront publicly humiliating George, George had not moved against deGraffenreid.

Insiders speculated that could be because, in George's 1957 kerfuffle with the feds over their court order authorizing them to examine voter records in Barbour County and in George's home town, Clayton, deGraffenreid had represented George as his attorney—one of the odd couplings for which politics is infamous.

DeGraffenreid, from an old money Alabama family, was also one of George's opponents in the Democratic primary for the 1962 governor's race that George won. Taking a cue perhaps from George's unceasing campaigning, deGraffenreid had not stopped campaigning for the governorship since 1962. Media described deGraffenreid as ambitious and aggressive.

If Lurleen declared as a candidate for governor to replace George, then deGraffenreid, an avid, vocal segregationist, would be Lurleen's strongest competitor in the primary.

George knew that deGraffenried's polling showed the articulate ex-football star at the head of the Democratic primary pack. There were other rivals, but deGraffenried would beat Lurleen in the May 3, 1966, Democrat primary, the polls showed.

Lurleen's defeat would embarrass George publicly and perhaps, as a ripple effect, diminish George's chances nationally at the presidency, by showing George as politically ineffectual in his home state. Always cash poor, George was counting on Lurleen's potential $25,000 a year governor's salary and free room and board at the governor's mansion to finance his national campaign for president.

CHAPTER SIXTY THREE
MANNA FROM HEAVEN

"...upon the face of the wilderness there lay a small round thing...
when the children of Israel saw it, they said...it is manna from Heaven."
Exodus 16:14,15

For George Corley Wallace, everything he ever dreamed about, lived for, worked for, and aspired to his entire life was at stake in those January 1966 weeks, plus everything in the wider future he was working toward: the presidency of the United States.

At 46 years old, he was right at the age cusp where he had to stand and deliver. Second chances were fewer.

His early successes in presidential primaries indicated the world's highest profile political office might be within his grasp.

In early February 1966, Lurleen had still not yet formally announced her candidacy. But she and George told folks that she had agreed to run for governor. The Alabama Democratic primary testing ground loomed May 3, 1966.

Wags began wondering what was the reason for foot-dragging? Ol' George usually liked to jump into a fray early. Why wasn't Lurleen announcing her candidacy formally? Was it Lurleen's health? It was almost as if George was waiting for something.

． ． ． ． ． ． ． ．

On February 9, 1966, deGraffenreid was in the Fort Payne Alabama airport with his pilot, watching and evaluating inclement weather. Independently wealthy, deGraffenreid was using a small plane to shuttle between campaign appearances. (Another source puts the date as February 25, 1966).

That 1966 late afternoon, shortly after takeoff, Ryan deGraffenreid and his pilot were killed instantly in the crash of the twin engine Cessna 310 on their flight from Fort Payne to Gadsden, Alabama. They were the only occupants of the aircraft. Obtainable accounts of the circumstances of the crash are brief, vary slightly and do not include the pilot's name.

One account discusses windy conditions and an approaching storm. The Gadsden destination was only 38 miles from the Fort Payne airport, but deGraffenreid worried that he was late for a speech.

Airport Manager Joe Dahl suggested that deGraffenreid choose driving to Gadsden over flying. Dahl's wife expressed disbelief that deGraffenreid intended to fly the 20-minute flight, given the questionable weather.

Spurning the advice, deGraffenreid took off.

Witnesses report the plane, "bandied about by gusts, never cleared the mountain." Torn-apart bodies were recovered.

Another separate account puts the Cessna's departure time as evening. A description attributed to an unnamed airport manager indicates that the (deGraffenreid) plane took off into gusty winds. It hovered over a mountainous area, corkscrewing suddenly as if caught in a blast of spiraling air, then plunged toward the rocks below.

A third separate account indicates that it was dark and adds rain as a weather issue. If it was dark and raining, the airport manager's account of actually seeing the plane at a distance hover the mountain, corkscrew and fall is questionable.

George attended deGraffenreid's funeral.

George issued a statement praising deGraffenreid as "truly one of the outstanding young men of our state."

Commericial pilots, given the scenario, speculate just from a description of events, that a fuel issue, like water in the fuel tank because someone left the cap off in the rain, could have caused the fatality.

. . . .

With deGraffenredi literally out of the picture, George no longer feared Lurleen losing, wrote Bob Ingram of the Montgomery Advertiser.

Sixteen days after deGraffenreid's death in the plane crash, Lurleen officially announced she would run to replace George as governor.

Forty five days earlier, she had had major surgery for uterine cancer.

CHAPTER SIXTY FOUR

LURLEEN OPPONENT CLAIMS FLIGHT SABOTAGE

Dr. Carl Ray Robinson, an Independent Party candidate opposing Lurleen in the November 1966 general election, was luckier than deGraffenreid.

Robinson, who was both a lawyer and a physician, survived a similar life-threatening aviation incident in an aircraft he, like deGraffenreid, was utilizing to campaign against Lurleen.

In the campaign's closing weeks, sometime before the actual voting, the helicopter in which Robinson was a passenger crashed into a suburban Birmingham shopping center.

Robinson suffered a back injury, which newspaper accounts said hospitalized him for a month, removing Robinson from the public eye just within the crucial time frame when candidates typically surge their campaigning and personal appearances and sometimes gain ground.

* * * * * * * *

Robinson is quoted in print accounts as requesting that the aircraft crash he survived be investigated for possible sabotage.

But the alarm he sounded appears to have been ignored.

Robinson's investigation request, which followed by nine months an aircraft crash death of another of Lurleen's opponents, Ryan deGraffenreid, drew a dismissive yawn from the media, who apparently never calculated the off-the-chart mathematical odds of the two crashes within the campaign framework.

215

Three years later, a third aircraft crash involving one of George's opponents would drive the mathematical probabilities further off the chart.

No one seemed to notice.

Lurleen and George's opponents might have considered staying away from aircraft or selecting different political races to run.

. . . .

Because of their design, helicopters can survive imminent crashes that airplanes cannot. Experienced, skilled helicopter pilots, despite malfunctions, can manipulate the rotor blades to guide the helicopter to drift down relatively slowly rather than dropping like a rock as regular airplanes do.

Print media quoted Robinson as saying that even though he ran as an Independent, he is really a Democrat. He said he ran because he didn't feel the Democratic Party was really represented.

Robinson was what politicos call a "spoiler" candidate.

With Robinson's candidacy detoured into a hospital stay, Lurleen would face only Republican nominee Jim Martin, a U.S. Congressman, in the general election. Alabama was a historically Democrat state in that era.

However, in a general election a "spoiler" candidate like Robinson could siphon off sufficient votes from Lurleen to allow the Republican Martin to win the governorship.

A contemporary example is the Green Party "spoiler" candidate consumer activist Ralph Nader in Florida, who analysts say drained enough votes away from Democrat Al Gore to allow Republican George W. Bush to win Florida and the 2000 Presidential election.

CHAPTER SIXTY FIVE
ADVICE: AVOID AIRCRAFT

Albert Brewer, who was initially a stalwart George Wallace supporter as Lurleen's lieutenant governor, then a vocal George Wallace opponent and detractor, was lucky he was not aboard a helicopter in 1970 when he ran against George for the governorship.

Brewer had moved from lieutenant governor to governor, serving out Lurleen's unexpired term after her death. He was instrumental in eventually changing the constitution to allow two successive governor terms.

Brewer's purpose in instigating the 1970 campaign flight was opposition research: to surveill George's brother Gerald's property and farm, rumored to be opulent. The occupants were the pilot and Brewer's press secretary.

That helicopter crashed.

But more discomfiting for Brewer's campaign was that it fell to earth on Gerald's property being surveilled! Neighbors saw Brewer's press secretary and the pilot bailing out of the helicopter, running across the field in Keystone cops fashion.

Brewer wasn't killed or injured physically the way deGraffenreid and Dr. Robinson were, because he wasn't aboard the helicopter. But he might as well have been.

The resulting publicity about the failed political reconnaissance embarrassed Brewer mightily, a humiliation perhaps with greater negative effect on his election chances than physical injury, revealing the lengths Brewer would authorize to obtain opposition research.

The relationship between Brewer and George soured Big Time when George, who had solemnly promised Brewer that George would not run against Brewer in 1970 if Brewer sought the governorship, retracted his promise and ran against Brewer.

Brewer was not amused.

Not only did George renege, but Brewer's 1970 Democratic primary race against George was called the nastiest in Alabama history. George won.

CHAPTER SIXTY SIX
FEAR OF FLYING

George could relate psychologically to aircraft crashes like those of Lurleen's opponents and his opponents because of his extensive personal experience with aircraft mechanics.

After returning from World War II, George professed a white-knuckle fear of flying that he asserted lasted all of his life. He forced himself on planes as a practical expediency required for candidates, he claimed.

However, during his four national campaigns for President, George gleefully flew all over America constantly. Press accounts describe him as unperturbed, jovially circulating among the press corps during flights.

In World War II, George served as a flight engineer, managing fuel consumption on B-29 bombers—one called "Sentimental Journey" and one called "The Little Yutz." In summer 1945, he flew as crew on bombing raids, turning Japanese cities into roaring infernos of mass shrieking death.

Although he was never a pilot, George was highly trained in the machine innards of planes. His war stories to a biographer detail times when military planes he crewed developed serious in flight problems, and he was able to jerry-rig the mechanics quickly enough to save the plane, the men, and himself.

Everything about fuel consumption was George's specialty.

One of the World War II instances, as George detailed to a biographer, seems somewhat similar to eyewitness descriptions of deGraffenreid's 1966 fatal crash in particular.

Flying at 9,000 feet in the dark of night, a wind updraft suddenly heaved the B29 to 19,000 feet, nearly overturning the plane filled with high grade explosives to be dropped on Japanese targets. Inside, debris careened everywhere around George and the other crew passengers.

"We've lost two engines!" the pilot screamed toward the back of the B29 as he struggled to control the pitching.

George shouted that he'd install a new voltage regular to try to surge the two silent engines back to full functioning capacity. He called to the captain, warning him not to instinctively push the throttle full forward.

With the new voltage regulator, a quick forward thrust on the throttle, such as would be used in a takeoff, might cause a crash.

Leave the throttle in present position until we see the effect of the new regulator, George advised the pilot.

Roger.

As George retrieved his helmet, blown off by the power of the upward spiral, the two once-downed engines coughed, coughed again, then sprang to life, transporting the soldiers back to their Mariana Islands base, a tiny dot of refuge in the vast empty blackness of the Pacific Ocean.

The airmen tried not to think how, if the two engines had not restarted, or if the captain had instinctively jammed the throttle full forward, they would have fared, spiraling downward, crashing into the roiling night sea, bobbing as invisible specks hundreds of miles and hours from any hope of rescue.

CHAPTER SIXTY SEVEN
SUCCESS HAS MANY PARENTS

Success has many parents. Failure is an orphan.
—Anonymous

Several sources are credited as providing George Wallace the idea of running his wife Lurleen as his surrogate candidate for governor.

Some identify President Lyndon Baines Johnson as giving George the idea by citing Ma Ferguson (1875-1961) who twice served as Texas' governor—once from 1925-1927, elected as a surrogate for her husband James E. Ferguson, who had been impeached and thus could not seek public office. She served again as governor from 1933-1935 when ex-governor James again ran her as his proxy.

Rebecca Beasley, editor of the Clayton Record newspaper, credits her mother, Bertie Gammell Parish, Record editor and Lurleen's long-time close friend, with giving Lurleen the idea of running for governor in George's stead.

"Mother made the suggestion to Lurleen. Mother had a lady in Clayton make a little bonnet, those kind with flaps on the side and ties, that pioneer women used to wear.

"Mother gave the bonnet to Lurleen and told her: Throw your hat into the ring," Rebecca remembered.

"Even before Lurleen announced, Mother told her: 'If you can have a Ma and Pa Ferguson in Texas, we can have a Ma and Pa Ferguson in Alabama.' "

But perhaps none of the above were catalysts for George's venture.

No one remembered—except George, who remembered it only too well—that he himself had suffered his most bitter political defeat at the hands of a family member running as surrogate candidate for another family member.

George lost his 1957 race for governor to young attorney John Patterson, who ran as proxy for his father Albert Patterson who was murdered by mobsters 17 days after being elected Alabama's Attorney General in 1954.

George saw first hand how successful a family member candidate with an already recognizable name could be, running for the same job the other family member held or vacated.

In fact, George, seeing how well it had worked for John Patterson, experimented successfully with that strategy himself in 1956 when he ran his brother Jack for George's judicial seat. It worked like a charm, just as it had for Patterson.

Jack Wallace won the judicial seat George was vacating— handily.

George's notorious obsequiousness to the truly powerful prevented him from telling LBJ: Thanks Lyndon, but I've already thought of running Lurleen myself.

Keeping public offices all in the family seemed to work advantageously for American political dynasties, state and national.

CHAPTER SIXTY EIGHT
PASS ME THE RUBBER STAMP

"There are two mays
and then a Must.
And after that a Shall.
How infinite the compromise
That indicates I will."
—Emily Dickinson

Even without knowing Alabama's political labyrinths, common sense analysis would illuminate why George selected Lurleen as his replacement.

George wanted a governor who would rubber stamp his ideas and policies unquestioningly. Other candidates with a stronger resume than Lurleen had a better chance of winning, but they might strain at or break away from George's very short leash.

George, who had separated himself for long periods from Lurleen during their entire relationship, not only perceived her as compliant, but was forthright in boldly proclaiming to all and sundry that he would tell her what to do and how to do it.

Had he spoken with Miz Henderson, one of Lurleen's teachers, George might have had second thoughts about how obedient Lurleen would be.

"As a student, Lurleen wanted to be a leader. She didn't want anybody else to outdo her," Miz Henderson remembered.

Then there was the power of Wallace name recognition in Alabama. Lurleen WALLACE. In political strategizing, name recognition is not one factor; name recognition is most often the only factor other than likeability.

Plenty of George's good ol' boy cronies such as Seymour Trammell (who would later go to prison) had political smarts and public speaking ability. But their backgrounds and second story activities could not withstand even a modicum of public and media scrutiny their gubernatorial candidacy would bring, George knew.

He remembered President Lydon Johnson's famous aphorism that in a political career, it is not so much your enemies who cause your problems, "it's your God darn friends!"

Much is made by biographers and researchers debating whether Lurleen jumped or was pushed into her 1966 candidacy. Both Lurleen and George bristled mightily at any even faint suggestions that George "forced" his wife to run.

Their defensive volley was an oft-related conversation in the governor's mansion when George, unhappy with a McCall's magazine negative feature calling her candidacy "petticoat bragging," told Lurleen she would not be running. He told her in front of several people who happened to be present that she would be going home to Clayton.

Those present agree that Lurleen responded emphatically in a vigorous end-of-discussion tone that she would run whether George wanted her to run or not. The speed and fervor of her response is often cited as evidence that she was not forced.

. . . .

One of George's male biographers concludes triumphantly that Lurleen ran because she loved her man. "She did it for George," he declares in a country singer Tammy Wynette fantasy riff.

Male-authored material on George is replete with pronouncements by academics and others as "fact" that Lurleen ran because she was so madly in love with George and wanted to please him.

But an alternative, more lawyerly analysis of the did-Lurleen-jump-or-was she pushed conundrum could be both, yes, she was forced to run, and, no, she was not.

If she did not run, Lurleen could easily see herself and her children collapse back into the financially strapped, rented-quarters life she escaped just three years earlier by moving into the governor's mansion in 1962.

The dark prospect surely flitted into her mind when George cited, in front of the others, the you-are-going-to-return-to-Clayton spectre as the fallback position.

CHAPTER SIXTY NINE
WHAT'S LOVE GOT TO DO WITH IT?

"What's love got to do with it?
What's love but a second hand emotion?
Music and lyrics by
Terry Britten and Graham Lyle
As sung by Tina Turner

While George might have perceived return-to-Clayton as an enticing carrot for Lurleen, Lurleen perceived it as an abstemious stick. On the other hand, George was a clever student of human nature.

Perhaps he intended the result he got from manipulating Lurleen.

The ignominy of moving out of the mansion into the unpleasant downgraded-to-coach past, loomed as an all too realistic possibility if she did not run.

If she declined, or ran but lost, there would be no $25,000 per year income—only whatever meager salary she might earn returning to work as a clerk, now with four children instead of three. George would be busy running for president and would thus earn zero.

In fact, George would want money for his campaigning, sometimes vacuuming from her meager salaries, as he always had.

She had to run. And, she'd better win, too.

Her older children were approaching traditionally expensive stages of life: college, marriage, starting careers. Her parents and brother Cecil had very modest financial resources and could be of no continuing financial rescue.

In the above senses, George did force her to run by his past personal and financial neglectful conduct, the memory of which must have hung over Lurleen's head like the dangling sword of Damocles.

Economic practicality trumps many variables. Or most variables. She had no other real-world option than to run.

But, in another sense, George did not force her to run.

Lurleen had very recently suffered through major cancer surgery. That hole punched in the hubris of immortality usually gets anyone's attention. When she decided to make the run, she may, or may not yet have known that her 1966 bout was actually a recurrence of cancer. But she knew as an aspiring nurse in high school that cancer survival rates at that era were not encouraging.

Cancer, then, was usually a death sentence.

Humans and even animals sense intuitively when they are dying, with or without a medical diagnosis. Because of her 1966 cancer surgery, Lurleen may have felt death's uncomprimizing presence concealed just around the corner intruding unbidden into her conscious thought.

Except for infrequent drive-bys, George had virtually ignored their children since they were born. Who would take care of them, and with what income at her death? As a former governor, George's salary would be zip. His only employment was practicing law, and he always disdained that.

Her daughter Lee was only 5 years old.

CHAPTER SEVENTY

WAS LURLEEN'S CANDIDACY *LURLEEN'S* IDEA?

Knowledge of impending death gives high-risk forays outside a comfort zone a why-the-hell-not appeal. Certainly, the life she might maintain if elected governor in her own right was far superior to the sad life that had been her burden during the acrimonious decades with George—a hardship life which circumstances would surely return her to as an ex-first lady.

George would still not contribute much or anything monetary to support his family. With only a high school education, she could qualify only for low-paid jobs.

Having lived for years in a mansion, a return to the farm might pale by comparison.

"Lurleen was an organized woman by nature," wrote Smith. "She approached solutions to her problems in a step-by-step manner. Here's the problem, she'd say to herself. Now what do I do about it? Step 1, Step 2, Step 3."

Lurleen didn't agree to run for governor because she loved George, nor even because she loved herself. She ran because she loved her four children.

By her candidacy she hoped to secure and preserve the best economic future for them in what was basically a one-parent family, with that one parent diagnosed with a recurring life-threatening disease.

For Lurleen, her decision to run was a no-brainer.

・　・　・　・　・　・　・　・

There was the possibility, too, that all along, George got the idea for Lurleen to run—from Lurleen—a possibility that has never been explored in print.

It is conceivable that Lurleen herself was the genesis, the spark: that Lurleen herself suggested her candidacy to George for all of the above practical, inarguable reasons.

Both she and George knew that in 1967 if the idea of her as surrogate was publicized as originating from Lurleen, it would go nowhere. From a political, societal and cultural standpoint, the suggestion of her candidacy had to seem to emanate from George.

To carry it off, Lurleen could not seem too eager, too willing. Lurleen had to project feminine reluctance evolving to gradual acquiescence.

CHAPTER SEVENTY ONE
ANSWER ONLY WITH YOUR EYES

Everyone who really knew Lurleen describe her as smart. Very smart.

In that era, women understood that being smart entailed being smart enough not to appear to be too smart. Men felt threatened by such uppity women.

She was also resourceful. Very resourceful.

Her two closest friends and role models were unusual in that time frame as independent women "out there" with careers: newspaper editor Bertie Parrish and home ec teacher Mary Jo Ventress.

Her close friends describe Lurleen as mischievous. She was skilled at putting people on. The comedic structure of her humor often was to conceal or veil her message by saying the opposite of what she meant or what she wanted.

Prior consent portrayed as hesitancy to be a candidate would integrate easily into her existing behavior pattern.

Lurleen— just as George did—observed the political victories of Patterson and of her brother-in-law Jack and others who ran with family names. Lurleen had spent years campaigning for and with George and knew the on-the-ground campaign ropes.

She and George also knew that her gender conferred a partial safe harbor shield for Lurleen. In southern culture then, and still, men hesitate to attack women publicly with the same vehemence and vicious comments they would sling against men.

Oilman-rancher Claytie Williams, a Texas gubernatorial candidate favored to win by a landslide saw his lead evaporate overnight when he refused to shake hands with his female opponent Ann Richards who extended her hand to him. She won handily.

. . . .

In carefully analyzing the oft-told anecdote about how in February 1967 George, as filing time neared for Lurleen's candidacy, told her she would not be running, multiple red flags pop up everywhere.

Just the fact that George appeared at the mansion at lunch time that day is inconsistent with his known habits. Lurleen is quoted often as saying that as first lady, because of his schedule, she saw George only at breakfast, and rarely even then because he was on the road.

Suddenly, George shows up unannounced for lunch, completely out of character for him, on a day when several of her friends, and family members were present.

George's topic du jour: "You will not be running," would seem to be one that would have been discussed privately between George and Lurleen alone. Even that February 1967 morning, before he left the mansion, they could have had a private conversation. Or, when he saw Lurleen had guests, he could have postponed that topic until evening.

Instead of discussing the issue with her privately, George approaches her almost as if having an audience witness their words was their choice. Staging comes to mind.

Their verbal interchange reads as possibly pre-scripted dialogue, to the point where it can be easily imagined written on a page: ENTER GEORGE: Hi honey!

When George is quoted as telling her he had decided she wouldn't run, part of her response is omitted in most renditions of the interchange.

"Yes, George, I want to run. And I'll be disappointed if I can't," reporter Anita, who spoke with the participants, quotes the language. Other sources quote similar language.

When Lurleen retorted that indeed, she would run, biographers omit her next sentence.

Lurleen added that if he would not support her decision to run for governor, she intended to be a candidate without his support.

BN reporter Anita Smith gets it right. In her book, Anita includes the quotes Catherine Steineker, Lurleen's social secretary—who was present—attributes to Lurleen:

"Now George, if you want to sit up there in that Capitol and not help me campaign, well…okay. But I'm going to run."

The additional quote casts the did-Lurleen-jump-or-was-she-pushed argument in a new light.

Maybe it was Lurleen's idea, not George's. Maybe Lurleen just made George think it was his idea.

CHAPTER SEVENTY TWO
ON THE ROAD AGAIN

"Ladies and gentlemen: I will be a candidate for governor of Alabama," Lurleen announced in a packed House of Representatives chamber where homefolks from all 67 Alabama counties waved banners and placards and 500 additional supporters milled outside on February 25, 1966.

Her additional remarks were brief, since George chomped at the bit as well as his ever-present stubby cigar, pacing nearby, impatient to seize the podium from her.

"If my wife is elected, I shall be by her side and will make all policy decisions affecting her administration," George professed.

Lurleen announced that she would pay George $1 per year to be her "No. 1 advisor."

In truth and fact, George had not been by his wife's side for more than two decades. Any marginally competent reporter seeking perspective could have characterized George's comments as hilarious comedy worthy of a "Saturday Night Live" spoof.

Throughout their entire marriage, George appeared to Lurleen and the children only very occasionally as a phantom apparition diverted by a mistaken turn from successive campaigns.

Further, after Lurleen's election, George was hoping to take a job that would move him even farther away from Alabama, president of the United States—hardly a passion that would allow him to place himself by Lurleen's or anyone else's side for more than a cursory moment.

And if he won the presidency, he would be relocated in Washington, D.C. in 1968, the second year of Lurleen's governor term in Alabama.

By her side? Uh-uh.

When questioned by an opponent about this "advisor" arrangement, George reportedly snarled a nonsequiter: "This is my day."

· · · · · · · ·

After the February 25 official announcement, Lurleen kicked off her campaign March 18, 1966, in Montgomery's City Auditorium.

The overflow crowd stood to their feet clapping and pounding their fists into the air for five minutes as George and Lurleen walked in arm in arm to the stage.

On stage, George veered away from the podium to sit with their four children.

Lurleen, alone, walked to the podium. For a woman in 1967, hers was a brave act.

"She had a flashing smile and high cheekbones. She had an unbelievable figure, particularly to have had four children. George thought she was pretty. And she was.

"She had drop dead gorgeous legs. George always talked about her beautiful legs. Her voice and manner were feminine" Anita wrote.

"It's gonna' be hallelujah time!" A man shouted gleefully from the audience just before she began speaking.

Somethin' was fixin' to happen.

Ooooohie Lordy!

CHAPTER SEVENTY THREE
YA' GOTTA' TOOT A LOUD HORN

The Lurleen Wallace campaign caravan rumbled into small towns across Alabama for the ensuing six weeks and four days. A literal, actual bandwagon.

Six or seven times a day, every day: It-t-t-t's-s-s-s-s-showtime! blasted from loud speakers, inviting a good time to be had by all.

Sound equipment, musicians, and instruments crammed the first truck. Lurleen, George, family members, and guests followed in a car, which was followed by two station wagons pulling trailers filled with folding chairs and flags. A red flatbed truck fitted as a stage in red, white, and blue bunting, with a speakers podium, trailed as caboose.

The high visibility entourage came to a halt at town squares in a swirling cloud of road dust, or in front of the courthouse, and quickly became the center of attention setting up.

What was termed "The Wallace & Wallace Road Show" would open with a warm-up act of a country and western band twanging from the flatbed truck about prisons, mother, trains, trucks, cheatin', lost love, and drinkin'. Sometimes their son, George Jr. 16,would shake tambourine with the band.

At the beginning of the Lurleen campaign blitz, alpha male George dominated.

Lurleen sat in a folding chair to the right of a speaker's stand. George would introduce Lurleen, who favored a preppy look ensemble of cream-colored longish skirt with conservative navy blazer. Lurleen would read thoughtfully from prepared remarks for less than 10 minutes, then sit down.

To mitigate the vocal strain of six or seven stops a day, she would choose from four alternating stump speeches.

Then the howitzer heavy artillery, George The Man roared out in Come-to-Sweet-Jesus-Have-You-Been-Saved meetin' style, whipping up the crowd for 45 minutes better 'n any preacher that could be named there and then.

When George Corley Wallace preached his gospel to you about hell (beatniks, atheists, Communists, strutting bureaucrats, pointy head liberals, and federal government overreach), you could right well feel the heat and those flames lickin' up round your toes -- headin' toward your legs real fast.

I tell you what.

Whatever anyone thought of his politics, as a speaker George had "it." He had no peer, wrote one biographer.

He was mesmerizing.

Gifted.

Great pre-Internet entertainment.

But George's Show Biz bling was a given—a well-recognized talent. His targets were predictable. Like a line of song an audience knows so well they can spontaneously sing along. Comfortable love.

Miz Lurleen was the new love, a new song.

A woman running for governor. Alabama's first lady. If she won, she'd be the only woman governor in America then.

Mothers and grandmothers brought their daughters and sisters

236

to meet this female phenomenon who'd stand there before speaking—and—afterward until every hand offered was shaken.

Campaign photos show fans approaching Lurleen with such awe that their mouths are literally gaping open.

I declare!

. . . .

Lurleen's brother-in-law Gerald often traveled with Lurleen's campaign entourage. He was one of the first to acknowledge and respect Lurleen's talents and effectiveness as a political campaigner.

"In the beginning of her campaign, people were voting for George. But as her campaign progressed and more and more people saw Lurleen, they were voting for her," Gerald said.

"People tried to portray mother as walked over by dad. And that may be the way it started. But it didn't end up that way," said her daughter Bobbie Jo.

"No it didn't," agreed her son, George Jr.

. . . .

The growing crowds Lurleen drew overwhelmed her opponents. One opponent, Carl Eliot, had 1,200 in attendance at a rally in Jasper, his home town.

In contrast, Lurleen attracted 4,000 admirers when she visited Jasper.

Those who blithely discounted her large crowds by attributing them as reflected glory from George stumbled badly in explaining: If that were true, why were her crowds larger than any crowds George ever drew in his 1958 and 1962 gubernatorial campaigns?

No one, except perhaps Lurleen, did the math.

She was, in best veteran politico playbook tradition, courting a voter base she had created over many years while George and his good ol' boys paid no mind to the female Cassius quiet and lean in the corner.

All over Alabama, the reality of Lurleen's incandescent star quality began erasing stereotypes of her as a mousy, shy housewife. Because Lurleen was a pioneer in women seeking high political office, or any political office, there was, at that time, no similar female with whom to compare her.

She had no contemporary role models.

In the late 1960s, Lurleen was the equivalent of a female astronaut landing on the Moon. One giant leap for womankind.

A trailblazer for women in politics.

CHAPTER SEVENTY FOUR
SLIPPIN' AROUND

"The concept that Lurleen didn't like politics and wanted little part of that kind of life wasn't a bit consistent with the picture of Lurleen which Alabamians witnessed in the spring and autumn of 1966.

"People who had heard and believed rumors about Lurleen's displeasure with politics lifted eyebrows as they saw her with their own eyes deftly criss-crossing Alabama as a poised, savvy campaigner," wrote one journalist.

"What had happened to first lady Lurleen? Had the rumors been false or exaggerated?

"Or had Lurleen really changed that much?" wrote Birmingham News reporter Anita Smith in analyzing whether Lurleen changed, or whether Lurleen was suddenly perceived as who she was all along.

Had Lurleen been layin' behind a log all these years?

The answer lay in how female resumes were perceived, like a magnifying mirror turned from "regular" to the high-resolution side.

On the high resolution side, Lurleen's factual resume would have read:

LURLEEN BURNS WALLACE:

1) Four years as first lady, governor's chief assistant, hostess, organizer.

2) 23 years managing small startup company (their family, their marriage and George's campaign business). Turned limited financial portfolio (her jobs were the family's sole support) into successful statewide enterprise.

3) Author of legal textbook used by judges daily on the bench. (Lurleen wrote Judging for Dummies to help George figure out what to do after he was elected judge.)

4) Multi-tasker, proficient in successfully handling—without supervision—difficult situations and difficult personalities (e.g. George Wallace & friends).

5) Familiar with day-to-day operation of state legislature, four years as enrollment clerk.

6) Familiar with policies and regulations of state department of agriculture, where she worked for years as a clerk.

7) Excellent social and organizational skills for events attracting thousands (first lady open house responsibilities).

8) Expert fisher, marksman horsewoman.

9) Aircraft pilot, skilled athlete, especially in water skiing.

10) Daughter of five generations of Alabama farmers.

11) Loves the Lord. Sunday school teacher.

"She wasn't out searching for herself. Lurleen had a basic core seed of strength," wrote reporter Anita Smith.

· · · · · · · ·

One of Lurleen's favorite country and western songs was "Slippin' Around," written by Floyd Tillman in 1949.

It was one of two introductory songs she requested be played at each stop throughout her campaign across Alabama, accompanying her and George as they materialized in the back of the crowd like magic, sprinting toward the portable stage.

George forbade their musician Hank Thompson to sing the "Slippin' Around" lyrics about marital infidelity, because George felt the words were too sexually suggestive.

Everyone knew the lyrics and what the lyrics were about: infidelity.

There were hundreds of razzle dazzle C&W songs that would have enhanced the upbeat mood of a Lurleen campaign intro number.

"Slippin' Around" was a curious choice by Lurleen.

If he were sure Lurleen's campaign stop intro song selection implied George's sexual indiscretions, George surely would not have allowed it to be performed at all. Certainly not connected with his wife's campaign.

But why did he allow this well-known song about cheatin'?

Why did Lurleen choose this song to hear over and over?

"Seems we always have to slip around
to be with you my dear, (slippin' around),
Afraid we might be found.

I know I can't forget you
And I've got to have you near.
But we just have to slip around
And live in constant fear.

Oh you're all tied up with someone else
And I'm all tied up too.
I know I've made mistakes dear—
But I'm so in love with you.

I hope someday I'll find a way
To bring you back to me.
Then I won't have to slip around,
To have your company."

Like the baby grand piano, and the lyrics of "Carolina Moon," the significance of the "Slippin' Around" lyrics remained a tantalizing mystery.

"Lurleen was very multi-dimensional. There was a lot besides Lurleen Wallace. She knew who she was," said Anita.

CHAPTER SEVENTY FIVE
COURTIN' HER BASE

Lurleen began creating her own voter base when she worked part time for several years as a clerk in the Clayton courthouse; then later for the Department of Agriculture Extension Service in Clayton. Both positions were conducive to meeting and assisting large numbers of the public—particularly at the courthouse.

At that time, agriculture was the main basis of Alabama's economy, essential to providing income for a high percentage of the population. Lurleen, daughter of a five-generation farm family, worked for the state organization that exemplified agriculture.

During the 1947 and 1949 legislative sessions, she worked in the state capitol as an enrollment clerk, a high volume, high stress job in the heart of the machinations, interacting daily with legislators, lobbyists, and visitors.

There she learned the sophisticated nuances of legislative politics that George had learned as a page in 1935: whose lever to press, on which political machine, for what desired result.

She taught Sunday school class at the Clayton Methodist Church, where she got to know Clayton residents and folk from small surrounding communities. She established herself as knowledgeable in the spiritual and religious currency at the essential core of southern culture for both blacks and whites in the Bible belt.

Loving the Lord mattered. Really mattered.

For her four years as first lady, Lurleen opened the mansion to the public all day every day. People could drop in unannounced at any time. And they did.

She entertained as many as 1,500 members of the public a week at open houses, teas, and socials she hosted at the mansion. Outside the mansion, at multiple civic venues all over Alabama, archival personal appearances photos depict her being warmly, affectionately received.

Alabamians who had previously met her over the prior years at those occasions were drawn to her campaign events, remembering First Lady Lurleen as poised hostess, speaker or special guest who had added exciting celebrity pizzazz to their small town's local event.

Lurleen was a draw.

However, a male reporter described her during her campaign as one would describe a naïve frightened child, revealing his almost insulting ignorance of who she was. "Lurleen learned to thrust out her hand and say, 'I'm Lurleen Wallace. It's good to see you,' " he wrote.

Lurleen didn't need to "learn" that basic, elementary social skill of self- introduction. She was long-ago savvy when the reporter was still mastering rolling his copy paper into his upright without getting it wrinkled in the carriage.

She'd been thrusting out her hand and saying "I'm Lurleen Wallace" for four years as first lady, as well as prior years on George's endless campaign forays, helping him in all 67 Alabama counties.

In fact, when a reporter asked her at the beginning of her campaign how she would figure out what to do, she snapped back that with 23 years experience campaigning for and with George, she already knew the ropes, thank you.

Even George credited his wife as his ready-for-the Big-Time polished student well before her campaign began.

"My wife is an old campaigner. Lurleen worked very hard in all my campaigns," he acknowledged.

Over the years, Lurleen, campaigning with George, had shaken hands with voters in all 67 counties. She'd been in areas with all those responsibilities when she was young, George Jr. said.

Lurleen already knew folk, and folk knew her. They admired Miz Lurleen.

· · · · · · · ·

Another male reporter wrote patronizingly that Lurleen was an easily startled novice who had to "acclimate to three or four thousand people, and the sound they made."

No, she didn't.

Again, she'd acclimated for four years as first lady, organizing and attending hundreds of events just like campaign events.

Sounds? Try bringing up four children by yourself. That will acclimate you to sounds.

CHAPTER SEVENTY SIX
A $2 SUITCASE IN A RAINSTORM

At the end of her approximately six-week, four-day grueling campaign, when Lurleen had won the Democratic primary by a historic margin, reporters continued to look down on her, subtly diluting her stunning achievement by describing her as physically weak: "exhausted," and "worn out."

In contrast, the press described alpha male George as macho — unaffected by fatigue, "going strong," "athletic."

The exact opposite was fact.

Reporters, covering for the first time a female candidate for the state's major office, never allowed solid facts affect their preconceptions and stereotypes.

Lurleen was a superb athlete who could slalom a zig zag course balancing on one water ski at high speeds. She could drive a speedboat expertly while pulling a water skier behind her. She could shoot dead reckoning as a skilled hunter. She could fish, then wield an expert knife, cleaning and deboning her catch without chipping her perfectly manicured fingernails.

She was a "walk you under the pavement" sprinter.

Her beautifully muscled legs that attracted George decades ago still, in her early 40s, attracted compliments.

During her campaign, George, her self-described would-be "No. 1 advisor," was unable to "always be by her side" as he promised voters.

#1 advisor George folded physically early on like a $2 suitcase in a rain storm .

In Talladega, the very first night of Lurleen's campaign, George fell ill with a virus. In April in Ashland, and other times, George fell ill and had to withdraw to rest. He said he had the flu.

Lurleen, only about eight weeks into recovery from major gynecological surgery, never, as far as is known, missed a campaign appearance because of illness, although she did miss one because of a schedule conflict.

The late 1960s were a time of readjusting long-held ways of thinking about the outside-the-home abilities of women, as well as how minorities were viewed.

Lurleen's intake of Menthol Benson & Hedges cigarettes increased exponentially in those seven weeks, shooting upward from her usual pack a day.

During speaking breaks, she'd slip off her shoes inside a vehicle, relax a bit, and smoke.

CHAPTER SEVENTY SEVEN
BECOMING WHAT ITS ESSENCE IS

When #1 advisor George fell by the wayside, unable to keep up the pace with her on her campaign stops, she blossomed, moving away from reading a prepared text.

In his absence, Lurleen began to sparkle. She spoke extemporaneously, even using mild humor at times to make a point.

At Pleasant Grove there was a Confederate cannon fired on special occasions. But no one had warned Lurleen about the cannon that suddenly thunder-boomed during her speech at a barbecue and fish fry.

One of her startled bodyguards actually jumped into the air.

Unfazed, Lurleen never missed a verbal beat.

She just kept right on speaking, ad-libbing: "That's the loudest reception I've had yet!"

· · · · · · · ·

"George wasn't there on the trail for a few days, so she had to take it alone at the rallies. She saw that she could really do it if she had to. She saw that the people were really listening to her speeches. So she took it and went.

"She had several stump speeches she used to rotate. But then she learned to take what she wanted from each one, to combine them. She'd say: 'Now, let's take this from this speech. Let's take this part from the other speech,' " remembered her friend Catherine Steineker.

Reporters deemed her improved speaking skill as evolution.

But perhaps the skill was innately hers all along, just waiting for an opportunity to emerge when her thoughtful, neighborly style would not be compared on the spot with George's masterful febrile delivery.

As she campaigned across Alabama, white male reporters persisted in describing Lurleen as "shy" in front of the adoring crowds that grew larger and larger, more and more enthusiastic.

The hundreds attending mansion social events and open houses hosted by Lurleen as first lady over the prior three years may have wondered: Who the heck are the reporters were describing as shy?

Not the Lurleen they'd met and knew.

"Mother grew as a person. Had she not run, she might never have realized that she had all this ability and talent," her son, George Jr., said.

On June 4, 1966, Lurleen and George were called up onto the stage at the Grand Ole Opry in Nashville. Venerable country-and-western icon Roy Acuff introduced them and said a few words of greeting over national radio.

That venue was pure gold campaign publicity.

Lurleen was adding to George's following during that time, reporters began observing.

CHAPTER SEVENTY EIGHT

WAS LURLEEN A HIGH SCHOOL GRADUATE?

An issue her opponents brought up about Lurleen died a quick death by voter disinterest.

But her opponents may have been correct.

In their opposition research, her opponents said they could find no record or evidence that Lurleen Burroughs Burns graduated from high school in Tuscaloosa or anywhere else.

She claimed to be a high school graduate.

State Attorney General Richmond Flowers, one of nine men whom Lurleen whomped and stomped in her campaign primary, advised a Boston, Massachusetts Herald reporter to research the issue: "Just go to the high school Lurleen went to in Tuscaloosa and see if you find a diploma. Ain't nobody come up with it," Flowers declared.

The time -worn political advice still applied: Never misrepresent anything that easily can be checked.

Flowers, who years later would serve prison time for corruption involving kickbacks, was correct about Lurleen.

No diploma or physical record or transcript confirming her high school graduation was made public, produced, or proffered for scrutiny, during her campaign or ever by Lurleen, George, Tuscaloosa High School, her children, or anyone.

Logically, if such a document existed, George or her family would have produced it years ago to end the controversy and disperse the doubters.

It never was produced.

Lurleen most probably did not graduate from high school.

Lurleen supporters, family, and friends always put forth an explanation that Lurleen had skipped a year of high school, or had done extra work and graduated early, or versions of that scenario. Friends and family state that Lurleen's graduation was at 15 or 16 years of age.

Her daughter Bobbie, as an adult, discounts the doubters.

"They didn't do their due diligence (in opposition research). Mother took summer school classes to graduate early because she wanted to go to nursing school. You couldn't get into nursing school until you were 18. She graduated from high school at 16, and so she went to work (at the Five & Dime). Then by the time she was 18, she was married to Dad. So that ruled out the nursing school.

"I know she did graduate from high school because she had a high school ring," her daughter Bobbie Jo concluded.

High school rings and other academic jewelry can be purchased easily by anyone from various companies and jewelers.

. . . .

"She always felt inferior because she didn't have a college degree," said Mary Jo Ventress, her long time confidante, who holds a masters degree.

"Lurleen, just because people have college degrees doesn't

251

mean they have any sense," her friend Catherine reassured her.

"Well, Catherine, you can say that because you went to college," Lurleen shot back.

Lurleen's daughter Bobbie recalls that during the time Lurleen served as first lady, they discussed how, even as an adult, it would not be too late for Lurleen to begin the college education she said she aspired to.

Lurleen always declined to explore that opportunity, citing the time crunch in her busy schedule as first lady.

"I said: Mother you could take some college courses now, perhaps by correspondence. I didn't realize she couldn't put herself out there like that as first lady. That was not really a viable option for her," Bobbie concluded.

"Mother did feel inadequate because she didn't have a college education. I was in college at the time. It probably was one of those things of mother saying to me: Be so glad you can do this."

Given Lurleen's often-expressed wistful wish that she had attended college, and the flex time for beginning college classes she easily could have made in her first lady schedule, her declination perhaps confirms the allegation that she did not graduate from high school.

Had she applied, college admissions offices might, and probably would, require written proof of high school academic records. By seeking to enter college, Lurleen herself could unmask any deception.

If it was an untruth, hers was an easily forgiven, small untruth — perhaps told originally years earlier out of embarrassment or yearning for it to be true.

Or maybe George suggested it to her to enhance his image.

As she moved increasingly onto a very public stage, perhaps Lurleen decided that admitting to her misrepresentation years later would be more embarrassing, and perhaps detrimental to the public image of her and of George.

She and her family just couldn't walk it back.

Lurleen and her advisors apparently never considered reframing the issue as an arms-akimbo, head-tossed-back, feet-planted positive: that in light of her personal and professional achievements as a 40 year old woman governor in 1967, not being a high school graduate made her life path even more exemplary—a message that would have resonated favorably nationally as an alignment of the stars, simultaneously extraordinary, gender-historic, and inspirational to everyone.

CHAPTER SEVENTY NINE
GEORGE, CLEAN OUT YOUR DESK!

George could not abide being upstaged.

As it became more and more evident that Lurleen's sun might be slowly eclipsing George's, he became the annoyed professor whose student has surpassed him in his field of expertise.

Lurleen usually spoke first at campaign rallies, very briefly. Maybe five minutes. About mid campaign, when she began extending the time of her remarks, plus deviating from her prepared text, Lurleen was intruding into time and turf that had always been George's private domain.

What the heck is she doing? George thought.

After about five minutes of watching Lurleen basking in the crowd's obvious adoration, George, sitting almost directly behind her on the stage, began reaching impatiently up to her skirt hem, tugging it in a silent command: "It's my turn. Move away from the podium!"

Lurleen ignored George.

At prior stops, she had spoken extemporaneously and longer only when George was absent.

This time, she ventured impromptu off script when George was right there with her.

Lurleen continued speaking extemporaneously as if she did not feel his hand jerking harder and more frequently on her hem, like one of her children pestering for ice cream. Delighted crowds who spied George's tugging gesture laughed, even applauding her audacity toward the man who told everyone that if they elected her, he would be by her side constantly as her "#1 advisor."

Maybe he had meant "by her side" as tugging on her skirt hem to give her some of that advice right quick during her speechifying?

Another version, related by her son, George Jr., has Lurleen turning to George and saying, in front of the crowd of several thousand: "George, when I am finished, I will let you know."

With either version, George was not amused. Too him, Lurleen was running off the rails.

His not-amused days were accumulating rapidly as Lurleen's campaign high-kicked into the home stretch.

Her daughter Peggy said Lurleen began realizing she didn't need George quite so much. "I think night after night she got a little more tired and a little more tired of George's speeches. Then her little speeches got a little longer and a little longer, knowing her.

"And then all of a sudden, it was her. The crowd wanted to hear from her. That was a game changer," Peggy said.

Concern about his decision to run Lurleen in his place began creeping more and more into George's thoughts.

Had she become this sassy woman recently, or had she laid behind a log for two decades?

Mrs. Ross Henderson could answer that.

If George had ever spoken with Mrs. Henderson, one of Lurleen's teachers, he would have had his answer. He might have evaluated Lurleen in a different light when he was casting about for a sycophant to replace him as governor.

"Lurleen as a student wanted to be a leader. She didn't want to let anybody else outdo her," Mrs. Henderson said.

. . . .

Lurleen's son, George Jr., relates another incident revealing of Lurleen's astute inner core.

George and Lurleen were on a state plane to Florence, Alabama. Lurleen had been quiet, looking out the window in deep thought.

"After it was clear she would be governor, mother told (George): 'George, it appears I will be the next governor. So what you need to do is go to the Capitol and clean out your desk.

" 'I might as well take over. So you go ahead and get everything out so I can move in,' Lurleen told George.

"My father and his friend Oscar looked at mother to make sure she was kidding. But she just stared back, not smiling a bit. Their laugh was an uneasy response.

' "As they exited the plane where the conversation occurred, (George) let mother walk ahead of him, out of her hearing.

" 'Oscar, let me tell you something. You know women change their minds a lot. I don't know if it is such a good idea her being elected governor.

" '(Lurleen) fixes you with that stare. I don't know how to take that sometimes,' " George Jr. quotes his father as saying.

256

Like most women of her era, in dealing with males, Lurleen had mastered the intricate art of direct confrontation or criticism clothed in humor.

Women confronting men directly invited not only a figurative slap down, but too much indirection also risked not getting what you wanted.

It was a thin tightrope.

But with remarks disguised as humor, male recipients were confused, thrown off their game. A classic passive-aggressive strategy.

. . . .

George Jr. always interprets any of his mother's confrontational comments, in all contexts, as humor. To do otherwise would, for George Jr., involve thinking of his mother in whole new ways that would upend his childhood analysis of her. His resolute inflexible concept of Lurleen only-as-mother would morph into someone he can't quite get his mind around in his adult years.

If Lurleen were serious in her comment telling George to surrender his governor's office to her early—and many other Lurleen remarks disguised as jokes—her sassiness is at variance with George Jr.'s image of his mother.

George began to wonder if Lurleen, whom he perpetually called "Sweetie," had, all along, been a woman he never really knew. A troubling awakening if he contemplated the answer as yes.

He had been absent from home a lot over the past two decades.

It was a disturbing equation George tried to push to the back of his mind as requiring analytical thought too complex. Campaigning for president of the United States was much more important.

CHAPTER EIGHTY
SHE HAD ME FROM HELLO

Albert Brewer, who ran successfully for lieutenant governor in the same election cycle as Lurleen, remembers how quickly it became apparent in her campaign how much the voters absolutely loved Lurleen. She was a smash hit early on.

"The crowd's (positive) reaction was just unbelievable. And when Lurleen saw that, it gave her confidence.

"The bitterest enemies of George Wallace still respected Lurleen. Everyone admired her for the life she lived, and what she stood for," Brewer said.

"She's everything that everybody admires, and would like to be like. Lurleen's the good guy," Brewer said.

·   ·   ·   ·   ·   ·   ·   ·

"My mother's charisma was just as strong as my father's. It was a different type, lower key.

"But during the course of her campaign in 1966, when she started deviating from her prepared text, people started feeling her personality, her warmth and goodness," said her son George Jr., who sometimes accompanied his parents on the campaign trail.

"It was just wonderful to behold. I think she developed a self-actualization, realizing a potential she never knew was within her. And it was just wonderful to see that as well.

"The exchange between my mother and the crowds was a real love affair," George Jr. said.

"When my father wasn't there, she would talk off the cuff. The reaction was very positive from the crowd. I think that helped her grow."

"Had she not been able to convey something of substance about herself, she would not have been elected. No matter how popular my father was, the people would not have gone for it. I think that's important to remember." George Jr. continued.

"The State of Alabama fell in love with Lurleen Wallace. They absolutely adored her," Smith said.

· · · · · · · ·

"People put mother on a pedestal, but it was a pedestal they could reach," Bobbie Jo said in analyzing the Love Lurleen fest that her mother's 1966 six-week, four-day campaign became.

"At 22, I was at an age where I was not that surprised at what she was doing. It's only as you get older, you realize…" Bobbie Jo said, her voice trailing off in thought.

"All this realization came to me in later life. What a treasure my mother had been to people. What a phenomenal thing she had done, and with no college education.

"Mother had lots of backbone," Bobbie Jo added.

The first vote Bobbie Jo cast after she became eligible to vote was for her mother in the May 3, 1966, Democratic primary.

· · · · · · · ·

As a campaigner for herself, Lurleen Wallace was indefatigable.

"Everyone thought George set a fast pace, but before the day was over, everyone wished for George," sighed one of her press people seeking respite.

"At lunch time once in Ashland, we all began looking for someplace to eat. Then someone said, No, you won't get to eat. Mrs. Wallace has scheduled another stop in Ohatchee." A campaign worker had suggested she could get some votes there.

Right in the middle of the lunch hour, Lurleen drove 30 miles of dirt roads from Ashland to Ohatchee, her press aide recounts.

The next day, George was still sidelined with a fever.

In her #1 advisor's absence, although Lurleen began her morning speeches outlining what "our" administration will do, by afternoon she spoke of what "my" administration will do.

George showed back up on the campaign trail early the next morning.

News travels fast even in a non-Internet age.

CHAPTER EIGHTY ONE
SOME USEFUL AND CHIVALROUS AGREEMENT
FOR THE OCCASION

"Life is easier if you plow around the stump."
—Anonymous

"Daddy, you aren't governor any more. Mama is," Lurleen's daughter Lee, five, reminded George as they were leaving the reviewing stand at Lurleen's inauguration.

Evidence of that seismic shift in power became reality the next morning as George and Lurleen left the Governor's Mansion for her first official day as governor.

The anecdote of their Goldilocks clash has two main versions and many permutations.

One version is that George walked ahead of her, climbing into the right rear seat in the limo where, until the day before, he had sat for four years as governor.

Left standing outside the vehicle, Lurleen opened the limo door George had just slammed in her face.

"Move over George. I'm the governor now. I ride in this seat. You ride on the left," she told him.

He slid over.

A second version is that for several days after Lurleen took office as governor, George continued to sit in the limo's right rear seat, traditionally reserved for the governor.

Lurleen let his obstreperous conduct pass for a few days without challenging him. Then, one day George was late getting from the mansion to the limo.

Governor Lurleen was on time. Or she purposely arrived early. She seized opportunity.

When George rushed up, yanking open the right rear limo door, Lurleen was sitting there in the right rear seat where he had sat when he was governor.

"George, I'm governor now!" Lurleen reminded him.

George had a "not pleasant" expression on his face. But he went around the back of the limo and took the left rear seat.

However the confrontation may have played out in several versions, the defining moment was not lost on the state troopers present, who smiled at her feistiness.

Governor Lurleen wanted what she had earned.

She refined the who-sits-where issue a step further. Not long after, she got rid of the ostentatious limousine altogether.

In mid-March, when legislators, on their own, wanted to purchase an unrequested new limousine for her, "commensurate with her high office," she respectfully declined.

Instead of a traditional big black limousine, she ordered a small car, cream colored, so it stood out humbly among the other state vehicles for top executives.

Lurleen had begun marching to her own drummer in small and large ways.

George had not anticipated that Lurleen would slip from his grasp quite so quickly. She was as frisky as a new colt.

. . . .

George had retained the key to a private entrance door to the governor's office, Room 100. His small office was down the hall. One day he used the key to quietly let himself into what was now Lurleen's office as governor.

He, as well as about 50 people with whom Lurleen was meeting, were mutually startled to see each other as George appeared as an unannounced intruder into their business discussions.

George was uncharacteristically flummoxed as what to do next.

Everyone's head turned toward Governor Lurleen, waiting to see how the new governor would handle the awkward moment with the former governor, her husband.

"What can I do for you, George?" Lurleen asked, seizing the room, but adding a small smile.

"Oh, I just came by," George responded, momentarily cowed.

"Well, we're busy now. But I'll be glad to see you later," Lurleen admonished him, as one would a child, in front of the group.

Perhaps she remembered the many times, when she was first lady, that he made her wait in the anteroom of his governor's office until he would see her.

Perhaps she remembered many things about George.

As George backed out the door, he could hear Lurleen and the others laughing.

Things definitely were not going the way the #1 advisor had planned.

"He thought he was going to get her governor's office. And Mother put George in a little office down the hall. She just put his butt across the hall! I thought it was the greatest thing I've ever heard in my life! He had it coming to him!" Peggy exclaimed.

. . . .

A day or two later, George still apparently hadn't gotten the message that his young daughter Lee understood on Lurleen's inauguration day.

Staffers watched bemused as a Governor Lurleen bodyguard carried George's razor, toothbrush, and other toiletries out of what had been George's private washroom off his office when George was governor. The bodyguard took the personal items across the hall to George's makeshift office in Room 101, a conference room used for the press.

Workers spent an inordinate time remodeling space carved out of George's conference room office area so that Lurleen's Social Secretary Catherine Steineker, who helped Lurleen process bushels of mail and speaking invitations arriving daily, could move out of an inconvenient basement cubbyhole to be nearer Governor Lurleen.

Underlings who inquired on Lurleen's behalf as to why the holdup got excuses from the workers centered on what they said was delayed carpet delivery.

Exasperated, Lurleen herself phoned the building superintendent, who repeated the excuse about carpets.

"Carpets nothing!" she told him. "Before I came to Montgomery, I didn't know what carpets were !"

Her social secretary's office was move-in ready the next day, which further reduced the space allotted to George's makeshift office.

CHAPTER EIGHTY TWO
GEORGE, YOU'RE NOT GOVERNOR!

Another day George scurried down the hall to tell Governor Lurleen the names of the men he and his advisors had decided would be appointed to various high level vacancies in state offices—political plum appointments that by law were made by the governor.

"Why tell me?" Lurleen flashed back, irritated at being presented with a fait accompli.

Al Steineker, Catherine's son, relates what his mother Catherine told him she witnessed as typical, frequent private verbal scrimmages between Governor Lurleen and George in the early months of her administration, before George wandered off to pursue full-time the bright, shiny object of his second presidential campaign.

"George, you're not governor. I'm governor."
And George would respond "Ah....Honey.."
Then Governor Lurleen would say: "Not, Ah, Honey! I'll talk with you. But I make the decisions."

• • • • • • • •

When she took office, she did not immediately remove George's nameplate from the solid mahogany desk. She moved it to one side. She added a white marble nameplate given to her by a solider serving in the war in Vietnam. It read:

Lurleen B. Wallace, Governor of Alabama.

A silver-encased Bible presented to her at a prayer breakfast the morning of her inauguration shared her desk space with an ever-present bust of Egypt's fourteenth century B.C. Queen Nefertiti, Lurleen's heroine.

She had had beautiful Nefertiti with her as silent companion for many years.

When newspapers did a feature profile of Lurleen, they often mistakenly called the bust Cleopatra. Lurleen told interviewers she always kept the statute because Nefertiti was interested in good government.

Lurleen added that she and Nefertiti had much in common, but reporters never delved deeper.

Where had a farm girl housewife from small town Alabama developed a knowledgeable affinity with exotic Nefertiti? Lurleen had never traveled outside the United States. Perhaps she discovered Nefertiti in teaching Bible class at the Clayton Methodist Church.

No one asked her that.

But the two women, 3,500 years and cultures apart, did have some experiences in common.

Nefertiti, whose name means "the beautiful one has arrived," ruled with her husband, Pharoah Akhenaten, in the 18th dynasty (1550-1292 B.C., alternatively given as 1370).

Nothing is known about Nefertiti's childhood or parents, but she apparently died in her late 30s of a terminal illness. Another version has her posing as a male under a pseudonym to retain her hold on power after her husband died.

She was one of the most powerful queens ever to rule Egypt, historians state.

In Nefertiti's reign, old gods were discarded, and religion moved toward monotheism, creating societal upheaval equivalent to societal upheaval in America's late 1960s during the time Lurleen served as governor.

Akhenaten put Nefertiti's name with his on his cartouche, a kind of personal identity "card" usually reserved for the pharaoh alone.

The most famous relic in Neus Museum in Berlin, is a 3,500-year-old bust of Nefertiti done contemporaneously by the Egyptian artist Tutmoses. The painted limestone depiction of the queen, if accurate from life, depicts a stunning, incandescently beautiful face seeming lit from inside.

CHAPTER EIGHTY THREE
SASSY REALMS/ SPEAKING TO
THE LEGISLATURE

It took Lurleen's lieutenant governor Albert Brewer longer than it took George to get used to thinking of the new boss as governor.

On March 22, 1967, Brewer introduced her as she moved toward the podium to address the Alabama legislature.

He began:

"Ladies and Gentlemen, I give you Governor Geor…," then realizing he was about to faux pas big time, Brewer paused, then stopped. He immediately rephrased, this time correctly speaking Lurleen's name as governor.

Brewer said when he made the gaffe on state-wide television, she turned toward him and hissed in a loud whisper: "I'll get you for this, Al." Most people then and still regard Lurleen's response as an attempt at humor rather than genuine pique at Brewer's verbal misstep.

The two always had an amicable, respectful relationship.

• • • • • • • •

A recording of Governor Lurleen's voice, available at the Library of Congress, seems to reflect a slight shyness or hesitation in her voice at the beginning of a speech. But as she picks up speed, her voice becomes stronger, more assured, just as her family and others described.

In the early days of her administration, whenever Lurleen took the chamber podium to address legislators, media—most of whom were male—automatically trivialized her as a fish out of water flopping around bewildered in the bottom of a boat that George was rowing.

One derisive reporter referred to Lurleen as a "housewife happiest wandering around a fishing cabin humming Hank Williams tunes."

That comment was one of several vicious publicly insulting remarks Lurleen ignored.

One of George's biographers, a top tier reporter himself, calls out in print his male journalism colleagues, reprimanding them for their routinely unfair, scornful treatment of Lurleen as governor.

He writes criticism of his fellow scribes' unabashed bigotry and misogyny: "Since they could find no evil in her, they snickered—meanly—at her lack of experience and education."

But Lurleen was not even close to being as clueless about the legislature or anything else, as snarky journalists and others implied.

In fact, before she took the governor's podium to speak as governor, she spent several years sitting at the enrollment clerks desks just a few feet away from the same podium.

Had she responded with that riposte, however, her violation of state nepotism laws would have come to light, opening the door to scrutiny not in her favor.

She, and probably George, who arranged her clerk job years earlier, decided that discretion is the better part of valor.

· · · · · · · ·

Lurleen had an insider's sophisticated familiarity with the written and unwritten rules of how the Alabama legislature really worked, not only the formal rules and mechanics, but also the idiosyncrasies of the various personalities elbowing into and backing out of power roles and klieg lights.

During the 1947 and 1949 legislative sessions, while employed as one of the House enrollment clerks when she was 21 and 23 years old, Lurleen Wallace sat for hours and hours, days and days in a small office a few feet from the House chamber, largely unrecognized as a legislator's wife. An intercom links the enrollment clerk office with the House chamber, so the clerks like Lurleen could hear everything going on and absorb the fine points of legislative process.

When an item passes off the House Chamber floor, the hard copy is hand delivered to the clerks' office, where they record the bill or resolution number.

Enrollment clerks, next in the chain, are called to accept the document. The enrollment clerks write the bill number down in a different ledger, then try to distribute copies as soon as possible, explained Julie Saint, chief enrollment clerk in present time.

The formal process has not changed much since 1947 and 1949, when Lurleen served, except for the use of computers. Frenetic, highly demanding daily protocols, and zero tolerance for error, require enrollment clerks who are intelligent, quick and diplomatic in dealing with more than 100 House legislators, plus lobbyists, media, and the general public. It is a sustained high pressure job, not a job for the incompetent, weak, faint of heart, or clueless.

When the enrolled bill or document is passed on a vote, enrollment clerks hand deliver it to each chamber, obtain a signature from the presiding officer, then deliver it to the governor's office. An official there signs a ledger called The Governor's Book, stating the date, time, and number of the bill or resolution just received.

So, unknown until decades later, Lurleen well knew The Governor's Book and the inside of the governor's office before she became first lady and governor. In some respects, her two legislative sessions as an enrollment clerk tracked, in up-close learning opportunity, George's 1935 stint as a legislative page.

During their individual campaigns, neither George nor Lurleen publicly disclosed that she had worked as an enrollment clerk in the statehouse or worked for state agencies in Clayton. Concerned about past violations of nepotism laws, they kept mum, allowing the media to portray her as a hesitant, unsophisticated housewife.

For Lurleen, it must have been painful to bear the brunt of the personal jibes. She took one for the team.

•   •   •   •   •   •   •   •

It was not until years later, in interviews with one of his biographers, that George finally disclosed and confirmed her employment as a legislative enrollment clerk during two legislative sessions.

George told a biographer the reason for their mutual secrecy was that Alabama had a nepotism law that forbade the state employment of relatives of state employees. Lurleen's other clerical jobs at the Clayton courthouse and Clayton office of the Department of Agriculture may have been subject to the same prohibition.

Employees of he current office of the enrollment clerk indicate they have no records and ledgers from the 1947 and 1949 legislative sessions. They speculate that those records were all sent to the Alabama state archives. An Alabama archives researcher said they cannot locate such records in their facility.

Some legislative records, including enrollment clerk ledger entries, which might have contained Lurleen's signature or initial or handwriting from that 1947-1949 time period seem to have disappeared, apparently some time ago.

In successive regimes, as one administration transitioned to another in that era, historical accounts indicate that lights were seen on all night in some Alabama statehouse offices, fueling speculation that perhaps incriminating documents were being destroyed in advance of the scrutiny of newly arriving office holders.

It was the equivalent of erasing a computer hard drive.

CHAPTER EIGHTY FOUR
QUICKER 'N A CHICKEN ON A JUNE BUG

Until Lurleen became governor, Alabama banks had never paid interest to taxpayers on state funds deposited in state banks. Alabamians were loaning money to banks for free, so to speak.

Four days after taking office, Governor Lurleen issued Executive Order No. 1 directing the state treasurer to deposit taxpayer money only in banks that would pay 2 percent interest on state funds deposited more than 30 days.

The frugal house wife who was forced to scrimp by for decades, supporting four children on small amounts of money she earned at various clerk jobs, was adept at budgeting and handling finances. Lurleen was incredulous as to why Alabama banks hadn't been doing that all along.

Why should banks get free use of taxpayer dollars? Why hadn't anyone questioned this before? she wondered.

While everyone, surprised at her audacity so soon, waited for bank heavyweights to commence screaming in protest, bankers agreed, even helping draft implementing legislation that passed at the next regular legislative session.

Governor Lurleen moved quickly in her individualistic initiatives, piling up her pioneering first-ever-for-Alabama achievements as if she were trying to fit her "to do" agenda within a limited time frame.

・ ・ ・ ・ ・ ・ ・ ・ ・

In February 1967, Lurleen Wallace became the first governor in Alabama history to visit the state's mental facilities, which had historically "sucked hind tit" when it came to funding.

The initiative for the spotlight she was to shine on the forgotten was hers alone.

No one can account for the genesis of her keen interest in the mentally ill. They were not part of any cache of potential votes, so they had never been on the radar of officialdom. Some attribute her focus to a remark made by a friend.

Her brother-in-law Gerald Wallace had spent time as a patient in state hospitals housing tuberculosis sufferers—facilities whose decrepitude mirrored the mental hospitals, he said.

Governor Lurleen announced her concern shortly after her inauguration. The chair of the state Mental Health Board and one of his assistants, plus a probate judge and two of Lurleen's friends, including a pastor, signed on to make the unprecedented visit with her.

A February 1967 photo depicts Governor Lurleen Wallace trailed by her entourage, exiting 250-bed Bryce State Hospital for the mentally ill and Partlow State School for the mentally retarded —institutions in Tuscaloosa. Partlow housed 800 patients in excess of its assigned capacity.

Governor Lurleen's face is grim, stricken, shadowed with troubled disbelief as if she were among U.S. and allied soldiers liberating Dachau or Buchenwald German concentration camps in 1945, reeling and gagging upon seeing the grisly, starved, emaciated corpses stacked high and the waiting crematoriums spouting smoke.

275

The conditions she saw that day in Alabama's state mental facilities were-beyond any horrors she had ever imagined. Something beyond a snakepit.

Mental patients and the mentally retarded were tied to their beds for hours, sometimes beaten and starved. They were warehoused in beds almost touching each other, receiving no treatment. They shrieked and screamed much of the time, as they did during her visit.

Air conditioning was expensive and still under development as mainstream economical technology, so the facilities were not all air conditioned in the debilitating Alabama heat. Bed "sheets" were plastic.

Because of understaffing and underfunding, mental patients were expected to take care of other mental patients.

What could go wrong there?

Although condescending media falsely described Governor Lurleen as tearful during several prior official visits to other types of state facilities, this time she really was heartbroken at what she experienced and saw.

As she passed a child housed in one ward, the child held out her arms toward Lurleen and called out, "Mama!"

The expression on her face in news photos of her leaving one of the buildings with an entourage speaks everything that words are inadequate to convey. She is grim, stunned, head slightly down, and even her skin seems dark with a level of sadness down into her very soul.

"It was a shocking experience," she told the Medical Association of Alabama a few weeks later.

"That night I got down on my knees and thanked the Lord that my four children were healthy physically and mentally. I also made a vow to God that whatever I could do, I would do to improve the lot of our mentally ill."

. . . .

Lurleen wasted no time fulfilling her promise to God.

She was quicker than a chicken on a June bug in asking the legislature for money to upgrade the ghastly dungeons confining Alabama's mentally ill and mentally retarded.

Al Steineker, son of Lurleen's social secretary Catherine, said the mental health issues were a catalyst for Lurleen—a personal concern that pulled her further into independence from George.

"She set her resolve that day to be the governor that she told people she was going to be. It was no longer 'I'm just a sweet demure little lady standing up here because George Wallace couldn't succeed himself.

" 'I am the governor. I will make these decisions. We will do something to upgrade the mental health facilities,' " Steineker quoted Lurleen as saying.

CHAPTER EIGHTY FIVE
LEGISLATORS YES-MA'AM the STEEL MAGNOLIA

A docent leading a contemporary time school tour of the state capitol building, told a group of 9 and 10 year olds that Governor Lurleen did not have enough time in office to do much.

While it is true that she didn't have much time as governor, it is not true that she did not do much. In fact, she did more in her short time, than George. Governor Lurleen maximized her many accomplishments that remain visible all over the state.

Governor Lurleen quickly called the Alabama legislature into special session on March 3, 1967, recommending increased financial support for state mental health facilities. A $15 million bond issue passed at the next regular session. Voters approved the bonds in December.

She narrated a Public Service Announcement film, made in Alabama, to increase awareness of mental health issues. The Medical Assocation of Alabama honored her with its highest award.

Ironically for Lurleen, she personally helped pay for the improvements. Some of the money for mental health facility upgrading came from a new 2 cent state tax on each pack of cigarettes.

Lurleen continued chain smoking at least a pack of Benson & Hedges daily.

"When Lurleen is for something, every legislator says: 'Yes, ma'am' right away," George whined, complaining that his program goals were less easily accepted for funding. Some snidely observed behind their hands, that George had no gubernatorial program goals as governor except continuous campaigning.

Lurleen governed over 3 million Alabamians, headed 157 agencies, 27 boards, and served as titular head of the Democrat party.

. . . .

Alabama, at that time, had virtually no state parks.

After winning the 1966 primary, Lurleen accompanied George to a southern governors conference in Kentucky. As they were being entertained on a steamboat ride, Lurleen seemed pensive, standing at the vessel's railing, looking out at the beautiful trees and flowing water gliding past.

She had grown up near the Black Warrior river. Fishing and water sports were her major athletic interests.

She suddenly turned to George asking him why Alabama didn't have land set aside for recreational state parks for public use the way Kentucky did?

"Well, you're going to be governor," George responded, smashing the legislative initiative ball into her court.

After being sworn as governor months later, athletic Lurleen returned George's serve challenge.

Game. Set. Match.

She immediately began pushing for setting aside Alabama land to be preserved for public use as state parks.

At her initiative, the legislature eventually voted $43 million to establish state parks across Alabama over the ensuing four years. In 1971, a 1625 acre park, containing a 250 acre lake, nine miles northwest of Tuscaloosa, was named Lake Lurleen State Park in honor of her dedicated work toward the state parks goal.

Governor Lurleen also began the initiative to bring a cancer center to Alabama. She didn't want Alabamians to have to go out of state to obtain sophisticated cancer treatments.

CHAPTER EIGHTY SIX
YOU AIN'T BEEN INVITED, GEORGIE

Governor Lurleen's wifely comeuppances to George while they were in Alabama, which Lurleen was highly skilled at masking as humor, could be kept mostly private in the pre-Internet society.

But George's uncontrolled chutzpah, and refusal to relinquish the reins, would maneuver Lurleen into taking their power struggle visible nationwide—right into the White House itself in front of all the governors as well as the president of the United States.

George's boorish lack of manners, which played better in the back room of Billie Watson's store in Clayton than at the White House, would go viral.

. . . .

Lurleen received an invitation from President Lyndon Johnson to join him and other governors at the White House March 18, 1967, for a governor's conference. Because she was the only female governor in America, Lurleen would be the only female there.

National attention would be focused on her. She would be the princess bathed in limelight.

George was not mentioned.
George's name was not on the invitation.
Governors only.

Undaunted, George boarded the plane to D.C. with Lurleen. One account states that George waited in a D.C. hotel room while Lurleen met with LBJ and the other governors and attended briefings.

Say what?

Adynatons abound.

That George idled compliantly in a distant hotel is contradicted, not only by George's well-known inapposite mode of operation, but also by an account provided by her son, George Jr., who writes of the Washington, D.C. kerfuffle:

Afternoon briefings for the governors were scheduled with LBJ's cabinet on topics encompassing economic development, as well as domestic and foreign policy.

Spouse guests were supposed to separate at that juncture to be hosted for other planned entertainments and activities.

As Lurleen joined the other governors filing into the White House room where the briefings were to be held, she was startled to see behind her George begin following her in.

Further, as George caught up with Governor Lurleen, he suggested in the most patronizing tones: "Lurleen. Honey, why don't you go in with the wives and I will go in with the governors?"

Lurleen paused momentarily, making eye contact with George in what her son George Jr. describes as "that tranquil way."

Any remaining puppet strings were cleaved asunder like an ax through a hog's neck in that tense moment in the doorway of a White House briefing room.

George had finally overstepped even Lurleen's commodious

boundaries. He picked a wrong fight at an inopportune time with the wrong person. Had she followed George's mandate, she would have humiliated herself publicly—a self-immolation.

"George, I am going in with the governors. I don't care where you go," Lurleen told him as governors filed past them, witnessing the revealing power struggle exchange.

By creating that bit of a scene inside the White House, George had marred Lurleen's debut on a national stage—as governor—by publicly portraying her in front of the other governors as out of her league intellectually.

George's subtext to Lurleen was: You don't belong Honey.

She did not want to compound his louche behavior by asking that he be physically barred from the meeting to which he had not been invited—an ejection that would have immediately made sensational national and Alabama news.

Unfazed by her rebuking him publicly, George continued following Lurleen into the governors' briefing where he remained unbudging.

As the only female governor in America, Lurleen was the only woman present. It had been three decades since any woman had represented any state as governor.

George was the only non-governor present at the briefing for governors.

There are some people who are impossible to insult.

. . . .

George told one of his biographers a different version featuring himself as gallant rescuer, casting Governor Lurleen in subservient-to-him role of a frail befuddled damsel in distress.

George claimed that the morning of the briefing, Lurleen was timorous because she would be the only woman, and that he tried to calm her. He assured her that LBJ would be "solicitous and kind" to her.

LBJ did seat her in the front row and stood next to her for group photos in the rose garden. When the governors headed for lunch with George as tagalong, George is proud that LBJ "took Lurleen aside and asked if she wanted to go to the little girl's room?"

LBJ then escorted her to Lady Bird's private bathroom, waited for her, and escorted her back to the luncheon.

That night at a gala dinner in the White House for governors and spouses, LBJ joked from the podium that maybe his wife Lady Bird would run for President in 1972 when he would be term-limited.

LBJ was too smart to intentionally ridicule Governor Lurleen or to alienate more than 50 percent of his potential voters.

But instead of seizing an opportunity to favor Governor Lurleen with admiring presidential accolades for her early term achievements in mental health, public parks, and cancer treatment initiatives, President Johnson's remark, at its core, indirectly mocked Lurleen as a caricature, publicly discounting her stunning election victory by making her political success humorous and attributable only to George, not to her acumen.

In some sense, LBJ's off-the-cuff attempt at humor before all of America's governors also mocked his wife Lady Bird (Claudia Taylor), a businesswoman executive who ran her family's multi-million-dollar Texas-based radio and television station empire. Johnson implied that Lady Bird was laughably incapable of the intellect required for high public office such as Lyndon had attained.

Claudia Taylor (Lady Bird) was first academically in her high school class. In 1933 she earned a B.A. degree with honors from the University of Texas. In 1934 she earned another B.A. degree cum laude (in journalism) from UT, Her father, a judge, was born in Alabama.

LBJ graduated in 1930 from Southwest Texas State Teachers College. No academic honors are noted.

CHAPTER EIGHTY SEVEN
PLEASE DON'T PULL UP THE LADDER

Governor Lurleen also wasted no time after being sworn in to begin publicly praising females who put themselves forward for elective office. She encouraged more women to do so.

She did not pull up the ladder, a phrase women use for women who achieve personal success but decline to assist or ignore, women who are struggling up ladders behind them.

On January 23, 1967, just three weeks after taking office, Lurleen attended a ceremony honoring Mabel Amos, who was the first woman to serve as Alabama secretary of state. Mrs. Amos had served 28 years as George's secretary, then resigned to run successfully for the secretary of state position.

At the event, Lurleen spoke tribute to five other females who held elective office in Alabama and sent a shout-out to women across America.

"I am pleased to see women trying their chances in politics, even if they are Republicans," she said. At that time, former child star actress Shirley Temple Black, a Republican, was running for a California Congressional seat.

. . . .

After Lurleen made a speech to the city of Auburn's Chamber of Commerce, the Lee County Bulletin was impressed. Although the newspaper did not support either Wallace in the election, they praised the initiative and direction of Lurleen's speech.

"...if she exercises at least a modicum of independence, Governor Lurleen Wallace might well be a leader of great accomplishment," the paper editorialized.

That "modicum of independence" would come via the same mode of transportation, as George did when Lurleen first met him in 1942 at Kress's: by truck.

CHAPTER EIGHTY EIGHT
I'VE MISSED YOU, BUT MY AIM'S IMPROVIN'

George favored a bill that would allow truck-tractor-trailer trucks to hook up piggyback trailers to double their hauling capacity and productivity.

But the proposed bill would also result in extremely long truck rigs that opponents charged would be a highway hazard for motorists and would increase wear and tear on the highways themselves, thus incurring higher road repair costs for taxpayers.

Lurleen remained impervious to the trucking lobby. which had won George's favor. Her only olive branch of compromise was to agree to the bill if the super-long trucks were confined to interstate highways. But the truck lobby pushed for allowing them on smaller roads and city streets to travel to and from the interstates.

George would often ask her in saccharine tones: "Honey, you haven't changed your mind on that trailer bill, have you?"

"No."

Lurleen dug in her heels. Only if the long piggybacks were confined to the interstates, she countered.

The probable reason for Lurleen's opposition was personal and undisclosed.

No one except perhaps her children would have recognized the connection between their childhood and their mother's intransigence in flaunting George regarding the piggyback truck legislation.

• • • • • • • •

In the 1957-1962 period of their corroding relationship, when George was almost always absent from the home and they had violent quarrels, Lurleen many times would put the children in her car at night, fleeing along side roads toward her parent's rural home near Lewisville.

"When we'd first start out to MaMaw's and Mr. Henry's, right away Mother would get behind a big truck. She'd just stay behind a truck as long as we could all the way there. Mother told us it was safer at night to be behind a big truck to protect us from oncoming traffic," George Jr. remembers.

When Lurleen considered what the trucking lobby wanted, she framed the effect of the proposed legislation within the context of her life's personal experience. She envisioned how scary it would be with the elongated piggy-backed trucks, swaying back and forth on the small unlighted rural roads, to stay behind them for miles in a standard size vehicle as she had done as a young mother not so many years ago.

George's repeated entreaties to persuade her otherwise fell on deaf ears.

CHAPTER EIGHTY NINE
THE TRUTH THAT FINALLY OVERTAKES YOU

The shocking truth about the realities of her medical history came to Lurleen Burns Wallace by happenstance, casually and from a stranger, after the fact.

Some reports say she found out in late 1961 when she was campaigning for George. Others put her discovery time at early 1962 shortly after she became first lady. And others put the revelation about 1963-64 during a social event she was attending.

Anita Smith, the Birmingham News reporter who covered Lurleen's medical issues, writes in her book Crusade of Courage that it is unknown the exact date Lurleen discovered that her first cancer alert occurred in 1961.

Whenever it was, she had to deal with the bad news in three aspects. The devastating information itself, being totally blindsided by the revelation, and the fact that George orchestrated withholding vital information about her health from her with the help of her friends.

She was furious.
Livid.
"Lurleen freaked out," remembered reporter Smith.

* * * * * * * *

A man at a social event came up to Lurleen and began discussing his own cancer, or the cancer of someone he knew. Some reports say the man was one of George's campaign workers.

Then the stranger said to her something like: "Of course, you'd know about that because you've had cancer, too."

What do you mean? Lurleen asked, stunned.

Then he told her about her 1961 test results, which were apparently known about and discussed by George's campaign workers, as well as several of Lurleen's closest friends, and many others in Alabama.

It was the first time Lurleen was informed about her personal medical information—by a stranger who obviously knew more about her medical condition than she did.

Actually, a few months earlier, another stranger had made a similar remark to Lurleen. But when Lurleen asked Nita Halstead what the woman meant, Nita, who knew the truth, said she didn't know.

To Lurleen's face, Nita at that time, verbally dismissed the woman as confused, misinformed.

Lurleen, trusting Nita Halstead then, accepted Nita's claim of ignorance.

Keeping a life-threatening illness from Lurleen when early treatment is essential and available for cancer is the only time she lied to Lurleen, Nita Halstead explained.

"Nita, George and Lurleen's friends went to all sorts of lengths to keep her diagnosis from her," Smith said.

Generally, cancer has a five-year recurrence factor. If it has not returned, after treatment, in five years—then the patient is deemed "cured." Lurleen's 1965 recurrence would have been within the time period when treatment should have been undertaken.

Lurleen's untreated cancer recurred about four years and eight months after her 1961 diagnosis.

. . . .

To Lurleen, George's withholding of the facts, and the efforts at continuing concealment by George in concert with those she thought were her friends, was a betrayal so monstrous, so devastating, she almost could not comprehend it. Julius Caesar's disbelief when he was face to face with his close friend Brutus as Brutus joined others in enthusiastically stabbing him to death in 44 B.C. would be a valid comparable.

After her daughter Lee was born by Cesarean section in 1961, doctors found "some suspicious tissue implanted on the inside wall of her abdomen." Test results on the samples indicated that the samples contained malignant or pre-malignant tissue. Other results identified the suspicious tissue as "a phenomenon associated with childbirth, but not cancer," according to Smith's book.

Her physicians told George about the adverse results. But they did not tell Lurleen, an omission and commission not uncommon with women's health care in that late 50s early 1960s era.

George, who within that exact time parameter was making his do-or-die fevered second run at the governorship he had lost in 1958, chose not to share the malignant results information with Lurleen.

Accordingly, she had zero treatment, a decision made not by her, but by George alone, on an issue whose consequences she alone would have to bear.

George later justified his conduct as altruistic and selfless by saying that because her test results conflicted, he "didn't want to worry her."

· · · · · · · ·

As an astute politician, George's justification for not telling his wife about her cancer in 1961 could have had many selfish facets, as did many decisions George made.

Some who knew George's blind ambition well, suggested that George declined to tell his wife that some 1961 test results indicated she had cancer because of motivation to protect his own political interests, not hers.

He was concerned that the adverse medical news about his wife might have an adverse effect for him—casting a shadow on his 1961 gubernatorial campaign.

Voters might have concerns that her cancer treatment would distract him from his 1962 term gubernatorial campaign. Or criticize him for continuing to campaign while his wife was diagnosed with a life-threatening disease.

If disclosed in 1961, Lurleen's cancer diagnosis might also provide his opponents ammo to wonder aloud whether, if elected, he could be a full-time governor if he had to share job focus with a seriously ill wife.

Or that, if they voted for George, Lurleen would not be able, if she were first lady, to carry out the heavy social schedule that role traditionally required while undergoing cancer treatment.

His detractors say George, in concert with Lurleen's trusted friends, went to such extraordinary lengths and lies to continue keeping her from seeking treatment because he feared that public opinion would favor him dropping out of the 1962 governor's race to care for his wife, a warm and fuzzy role George may not have wished to sign up for, particularly given that in the 1959-61 same general time frame, Lurleen had left him and filed for a formal separation.

Would Lurleen have returned to George in that 1961 time period, as she eventually did with Gerald as negotiator, if she knew that some of her tests revealed cancer? Would knowledge of her medical situation in 1961 have affected her decision on whether to convert the formal separation agreement into a divorce or into reconciliation?

Whether George's reasons were altruistic or selfish, many others across Alabama did acquire Lurleen's personal, intimate medical information without her permission or knowledge. George himself was the No. 1 suspect as probable source and conduit for the disclosures, since presumably, her physicians told only George in 1961.

At whatever time George or someone violated Lurleen's privacy, her closest, dearest friends set into motion a four-year conspiracy—approximately during the years she served as first lady—to keep the 1961 cancer red-flag warning information from her.

Nita Halstead said she constantly worried that Lurleen would find out.

Why didn't Nita tell Lurleen?

If George's proffered excuse for withholding her 1961 medical test results from Lurleen was that there were conflicts in diagnosis within her medical reports, why did he encourage and cooperate with others to continue the deception so elaborately for so many years?

George, as a lawyer, must have understood the probable medical consequences for Lurleen. If even one of the 1961 reports was correct, and she did have cancer, she was, because of George—receiving zero treatment—increasing the likelihood that within five years, her cancer would recur, as it did.

CHAPTER NINETY
HUNTIN', FISHIN' and LINGERIE

Lurleen's father nicknamed her Mutt because as a child she followed him everywhere, perpetually asking lots of questions.

But the Mutt nickname could have other applications to Lurleen's persona, which was a mutt-like mixture of disparate tastes and interests.

She enjoyed clothes. But only after she became governor did she have money for anything other than basics.

Editors told their reporters to always write what the governor was wearing. The edict caused some consternation among the hard bitten male scribes.

One nationally popular male who was only too glad to discuss what Lurleen was wearing was the fey Mr. Blackwell. As a designer ordained by the media as arbiter of all things fashion in the late 1960s, including who was "best dressed," Mr. Blackwell delighted in trashing Governor Lurleen Wallace's fashion efforts and taste.

In a May 6, 1967, national television show hosted by comedian Joey Bishop, Blackwell criticized Lurleen's clothes as "looking like last Monday's wash hung out to dry." Blackwell included Elizabeth Taylor, Julie Andrews, Lurleen and others as dismal fashion failures relegated to his worst dressed list.

Later the Birmingham News noted wryly that Mr. Blackwell himself was the designer of a few of Lurleen's wardrobe items.

George reluctantly modeled one of her clothing items—an apron Christmas gift from Lurleen—in photos released nationally in December 1967. Governor Lurleen, laughing in the photo, said she meant the gift as a sort of public joke about George being "first lady" when she was elected governor.

Mr. Blackwell did not comment on George's apron.

George is not smiling in the photo.

. . . .

Lurleen's flexible multi-faceted personality retained traces of her tomboy youth in her love of hunting, fishing and athletics. But in contrast, also she loved very feminine lingerie. The lacier, silkier, and softer, the better.

She collected lingerie.

Friends, knowing of her preference, gifted her with more lingerie on birthdays and holidays. She particularly fancied, frilly underthings and bed jackets—soft, lacy, long-sleeved loose jackets to be worn while sitting up in bed.

As a physical remembrance of her mother, Lurleen's daughter Bobbie Jo has saved pieces of the lingerie, including the bed jackets her mother enjoyed. Each item is delicate and beautifully made.

. . . .

The media discovered her tomboy youth side: that Lurleen was an accomplished hunter and went fishing whenever possible — both pursuits traditionally male territory into which, in that historical era, only very self confident, independent women veered at their social peril.

A ubiquitous photo of First Lady Lurleen in field clothes,

holding up a 15-pound wild turkey she had just shot, is displayed proudly all over Alabama. She did really shoot the turkey, of course —at daybreak in Lowndes County.

But if the number of people who later claimed they were with her when she bagged the bird is true, humorists note that about 6,000 people must have been tromping through woods and fields with the first lady at the time, the commotion scaring off every wild creature for many square miles.

A man who was present at the shoot wrote in the Birmingham News of Lurleen's prowess as a hunter: "The dainty hand that wields the pen can also pull a deadly trigger."

CHAPTER NINETY ONE
WEEPING ENDURES FOR A NIGHT

"Weeping endures for a night. But joy, joy cometh in the morning."
—Psalm 35, Verse 5

From her swearing in on January 16, 1967, until June 20, 1967, Lurleen experienced what she described later as "my happiest days."
Surely she had earned that happiness many, many times over.

She was growing into the governor's job well.
George was absent a lot running for president again. Mutt was off leash.

Alabama newspapers that relished attacking George had begun to sing her praises.
People loved her personally, and she reciprocated.
The racial issues and resulting violence continued throughout the South. She condemned the "night rider" bombings of homes and businesses in Alabama and elsewhere as "despicable, cowardly acts" and offered monetary rewards to those who helped apprehend the perpetrators.

Lurleen had mastered the skill of tuning George out on racial issues. Reporter Anita Smith of the Birmingham News wrote that "while George was ranting about civil rights issues," Lurleen ignored him. She kept knitting, murmuring an occasional H-m-m-m-m."

Her daughter Bobbie Jo remembers: "Mother always taught us that nobody is better than anyone else."

·　·　·　·　·　·　·　·

These were halcyon, personally serene weeks for "Mutt" from Northport.

There were some glorious days at the governor's beach house near Gulf Shores where she baked herself for hours in the sun's strong radiation as she always had, while keeping her lungs filled constantly with the smoke of endless Benson & Hedges cigarettes. She fished and went crabbing with friends.

"The last time Governor Lurleen went fishing, I went with her. I was 13 years old," remembered Al Steineker, son of Lurleen's Social Secretary Catherine. It was a deep sea fishing in June out of Orange Beach, Alabama, across the bay from Mobile.

"She asked me if I wanted to go fishing with her and her security guards, and I said yes. The weather was horrible that day. The seas were rough. I'm not talking two or three feet. I'm talking 10-12 foot ocean waves.

"Miz Lurleen and I took turns getting sick in the head (bathroom). It was that bad.

"We didn't catch one fish in the entire four hours. That's about as much fun fishing as any of us could stand," Al said.

"That same week in June, 1967, I remember going crabbing with Miz Lurleen in the afternoon three or four times. I always called her Miz Lurleen instead of Governor Lurleen.

"We'd take a line and have a little weight on it. We'd tie a piece of chicken liver to it and toss it out into little pools along the beach area that had filled up with water. We'd feel the crab eating on it, and we'd pull it back in." Al said.

Although George Jr., Peggy, and Lee were there that week, they did not join young Al and Lurleen in the fishing adventures.

"Governor Lurleen and I just hung out a lot together," Al explained.

Peggy, a 17-year-old high school senior, said she was there at the beach because Lurleen had grounded her. "She said, 'You are boy crazy, so you have to go with us to the beach. I cannot leave you in Montgomery because you will be on the phone the entire weekend.' She was very right about that."

Lurleen's mind was on the betrayal.

CHAPTER NINETY TWO
BIG GIRLS DO CRY

In June, Lurleen's cancer, operated on in early 1967 just before she announced her candidacy for governor, returned.

In the beautiful delicate lingerie she enjoyed, one morning there was her blood—bright and red. Small hemorrhaging clots in her underwear. Since her uterus had been removed in early 1966, the blood wasn't coming from her uterus as menses.

As an intelligent woman, Lurleen understood the worst without having to look at any medical reports.

Her cancer had not only returned. It had spread.

· · · · · · · ·

On June 20, 1966, she entered St. Margaret's Hospital in Montgomery.

Then something unexpected happened.

The tests were negative. She did not have cancer.

Hope sprang, followed quickly by sorrow.

A referral to a specialist resulted in a diagnosis that her cancer had returned. The stark discrepancy in the test results tracked the same discrepancy as in her 1961 results.

And, as in 1961, the no-you-don't-have cancer-yes-you-do-have-cancer disparate, conflicting conclusions from the same physical evidence were never explained publicly.

Alabama physicians recommended she travel to M. D. Anderson Hospital in Houston for further testing.

She fell into a deep despondency.

Bobbie Jo, her confidante, her hero child, accompanied her to Houston July 4. George went, too.

Surgeons removed an egg-sized malignant growth and an 8-to-10-inch section of her colon on July 10. Doctors expressed confidence in their work. She remained hospitalized until July 25 when she returned to Alabama.

"I won't be here a year from now," Lurleen told her social secretary Catherine Steineker as they sat together in the sun those last June days on the beach before she went in for her July surgery.

"Now Lurleen, I'm just not going to hear any more talk like that," Catherine responded.

"But the way Lurleen said it, so matter-of-factly, there was really nothing much left to say. And you certainly couldn't make up a lie to tell her and get away with it," Catherine said.

CHAPTER NINETY THREE
WHEN YOU'VE GOT THE WOMAN,
YOU GOT THE MAN

Mid afternoon on Tuesday July 5, 1967, Anita Smith was sitting at her desk at the Birmingham News. Outside the cicadas whistled their shrill sustained cries signaling the temperature was soaring upward to a temperature where the air conditioning would be virtually useless.

Manual typewriters clacked all around her, bells binging each time a reporter hit the carriage with his middle finger to send it flying back flush left.

Small or large, dailies or weeklies, newspaper newsrooms across America in the 1960s shared a clattering ambience of sound and flurry, reflected in whole or in part by the Birmingham News.

Sounding like deafening freight trains, grey metal Associated Press and United Press International machines chugged nonstop side-by-side 24/7/365 as story after story from correspondents in far flung locales in America and worldwide spewed downward on thin yellowish copy paper toward the ink-stained wooden floor, like toilet paper rolls unrolling very fast.

A teen-age boy wielded a ruler against the engulfing paper tide feed, using it as a tool to separate each story by deftly ripping the paper with his right hand against the metal strip on the ruler in his left hand.

The boy hurriedly sorted the wire service copy according to the desk it was destined for by bashing the paper sheets down onto a series of metal spikes protruding upward lethally on a battered table.

Sometimes men typing loudly at the rows of battered wooden desks screamed "Copy!" while holding up their left hand filled with paper. Sometimes they could yell "Copy!"and still keep typing with the right hand at the same time, while speaking into a phone receiver cradled between their shoulder and neck.

The boy had to run from his hard wooden chair by the clattering AP and UPI machines over to the man holding up the paper, grab it, then run to a man sitting in the middle of another bigger horseshoe-shaped desk.

He had his tie flipped over his shoulder, a tender mercy to those with fashion criteria.

A chocking thick cloud of cigar and cigarette smoke hovered, perpetually obscuring the patterned tin ceiling stained to a muddy brown. A cigarette hung from nearly every lower lip or burned to a long ash in nearly every ashtray.

White men with pencils, their ties loosened, sat at the rim around that desk, so intent on scrutinizing piles of the copy paper accumulating before them they did not converse with each other except in monosyllables or grunts known to each. Some wore green eye shade visors and had black elastic bands holding back the long sleeves of their white dress shirts.

A few of the articles the men were editing extended 10 to 12 feet long as letter size pages the copy boy had pasted together using a small brush oozing a clear, gelatinous glue.

Two metal tubes, bound together, snaked from the ceiling across the room, ending near the left elbow of the man with thick eyeglasses in the center of the horseshoe desk who kept one eye perpetually on a very large plain clock on the wall facing him. Periodically, he'd open a brown canister from the unstable pile inching off the table on his right, insert rolled up copy paper inside, stuff it in the tube, and snap shut the lid.

There was a distinctive sucking sound as the cartridge tubes traveled to the basement linotypes, huge typewriters where each letter of each word was cast in hot lead simmering as bubbling gray liquid in pots underneath. Men sitting at the linotypes wore small hats of newspaper pages, folded like origami figures into squares.

When deadlines neared, a low vibration began through the newsroom floor, better than a clock, warning that the ceiling-high monster steel presses underneath the building were cranking up about to roll within 30 minutes. Sometimes staff could even hear the big buzzer signals, almost like a horn, on the presses warning mere mortals to stand away from the rapidly rotating potentially dangerous mechanical parts.

When that distinctive rumble began under everyone's feet, one of the men at the horseshoe desk got up, walked quickly over to another man hunched over an upright typewriter, lifted the carriage bar, yanked the paper out unceremoniously, walking away with it expressionless, back to the desk.

A 1967 newsroom was a stimulating place.

· · · · · · · ·

At her desk, Anita was reading about Governor Lurleen's latest medical travails shuttling from Montgomery to Houston for cancer treatment.

Her phone rang.

"Anita, can you come up to the front?" her managing editor, John W. Bloomer, asked. She took a seat inside his small, glass walled office that overlooked the entire frenzied newsroom.

Anita Smith had worked at the Birmingham News for three and one half years beginning right after she graduated in journalism from the University of Alabama. She had just accepted a job offer from a newspaper in Portland, Oregon.

She planned to move on to where there might be more opportunities for women journalists.

Maybe Bloomer wanted to talk to her about that.

CHAPTER NINETY FOUR
DO YOU WANT TO GO TO HOUSTON?

Bloomer got right to the point quickly.

"Do you want to go to Houston?" Bloomer asked Anita.

"I was still green at the gills. I was delighted. Pleasantly surprised," Anita remembered.

"We want you to cover Governor Lurleen's cancer battle for us," Bloomer explained.

Anita said yes right away. It was a plum assignment with byline potential.

The Portland Oregonian job could wait.

"The reason they decided to send me to Texas was that the Birmingham News was very, very politically opposed to George Wallace. They had George in their crosshairs.

"I think their (bias) tended to spread over into their news pages. They were very aware of this. So when Governor Lurleen was diagnosed with recurring cancer, they did not want the sensitivity of her illness to be reported by (political) writers who were so anti-George Wallace," Anita explained.

"The Birmingham News wanted coverage of Governor Lurleen Wallace's illness to be an objective assignment for someone who was not associated with anything anti-George Wallace. Their political writers, who were very high profile in the state, agreed with this.

308

"I had never met Lurleen or George Wallace. I was apolitical. About a year earlier, BN sent me to cover a Governor George speech at the Alabama Theater in downtown Birmingham. I have pretty close to a photographic memory. So I memorized his speech.

"When I began at BN, I told them I wanted to do serious stuff. I did not want to do what at that time was called Women's Department.

"But they were afraid to use me, because they did not have any other woman doing general news. They didn't know what to do with me. I could type very fast, so I ended up taking dictation for awhile, doing odds and ends. They had one female doing Metro, which they had just started, one woman college graduate at the desk, and me.

"Eventually BN offered me the medical beat, which was not big at the time. But medical news coverage became the biggest thing in Alabama. So the medical beat, which I had been on when I got the Governor Lurleen assignment, was a gift," Anita explained.

"So I turned 25 years old on Saturday July 1, saw Bloomer and got the Houston assignment on Wednesday July 5, and on Thursday July 7, 1967, I was on a plane to Houston, Texas.

. . . .

On the back of Anita's desk chair at the Birmingham News there was a sign that said "Nita Baby," put there by male staffers.

"They were very protective. They were very paternal. I think if BN had really thought about me going to Houston, I'm not sure they really would have assigned me. 'Nita's a woman, a girl, and we're sending here out there?' The assignment to go to Houston and write about Governor Lurleen was because I had experience covering medicine.

"Also those years when I worked there included the civil rights era when they were very busy. The allocation of labor was very tight," Anita said.

The July late afternoon she arrived in Houston, Anita first met George and his entourage as the group was having dinner at Trader Vic's, an "in" trendy restaurant near M.D. Anderson hospital. Lurleen was in the hospital for more tests. A seasoned political reporter from Montgomery introduced Anita to George, to some of his staff, and to some political supporters at the upscale eatery in the storied Shamrock Hilton Hotel.

Other reporters were there from national publications like TIME, Newsweek, as well as London. There were press conferences almost every day. News coverage wasn't only about Governor Lurleen. "You had George there, a presidential candidate on a third party ticket who had raised quite a ruckus with all his goings on.

"The coverage was huge. I was very ambitious.

"Maybe two weeks later, after her surgery, I met Lurleen in her hospital room. I don't remember who introduced us. But it was 'This is little Miss Smith from the Birmingham News.'

"George was out in the hall. But he came in and said to Lurleen: 'Sweetie, she (Anita) is a real sweet little girl.'

"Governor Lurleen had just had cancer surgery. They had reason to be hopeful. She was very upbeat," Anita remembered.

"Governor Lurleen had on a very lovely, gorgeous negligee and bed jacket. We had a very brief meeting that first time.

"And I remember thinking when I looked at her: 'You're pretty,' " Anita said.

CHAPTER NINETY FIVE
PAYIN' TO PLAY. LOOKIN' THE OTHER WAY

"I was paying off people for access.

"I spent a lot of the Birmingham News' money on paying them to give me access to search for such and such," Anita revealed.

"It was sort of an understanding with M.D. Anderson staff, that if they didn't know, they weren't going to tell.

"George's Alabama staff also looked the other way. And the staff there at M.D. Anderson looked the other way too. I became friends with them very quickly.

"George was very nice to me and his entourage was very nice to me. By George's entourage I mean the three doctors who were her doctors from Montgomery.

"The Alabama doctors had made a commitment to Lurleen that they would come to Houston and be in the operating room when she had the surgery. I had breakfast with George's entourage. I was at the hospital all day long," Anita said describing her daily routine.

"I was having interviews with the M.D. Anderson doctors about what (medically) they found, what they planned to do. It was a full time thing. I wasn't hanging around the hospital rooms waiting for someone to call me.

"I was out there competing," Anita said proudly.

"I could not afford at that stage for the Birmingham News to send me to Houston and be a tagalong. I just couldn't do that.

. . . .

"I had money from the paper. It was the Birmingham News' money."

Did the Birmingham News give Anita an expense account?

"They just gave me money."

Did the BN tell her what to do with the money they gave her?

"I knew what to do with it. I asked for the money."

Was the money to be used as a bribe?

"I said: I need money. Ok?"

Anita does not provide more specifics.

George's July 1967 Houston entourage included his legal team, bodyguards, security people, press secretary, two or three political supporters, and state finance director Seymour Trammell.

Although George was no longer governor, he was basically running Alabama while Lurleen battled for her life, Anita said.

Trammell came from an impoverished family of whites who had been the only whites in a group of black tenant farmers with whom Trammell grew up in dire rural poverty. Trammell had somehow gotten admitted to the University of Alabama law school, based on his life experience or something similar, instead of having to meet the law school entrance requirements of an undergraduate degree.

Eventually Trammell, a long-time close George Wallace hanger on, would go to prison for financial shenanigans.

Anita derisively imitates Trammell's low, slow creepy bass voice, describing how while she was in Houston, Trammell made her skin crawl when he phoned her in her room late one evening, suggestively inviting her to visit him in his room.

Anita declined.

Something about having to sort her sock drawer.

. . . .

After returning to Montgomery from Houston in July, Governor Lurleen worked as often she could, but also recuperated, chain smoking, again with hours in the sun at the governor's beach retreat near Mobile.

Sunshine is radiation from the sun. By spending hours in the sun, Lurleen was unintentionally quadrupling or more the amount of radiation into her body. She was combining radiation treatments from the hospital with additional self-radiation from the sun.

September 10, 1967, Governor Lurleen returned to Houston for what was termed "precautionary treatment" at M.D. Anderson.

Male reporters described her as looking "brisk and chipper" when she left for Houston Sept 10.

Anita, one of a very few female reporters, sounded a more solemn, foreboding note, describing Lurleen succinctly as "thin, very thin."

"Early detection has meant a lot to me," Governor Lurleen added in her remarks to reporters, perhaps as a public swipe at George and some of her woman friends, who for about four years cooperated in elaborate efforts concealing her 1961 cancer diagnosis from her at George's behest and with his guidance.

Reporter Anita quotes medical authorities as saying their examinations on September 11 "reveal no evidence of cancer activity."

Apparently they were identifying her four-and-one-half-hour July 10 surgery as a success.

Nevertheless, despite her "good report," the physicians decided to subject her to Cobalt 60, a radiation technique developed in Houston between 1946 and 1953. The physicians justified the aggressive treatment by saying they did not want to wait and perhaps find evidence of larger cancer masses later on.

After the September 7 treatments in Houston, she flew to Montgomery Sept 15, 1967, where a large crowd greeted her at the Alabama airport.

"I told the doctors from the beginning to tell me the whole truth. I don't want anything hidden from me about my condition," she told reporters. She advised other women to see their physicians regularly.

She had followed her own advice. She had seen physicians regularly about her health.

But the Montgomery physicians who attended her for her Cesarean surgery in 1961 had followed George's lead in ignoring cancer warning signs. She had never had an opportunity to make a decision about her own health issues.

• • • • • • •

"Governor Lurleen and I really got to know each other when she returned to M.D. Anderson hospital in September for followup radiation and treatment. The Birmingham News had decided they wanted me to expand my coverage beyond just her illness. They wanted me to do a series of articles on her life. She was staying at the Mayfair Apartments across from the hospital. I would go watch her radiation treatments. After, we'd just sit there and talk."

Lurleen celebrated her 41st birthday September 19, 1967. "I was about the age of her oldest child, daughter Bobbie. So sometimes Governor Lurleen's attitude toward me was mother-daughter," Anita said.

Lurleen was not completely candid with her younger children about the extreme gravity of her illness. Although Bobbie Jo, 23, her oldest child, knew and understood. She had dropped out of the University of Alabama to be with and comfort her mother during Governor Lurleen's last months and weeks of horrific suffering.

Lurleen particularly tried to shield her youngest child, her daughter Lee, 6 years old. Lurleen is recorded as expressing regret that she was not more blunt with her children about the very short time she had left to spend with them.

George was somewhere flying around America campaigning for president. But he did come to Houston for the opening of his Texas presidential campaign headquarters and periodically spent some time with his wife when she was at M.D. Anderson.

• • • • • • • •

With the exception of some small town weeklies, many newspapers, statewide and nationally, routinely vilified or, at the most, tolerated George during his life of nonstop campaigning and acerbic confrontations over racial issues.

But Lurleen, whom local and national media initially dismissed as a dime store girl joke, they had grown not only to admire, but to love. Not many public figures then or since reached that lofty status with the pre-Internet press.

Governor Lurleen had become family.

With the media, that is not an easily given, easily won affectionate embrace.

"Even those who snipe at George's presidential hopes find it very difficult to fault Lurleen Wallace, either in her official or her private life.

"Here is a woman, with her very life at stake, who has demanded that her physicians tell her all the facts so that she can keep the people of Alabama fully informed," the Alabama Star News in Andalusia editorialized.

George did not accompany Lurleen when she returned to Houston September 18, although he did fly into Houston for her birthday, September 19.

She was 41 years old.

George didn't stay long with Lurleen.

He never had.

Metaphorically, he was still leaving the motor of his truck running while he dashed inside a store, exactly the way he'd done the July day he first met Lurleen 25 years earlier.

With 14 months remaining to campaign for President, George zoomed off to public appearances in Portland, Reno, and Seattle and opened his national campaign headquarters in Montgomery with cheery hoopla.

CHAPTER NINETY SIX
DON'T YOU THINK SHE'S SMOKING TOO MUCH?

Lurleen became more ill at the end of her second week of Cobalt 60 radiation treatment in Houston. She suffered side effects of dehydration, stomach pain, and nausea. She had not until then been technically admitted to the hospital because she had rented an apartment across the street, spending nights there instead of at the hospital. Her daughter Bobbie Jo, Anita Smith, Nita Halstead, and others were loyal companions, contributing what small comforts and encouragement they might be able to provide Lurleen just by their physical companionship — just by being there.

Bobbie Jo eventually took a leave of absence from her studies at University of Alabama to be with her mother.

On October 9, 1967, Lurleen was readmitted to M.D. Anderson hospital to "supervise her food intake." The Cobalt 60 treatments were suspended temporarily.

"Don't you think Lurleen is smoking too much? Don't you think Lurleen should cut down on her cigarettes?" George asked one of the doctors in Lurleen's presence.

"Oh, I don't know. We don't want to take all her pleasures away from her," the doctor responded.

His words were a bolt of lightning.

According to reporter Anita, Lurleen's face immediately registered her understanding of the not-good-news significance of what the doctor said.

It was an ominous subtext: It doesn't matter if Lurleen smokes now. It doesn't matter what or how Lurleen does anything now, because her death is imminent.

"I saw the look on Lurleen's face. She had caught the meaning," said her friend Nita.

· · · · · · · ·

State health insurance covered a portion of the huge expense of her treatment. But Lurleen had to pay most of her medical expenses out of her $25,000 per year salary, which was being drained fast.

George was unemployed, or, as he proudly told reporters who inquired about his finances: "My wife supports me."

Because she was able to conduct some state business while in Houston, the Governor's Emergency Fund was used to pay for her apartment rental.

Alabama law required that the lieutenant governor assume her duties if she remained out of Alabama more than 20 days. She flew back to Montgomery in October for a weekend, tolling the 20 days. Reporters greeted her at the airport with obvious questions. How much longer would she be in Houston?

Lurleen answered the press with a positive outlook.

But the physician's comment about her cigarette addiction stayed with her.

Anita reported that Lurleen had "lost weight" downward from her normal 100 pounds, and "wore more makeup than usual"

. . . .

On November 1, after completing seven and one half weeks of medical treatment in Houston, Lurleen had a special request about going home to Montgomery.

She did not want to fly this time. She wanted to be driven by car from Houston to Montgomery to "see the country."

She and George never had a real honeymoon. Just the room in the railroaders boarding house with the single light bulb dangling.

And not once during their two decade marriage did they travel anywhere together that was not connected with politics—travel that was just for sightseeing or fun. So the brief, relatively leisurely drive from Houston to Alabama with friends and security guards, where they stopped for local food and peeked at local historic attractions, was sort of a honeymoon-for-one for Mutt.

It was the only real vacation Mutt ever had.

Clearly, Lurleen Wallace knew she was dying. She would repeat that directly weeks later to friends.

By driving, she was trying to see that which she had always wanted to see, but knew she would never have an opportunity to see again. She also spoke to friends of her long-time wish to see the mountains near chic Aspen, Colorado.

George Wallace would see the Colorado those mountains during his presidential campaigns.

But that would never happen for Mutt.

. . . .

Lurleen's once beautiful auburn hair had begun to turn to silver when she was physically able to return to her governor office for short periods beginning November 20 and in December 1967.

During that time, the state Mental Health Board announced that the first of four proposed mental retardation facilities would be built in Decatur and Mobile.

Without Lurleen's persuasion, those improvements might have happened years later, or maybe never.

Aides brought Lurleen in through a back entrance to the capitol and up inside the building to the executive office section, which is a separate wing to the left of the west entrance. She was not physically able to climb the side entrance steps as she usually did.

The beautiful muscled legs that attracted George's attention the first day they met were withered.

News photos showed deep, darkened lines on her face. She was rail thin.

. . . .

Incredibly, she flew November 22, 1967 to California, where George was campaigning for president on his American Independent Party affiliation. Some said by the trip, she wanted to show Alabamians that she wasn't as debilitated as the press indicated.

Cynics said George had asked her to help him campaign.

According to his son, George Jr., his father did ask Lurleen, whom he had every reason to understand was dying, to wash his socks.

In a California hotel, they were all "talking up a storm when George remembered he didn't have any clean socks," George Jr. said.

"Lurleen Honey, would you mind washing me out a pair of socks?" George asked his wife.

Even Oscar Harper, one of George's good ol' boy cronies for years, was stunned at George's insensitivity. Harper intervened. "Wait a minute, Lurleen. You're the governor. You shouldn't be washing his socks. Let him buy some or send them to the laundry," Harper interjected.

George said he feared Lurleen was going to hand him her hose to rinse out. But Lurleen laughed, according to her son.

While she was gone to wash George's socks, George reprimanded Harper for Harper's comments standing up on behalf of Governor Lurleen.

"Don't you go setting Lurleen off. We've got enough to do (with my) running for president without you getting Lurleen mad," George told Harper.

· · · · · · · ·

December 9, 1967 she flew again to California to join George, but felt too ill to keep speaking engagements that had been booked for her.

At that juncture, The Tuscaloosa Graphic newspaper called George out in print as a reprimand. The TG asked editorially why George and his entourage were off "gadding in California and elsewhere when Lurleen was so gravely ill? She is entitled to their assistance in these tragic days."

On December 23, 1967, after George got enough signatures to get on the California ballot, he flew to Montgomery to be with Lurleen during the Christmas holiday he said.

Intra-family, George had a notorious past during Christmas, described by his children as being perpetually grumpy, and more-than-usually disengaged with them during the holidays.

He would arise late and barely glance at their gifts they excitedly tried to share with him. Lurleen had purchased the gifts. Everyone knew Christmas was Lurleen's favorite time.

For George, Christmas was an unavoidable annoyance, something to be endured, to be tolerated until he could get back on the campaign road.

• • • • • • • •

On January 2, 1968, Lurleen returned to Houston for more tests. The news was bad: a new nodule, which physicians said was possibly malignant. On January 8 she resumed a more powerful Betatron treatment daily at 2 p.m. in Houston.

On January 31 she thought she could go home to Montgomery. But on February 1, 1968 she suffered severe pain and was readmitted to the hospital. On February 4, she was able to be transported to Alabama.

• • • • • • • •

On February 8, 1968 in Washington, D.C. George Corley Wallace made the formal announcement that he would run for president of the United States. It was his second run at the job.

George told spectators that Lurleen wanted him to announce.

In Montgomery, Lurleen announced that he had her "blessings" to run for president.

Some Alabama media cried foul, describing George as a selfish cad and epithets equivalent to SOB.

"George's decision to run for president while his wife is still sick is likely to be the biggest item George will have to explain to the people of Alabama," said one TV commentator. He hadn't heard about washing George's socks.

Another journalist Hal Steward wrote: " His enemies repeatedly accused George of furthering his political ambitions at the expense of a critically ill wife."

Lurleen's press secretary at the time refuted George's claim that Lurleen wanted him to run. The press secretary wrote in a 1969 book: "Lurleen apparently lost some of her will to live after her husband formally announced (for the presidency)."

CHAPTER NINETY SEVEN
UNTIL DEATH DO US PART

February 22, 1968 Governor Lurleen Wallace was rushed by ambulance to a Montgomery hospital and underwent four hours of surgery, her third surgery. Estimates of her body weight ranged from 60 to 70 pounds.

Henry Fairlie of the London Express News Service added his public voice to those of critics were increasingly offended by George's apparent crass detachment from Governor Lurleen's impending death.

Fairlie wrote: "That Governor Lurleen Wallace knows her illness is, as the doctors say, terminal, is public knowledge. That she craves peace in whatever time is left, is known to all around her. Her life, especially in recent years, has been one of total self-sacrifice to the ambitions of her husband.

"To the journalists covering Alabama, the story is harrowing."

George had announced that he planned to attend a March 4 American Party convention in Omaha. It is unclear whether he went.

But on March 11, Lurleen's condition worsened. She endured a fourth surgery to drain an abscess. George was there then. He canceled his presidential campaign appearances in Texas and Oklahoma.

Weeks earlier, her daughter Bobbie Jo had withdrawn from the University of Alabama to be with and comfort her mother in Houston and in Montgomery.

. . . .

In the last few weeks of her life, Lurleen asked her state trooper bodyguards to drive her to the four-bedroom brick house on Farrar Street that she had, with great difficulty, persuaded George to purchase for the time when she would transition from governor to private citizen.

She went alone, except for the troopers. It was a private goodbye.

For many months before her condition deteriorated, she reveled in purchasing furniture, rugs, lamps, and other items to place in the house with items she had collected over the years. "I've never had a beautiful house of my own. It is brick, too," she told friends proudly.

George, who had for years successfully spun himself to a gullible press as the "son of a poor dirt farmer," grew up in a beautiful brick house like the one Lurleen selected on Farrar Street.

The wood farmhouse she grew up in had an outdoor toilet.

The troopers helped Governor Lurleen walk into her beloved Farrar Street house, and ease her into a soft chair in the parlor. She would sit there, alone, just looking around the room quietly at the items she selected to display. "I like to feel my home." she explained.

The troopers usually waited outside for an hour or so, then knocked softly on the front door to check whether the governor was ready to leave?

The last time she visited, perhaps sometime in March, 1968, the troopers had to almost carry her from the Farrar Street house to the car, she was so weak and frail. As they drove her back toward the mansion, Governor Lurleen did not turn slightly in her seat to gaze back at the Farrar Street house the way she usually did.

She would never get to live in the brick house, although her children would for a short time. The few quiet, private sojourns in her last days were as close as Lurleen would ever come.

Her thoughts were her own.

Back at the mansion, she was able to spend the last 25 days of her life in her freshly decorated bedroom on the second floor.

The newly painted walls, heavy drapes and new carpeting were in various shades of turquoise and purple, her favorite colors.

"Things we didn't get to have as children we finally get as adults," Bobbie said.

But for Mutt those things would be only on loan.

CHAPTER NINETY EIGHT
NUNC DIMITIS SONG OF SIMEON

On March 27, 1968 she developed blood clots in her lung.

George canceled his presidential campaign press conferences in Mississippi, Tennessee, and North Carolina, and returned to Alabama to attend his maternal grandmother's funeral.

On April 2, Governor Lurleen's condition suddenly improved.

Physicians explained that sometimes very gravely patients can, against all explainable odds, will themselves to rally in anticipation of a very special event.

On April 13 Lurleen helped her daughter Lee celebrate her seventh birthday. Lee had continually asked Lurleen if Lurleen would be with her on her seventh birthday.

Lurleen had promised that Lee that she would be there.

She was.

On April 20 Lurleen asked to be driven to her parents' home in Knoxville.

It was a drive she knew well—over what her daughter Peggy called "the broken road to a place of safety," fleeing her miserably untenable relationship with George.

Mutt knew it was her final trip home to Knoxville.

· · · · · · · ·

On May 1, six days before his wife died, George issued a press release that he was dispatching coordinators to all 50 states to try to get on the ballot in each for president.

On May 6, Lurleen's condition became extremely grave. George did not appear at a campaign press conference.

Ironically, it was the same evening two years earlier, on national television, that snide Mr. Blackwell, a self-described fashion expert, had, on the Joey Bishop talk show, mocked and trashed Lurleen's clothing style.

She asked George and her physicians to remain with her during the night of May 6.

Her once muscled, athletic body that had soared joyously atop the water on skis, weighed 60 pounds.

Her entire family was there with her. "I have a strange feeling," she told them.

Later she lapsed into unconsciousness.

Lurleen Burns Wallace died in the early hours of Tuesday May 7, 1968, almost exactly two years from her history-making victory over nine opponents in the Democrat primary, a still unequaled feat.

Ironically, May 7 was election day.

But death was not a defeatable opponent, no matter how much money was raised or how ardent or dexterous the campaigner.

• • • • • • • •

The same morning Governor Lurleen died, The Poor People's March from Selma to Washington, D.C. was scheduled to pass through Montgomery in less than 24 hours and stop at the Capitol building, which was being prepared for Governor Lurleen's visitation and memorial in the same location and time as the march. A military band was spending the night there rehearsing for Lurleen's funeral events.

Albert Brewer, who became governor on her death, had declared the entire city in official mourning.

The SCLC leadership declined a request to by pass Montgomery. But they did agree not to march on the Capitol building.

Dr. Ralph Abernathy of the Southern Christian Leadership Conference, who had pastored a church down the street for many years, released a statement to the press praising Lurleen's life of example.

"A dark shadow has been cast across the horizon of America by the death of the Honorable Lurleen Wallace," Rev. Abernathy said.

His deliberate use of her title Honorable was not a coincidence. Lurleen had passed. Mutt was going home.

George told Lee that her mother had gone to heaven.

"Dear Mama: I love you. I didn't no (know) that you were going to Heaven so soon. I thought we were going to the lake to fish." Lee block printed in a note she left for Lurleen.

Her daughter Peggy would graduate from high school the next week.

Throughout her life, George never went fishing with Lurleen. Not once.

Fishing was Mutt's favorite pastime.

"She'd get up early, make a thermos of coffee, get bait and pole and troll the slough. She'd be there waitin' for you," Peggy remembered.

. . . .

Where did Lurleen get her undaunted courage and independent spirit?

"I think she was born with it. Then it slowly evolved. And then when she started to really find it, she passed away," Peggy said.

"There were programs she wanted passed: mental health, state parks, a cancer hospital. Rarely did the Alabama legislature tell that woman no. But if they did, Governor Lurleen went back to them, and she usually got what she wanted. She said: Guys, we are going to do this. Not for George Wallace's wife, but for the state of Alabama," Al Sheineker said.

"When mother died, people were talking about how young she was. And when they are saying that, I'm thinking: No! Forty one? That's not young! That's pretty old. Which it isn't of course," Bobbie Jo reflected.

"All of this understanding came to me later in my life. What a treasure she had been to the people. What a phenomenal thing she had done with her success and with no college education. Extraordinary. Running, being so humble.

"Her personality fit the time," said Bobbie Jo.

CHAPTER NINETY NINE
LET THY SERVANT DEPART

"A nation reveals itself not only in the (women) it produces,
but in the women it honors; in the women it remembers."
—President John F. Kennedy

For Lurleen Burroughs Burns Wallace 41, lying in state that afternoon in the governor's mansion, the alpha and the omega, the happiest and the most painful aspects of her life had often coexisted in the same time framework.

Historically, too, in 1968, the most tumultuous year in America's history, intersected with the omega end of many aspects of American culture and society. There was sudden end by assassination of the lives of two extraordinary men, Robert Kennedy and the Rev. Martin Luther King Jr., and the alpha beginning of an era where nothing would ever be the same in American culture.

Had Lurleen lived longer into 1968, she would have, as governor, faced many difficult challenges involving race and civil rights.

· · · · · · · ·

While her body lay in state that afternoon of May 7, 1968 in the Governor's Mansion, to be viewed by close friends, family and public officials, she had a young caller who came alone to pay his respects after everyone had gone.

"I remember Dad took me to the mansion to pick up mama (who was Lurleen's social secretary) for dinner. I said, 'Daddy, I'll go and get mama.' But in my head I said: I want to see Governor Lurleen one last time. Of course I didn't tell Daddy that," Al Steineker remembered.

"I went to mother's office. I asked her if I could go in and see Governor Lurleen? Mother had been with her the previous night when she died.

" 'Yes. Go ahead, son.' "

"Her casket was in the mansion sun room. When I walked in, the casket was centered on a carpet—maybe it was a red carpet.

"The minute I walked into the room, the four military corps honor guards, who had been in at-ease status, came immediately to strict attention. They had rifles. They stayed that way as long as anyone was in that room," Steineker said with pride.

She could be viewed through a protective sort of glass bubble.

The young boy approached the casket slowly, reverently, respectfully to say goodbye to his fishing buddy. He looked over the edge. She seemed to be clothed in something white or cream colored.

"She had on her inaugural gown." Al said.

It was the same gown Lurleen folded and put away unworn when her inaugural evening gala was canceled.

She had said then that she would save her beautiful gown to wear for another special public occasion.

CHAPTER ONE HUNDRED
BEND AND TELL ME THAT YOU LOVE ME

The next morning, May 8, as a motorcade escorted her remains away to the state Capitol building, an Army band played. There were muffled drums.

Draped in the white Alabama flag with the St. Andrew's Cross, the casket was placed in the Capitol rotunda. Until then, only Jefferson Davis had been so honored before.

Brother in laws Jack and Gerald Wallace, Lurleen's children, and her parents and brother were present with George.

Lurleen had specifically requested that her casket remain closed because she did not want her remains—in what she called her deteriorated condition—to be publicly displayed.

George overrode her dying request because in his view, the undertakers had restored Lurleen's appearance. Her casket remained open with Lurleen "ensconced in a protective glass bubble," like the drawings of sleeping Snow White in children's books of that time.

• • • • • • • •

More than 30,000 persons, black and white, at 1,800 per hour, filed slowly, quietly and respectfully past the open casket to pay their respects until the building closed at 1:30 am. May 9.

Toes of the pink satin slippers she had requested peeked out from the white inaugural gown that was her shroud.

At 7 a.m. the next morning, May 9, 1968 thousands more waited in a queue down the Capitol steps for blocks and blocks. At 1:30 the cortege left for services at St. James Methodist Church.

Reverend Vickers read a poem Lurleen had requested. One of the lines referenced "...all the beautiful belongings that no one else had looked quite far enough to find."

Her remains were taken to the highest knoll in Montgomery's Greenwood Cemetery. Overhead, jets flew in the missing plane formation, signaling the loss of a comrade pilot.

Lurleen and George are interred several feet apart, in front of a tower. Their headstones are small and simple, carved with only their names and years in office.

. . . .
.

June 11, four weeks after his wife's death, George resumed campaigning for president.

He never turned off the ignition. His engine just idled awhile.

Some print media, including the New York Times, alluded obliquely to what they termed George's insensitivity to his wife's suffering and death.

CHAPTER ONE HUNDRED ONE
VOICE FROM THE GRAVE

"Death ends a life. But it does not end a relationship,
which moves on toward a resolution which it may never find."
Movie dialogue, I Never Sang for My Father, 1970

Lurleen was a clever woman. Very smart. She left a last surprise for her family and the public. Something they could puzzle over for years after her untimely death.

She requested that an autopsy be performed on her remains.

Autopsies are usually performed when there is some question, some inconsistency as to a cause of death.

The probable cause of Lurleen's death, as everyone knew, was cancer.

Did Lurleen herself have doubts about her own cause of death? Maybe once she learned that her 1961 cancer had been concealed from her by George and her friends, she no longer trusted the concealers.

Autopsies also are done when criminal acts might be a possibility. But how would criminal acts relate to Lurleen's long public battle with cancer?

What did Lurleen speculate, hope, or know would be found in an autopsy? Was her request intended to be, in some way, her voice from the grave?

Some reports indicate an autopsy was involved because of Lurleen's interest in donating her remains for scientific research. But this explanation is unsubstantiated.

Reporter Anita Smith gives a partial second-hand peek at the autopsy results by quoting what Lurleen's attending physicians said about the reports. Smith did not see the actual autopsy records.

"...the autopsy revealed that Lurleen's cancer had spread in considerable proportions, to the liver, even to the lungs. It showed that a tumor, not an abscess had caused the intense pain during the final days of her life"

No further details of the autopsy have ever been disclosed publicly.

• • • • • • • •

"The day I turned 41, the age when mother died, Bobbie phoned me. Bobbie asked me how do I feel? I said I can't believe mother passed away at 41. Think of all she missed. Us children growing up, grandchildren," her daughter Peggy said.

"At the end of her life she knew that she could slip away be-cause all of her children were strong, and could take care of them-selves. That's how I feel," Peggy added.

Daughter Lee sent word through her sister Bobbie, that she did not wish to be interviewed about Lurleen. Because she was 7 years old when her mother died, her memories are few she said. And, at interview time, she was making care arrangements for her Down Syndrome son.

• • • • • • • •

When history graded each of them, fiery George and the dime-store—America's Evita, Governor Lurleen Wallace—would be forever remembered with cancer hospitals, roads and schools and public buildings named in her honor.

George would die as a self-described "ugly old man" whose public repentances for his racially charged rhetoric in his early life were always suspect as just another pivot of convenience cut to the changed fashion of the time.

· · · · · · · ·

There is a subtle irony in the placement of the oil paintings of Governor George and Governor Lurleen Wallace in the Alabama Capitol rotunda, directly across from each other, on either side of an archway leading to the wing housing the governor's offices and support staff offices in Montgomery.

The large painting of Governor Lurleen is the first one visitors see entering the west door.

A three-ton white marble bust of Lurleen facing west, surrounded by four white marble plaques with quotes, centers the rotunda floor, the place of greatest honor.

George's portrait is invisible when entering the west door. It is easy to miss, partly hidden to the left around the rotunda wall, somewhat shadowed.

Governor Lurleen, who faces George's painted image, is wearing the elegant cream-colored long gown with ermine collar she never got to wear to her gala 1967 inauguration ball, which was canceled while George met with his political operatives.

· · · · · · · ·

Christina Fernandez de Kirchner, in 2007 the first female elected president of Argentina, says that women of her generation (from all countries) "owe a debut to Evita Perón for her example of passion and combativeness." Kirchner was re-elected president in 2011.

American women and all women can find in Governor Lurleen Wallace an inspiring woman who managed to successfully juggle her role as mother of four children, working in low-level jobs outside the home, a marriage to a very difficult man, the betrayal of trusted friends, a grim, unsuccessful battle with cancer, and the governorship of a southern state in 1967-68: the most tumultuous years in American history.

. . . .

Why was Lurleen attracted to George Wallace?

"You'll have to ask her when you get to heaven. Because I don't know," said Al Steineker, shaking his head side to side in disbelief.

CHAPTER ONE HUNDRED TWO
HOW CLOSE WAS GEORGE TO BEING ELECTED PRESIDENT?

Buoyed by standing-room-only audiences for his West and Midwest speaking forays, George C. Wallace decided at the last minute in 1964 to enter three Democratic primaries outside of the south. Despite his segregationist baggage, Wallace's fiery charismatic rhetoric against big government and Communism attracted 25 percent of the Wisconsin primary vote, 30 percent in Indiana and 43 percent in Mayland—way above expectations.

However, despite his populist appeal and high vote totals, he won few delegates to the national convention because of lack of money and organization. When the Republican nomination of conservative Senator Barry Goldwater promised to undercut Wallace's support in the South in the general election, he withdrew from the Democratic primaries. Lyndon Johnson overwhelmed Goldwater in the general election.

Wallace changed strategy in 1968. He organized a third party, the American Independent Parry. Wallace reasoned that he would have little chance in the Democratic primary against incumbent Lyndon Johnson, and that if no presidential candidate received a majority of electoral votes in the general election, the election would be decided in the House of Representatives, where he and the conservative South could extract concessions from the major party candidates.

Wallace's name was on the ballot in all 50 states. He got 13.5 percent of the popular vote and 46 electoral votes from five southern states, not enough to prevent Richard Nixon from winning a majority of the electoral votes.

Analysts agreed that Wallace would have done better; but many of his supporters didn't vote for him because they thought he couldn't win as a third party candidate.

In 1972, Wallace's strategy reverted to competing in the Democratic primaries again, where there was no incumbent Democrat running for re election.

His results were extraordinary. Against 11 opponents, Wallace received 23.48 percent of the popular vote. He came in third, but within reach of George McGovern's 25.34 percent and Hubert Humphrey's 23.77 percent.

Wallace took first place in five southern states as well as Nebraska, Maryland and Michigan.

He placed second in Wisconsin, Pennsylvania, and Indiana.

By May 17, 1972 he had accumulated 327 delegates, significantly ahead of Vice President Hubert Humphrey and slightly behind Senator George McGovern.

Tragedy struck May 16, 1972, the day before the Michigan and Maryland primaries. As George Wallace moved toward the rope line in a Maryland shopping center parking lot, Arthur Bremer shot the former governor, permanently paralyzing him from the waist down. Although he still won Michigan and Maryland May 17, his personal campaigning was sidelined for the remainder of the primary campaign season.

The attempted assassination slowed his delegate vote accumulation to a crawl. At the Democratic convention, he placed third behind Senator Henry Jackson and McGovern, the 1972 nominee.

• • • • • • • •

In 1974, after winning the Alabama governorship in his wheelchair, George made a fourth and last presidential try in 1976.

The must-win Democratic primary was Florida, where he won every county in 1972. Although initial polls showed him leading with 40 percent of the vote in a three-candidate race, Wallace's vote total dropped to 31 percent, behind fellow southern governor Jimmy Carter. Wallace then fell far behind other candidates in other primaries where he had done well in 1972.

Analysts attributed his evaporating support to voter concern that his medical condition might hinder his service as president.

Had he not been shot, Wallace was well on his way to being the Democrat's nominee, and perhaps being elected president.

Like his brother Gerald, he was married three times.

After Lurleen's death, George later served three four-year terms, ending in 1987, as Alabama governor. He died in 1998 and is buried near Governor Lurleen.

His mea-culpa, teary public repentances for his racially charged rhetoric, which launched his political career, were always suspect as just another pivot of convenience cut to the fashion of a changed time.

(This chapter was researched and written by Donald O. Jansen)

CHAPTER ONE HUNDRED THREE
AUTHOR'S NOTES

People often ask me: How did you get the idea for writing about Governor Lurleen Wallace?

And the answer is: I don't know. The idea just came to me. Maybe because of talk about Hillary Clinton, the wife of a southern state governor, Bill Clinton, running for president?

Nonfiction authors always seek to write about someone or something that hasn't been written about much previously. Lurleen is ideal. Although there are a few thin, small books about Lurleen and passing mention of Lurleen in books about George, there was nothing comprehensive about her life and legacy.

Existing publications portrayed Lurleen as one-dimensional: nurturing, clueless, vapid, "giggling" at every opportunity. Surely there had to be more depth to this woman whom Rev. Ralph Abernathy thought worthy of public praise in a turbulent time.

And I don't know how I thought of the similarities between Evita Perón and Lurleen, either. But when I began comparing the life trajectories of the two women, their similarities in a generally compatible time frame were uncanny.

I had to accelerate my interviews and research because many of the people who actually knew Lurleen are elderly. Coincidentally, just after I got the idea for *American Evita: Lurleen Wallace*, my husband, also an attorney, got a speaking engagement in Birmingham. It was meant to be.

So I set up interviews on which he could accompany me, we rented a car, and we drove around Alabama.

I was ideal to write Lurleen's biography, paired with Evita Perón's, because we have commonalities. I, too, am a woman who sought and won political office. I, too, campaigned with my husband, a veteran political operative. Before I became an attorney, I was a print journalist. So interviewing the journalists and press folks about Lurleen and reading journalists' accounts of Evita Perón was a walk down memory lane.

I noticed that nearly all books and other material about Evita Perón, as were books about Evita, were written by males.

I worked as a print journalist in the late 1960s, the same years Lurleen served as governor.

I traveled across America with a group of male journalists from major national publications. We were assigned to cover religion, but because the civil rights movement began in churches, we really covered civil rights. It was a very, very exciting time to be a print journalist.

After I got the Lurleen book idea, I was sorting through some really old papers and came upon a feature I wrote on February 4, 1976 when I covered George Wallace campaigning in Florida while I worked general assignment at the Fort Lauderdale News.

I feel enormous respect and affection for the South: southern people, southern humor, southern cuisine, southern manners, and southern writing, particularly Eudora Welty's work.

Although I was raised a Yankee, I moved to Southern Georgia in 1964, during the south's most violent and challenging times. I worked at what was then Valdosta State College and wrote features for the Valdosta Daily News. I've lived in the South ever since. It is where I feel at home.

People also ask my opinion of whether there was mutual love

between George and Lurleen, Juan and Evita?

That question is answered for George by his conduct on many occasions. To cite only one: He paused his campaigning for president only shortly before her imminent death and resumed campaigning shortly after.

Lurleen loved George for a year or so after their marriage, until the reality of what he was and what he wasn't, dawned on her about age 17. Then she forced herself to tolerate him because she had three children at age 24 and no money, no high school diploma. She came to dislike him intensely—the formal separation agreement confirms that. At the very end of her life, she tolerated him again because it was futile in the short time remaining for her to do anything about the unhappy marriage.

People who say of Lurleen "She loved that man" have confused reality with a popular country western song title.

• • • • • • • •

Evita Duarte and Juan Perón were a true love story, a perfect match. Popular press have written, without evidence, that it was a sexless, mutually convenient marriage of two extremely ambitious, talented people, lacking even pretense of affection.

To the contrary, Evita and Juan complemented each other in personality and understood each other at the deepest political and sexual levels. Juan's support for and promotion of a female leader in that era in Argentina was extraordinary. Isabel, a subsequent wife, did become president of Argentina when Juan died in 1974.

CHAPTER ONE HUNDRED FOUR
DRAMATIS PERSONAE

MARY JO VENTRESS: If you emailed Central Casting requesting a quintessential "southern lady," Mary Jo Ventress would appear at your office door. Just hearing her Alabama speech, the musical southern patrician cadence, is like slow water over smooth, mossy rocks in a sunlit stream. Her grammar and diction are perfect.

She was Lurleen's life-long, devoted companion and friend. She gave me a thoughtful interview, carefully pondering each question before responding. Although her health was very frail, I had the feeling she made a gracious effort to speak with me in person because she wanted to do everything she could to maintain the memory and career of Lurleen. It was truly an honor to meet Miz Ventress. We will all be culturally poorer as her generation, sadly, passes from the scene. She is what is called in the South a Great Lady.

Working her way through college, Mary Jo earned a Bachelor of Science degree from Auburn University in 1944, and a Master of Arts from Auburn in 1964. Her parents did not attend college. She and her husband had no children.

AL STEINEKER: Charming, ebullient, sharp, quick-witted, and canny. Humorous. Another great interview because he was not a family member and could interpret events more objectively. His mother served as Lurleen's social secretary and scheduler.

Although he was a child when he knew Lurleen, he provided an adult's sophisticated insight into Lurleen's personality and thought processes both through his child's eye perspective and his later adult perspective. "I'm going to tell you, Governor Lurleen Wallace was something else!" Al said. He is part owner of King's Table Catering in Montgomery.

He was present in the Montgomery, Maryland parking lot at the exact moment when George Wallace was shot there on May 15, 1972.

ANITA SMITH: One of the pioneer women reporters at the Birmingham News in 1966, she was a fulfilling interview because she was an outsider, not a family member. And she is one of the few women who actually knew Lurleen and wrote about her when both were adults. Anita's 1967 book The Intimate Story of Lurleen Wallace, Her Crusade of Courage is outstanding reporting, accomplished writing that should have won journalism prizes.

Anita, a serious all-business personality, expertly captures the Lurleen Wallace dynamic and provides insightful details missed or ignored by male authors. Most of the Lurleen books, like the Evita Peron books, were written by men.

Anita began working as a journalist about the same time as I in what is now known as the "golden era" of American journalism.

GEORGE WALLACE JR.: When he walked into the lobby of our Birmingham Alabama hotel for an interview, my husband and I recognized him instantly. George Wallace Jr. looks exactly like his father, who was an igneous national television and print political staple for three decades.

George followed in his father's political footsteps and served as Alabama state treasurer and has been active in Alabama politics. He had a brief music career as a teenager, three marriages, two divorces.

Even though I kept reminding George Jr. that my nonfiction

346

book would be about his mother Lurleen, it was difficult to keep him from drifting often into talking about his father. He desperately wants to, and he wants others to, portray his father as a wonderful person. He gets angry if they don't. George will never be able to accept that his father was not a nice person, however much George might wish that he were. Only Richard M. Nixon was more ruthless than George C. Wallace.

Because George Jr. knew his mother Lurleen when he was a child (obviously), he thinks of her still frozen in that maternal context only, as one of those plaster of Paris blue and gold statutes of Mary in Roman Catholic churches, particularly popular in Mexico. To him, Lurleen remains solely a mother, not a woman who struggled with a woman's flesh and blood choices.

BOBBIE JO WALLACE PARSONS: Bobbie died at the age of 71 years on February 13, 2015. The obituary did not list a cause of death. Although she was the oldest child, she deferred to George even when both she and George recognize that her knowledge exceeds George's on any given topic. Psychiatrists would call her the "Hero Child" in the troubled George and Lurleen marriage.

She was editor of her high school paper and majored in home economics and minored in journalism at University of Alabama. Because of helping Lurleen through her cancer and death, and her own health issues, it took Bobbie Jo eight years to get a college degree.

After graduation, Bobbie worked for a time on the Livingston. Alabama Home Record, a weekly newspaper. She covered city and county commission meetings, wrote news and general features.

She lived with her husband, Jim Parsons, with whom she had two sons, in the low rolling hills of 500 acres outside Birmingham. Their magnificent estate has artificial lakes and several guest houses, one of which is occupied by George Jr. Her hobby was killing African game animals such as leopards, lions, elephants, rhinoceros—and quilting. She was also an avid horsewoman. She battled kidney stone ailments that began at 16 and continued throughout her life.

She is much more realistic than her brother George Jr., about who her father was as a person, but she seems to hold back on expressing that realism, particularly in the presence of George Jr. Although Bobbie and her father were estranged for many years while Lurleen lived—as well as after Lurleen died—George Jr. says Bobbie and her father eventually reconciled.

Bobbie however, does not say that in an interview.

She loved her mother utterly. Although she understood Lurleen when others didn't, she regrets that she was not appreciative enough of the woman-out-of-her-time that Lurleen was.

Bobbie Jo was old enough to see first hand, as well as understand, how disrespectfully her father treated her mother. Her younger siblings, as children, could not be as observant as she because of their age. Bobbie Jo witnessed it all.

When I arrived for the interview, I had gotten caught in a rain, and my clothes were soaked. Bobbie immediately gave me some of her clothes to wear until her assistant dried my clothes. Southern hospitality is something to behold. I hardly recognized my clothes when they were returned because they were ironed to a perfection I did not know existed.

Bobbie looks exactly like photos of her mother. Her persona is very serious, as if there is a trailer script of sadness always running on the back screen of her mind that nothing can alleviate.

Both she and George are guarded. That is understandable.

For the children of the famous and infamous, their inherited life is always difficult. They did not ask to be born, thrust into national turmoil, but they are left to cope somehow, with the detritus of a controversial family heritage.

PEGGY WALLACE KENNEDY: She was the most candid of the Wallace children, and the most sensitive to subtleties of human behavior. In her mature years, she seems to have decided to "let it all hang out" and say what she really feels about everything, including growing up with her father George.

While George Jr.'s overriding goal is to put a better, kinder face on George, Peggy seems more realistic about who George was and is willing to say so unabashed. She doesn't hesitate to criticize her father when she feels criticism is warranted.

She and her husband retired Judge Mark Kennedy collect "folk art."

Among their eclectic collection is a 1987 oil painting by Elizabeth Kimbrough entitled "You Can Be Anything," which seems to exactly exemplify her mother Lurleen's extraordinary achievement.

In the artwork, a female figure stands alone in the middle. At the outer edges are arrayed symbols exemplifying all the possible life paths and careers the woman could choose for her life.

Peggy and her husband hadn't noticed the connection with Governor Lurleen Wallace's life until brought to their attention.

ED EWING: Ed's an affable old-time political operative, with Gentleman of the Old School manners, who hasn't yet become cynical about politics. He arranged access for me to many interviewees and was extremely helpful.

HOW MANY EVITA/LURLEEN SIMILARITIES CAN YOU ADD TO THIS LIST?

1. Born in rural villages with modest family incomes.
2. Left their homes at ages 15 and 16 years old to venture to "exotic" places.
3. Married steely-eyed men who were very politically ambitious.
4. Non high school graduates who married "up" socially, to men more educated than they.
5. Achieved all of their fame and accomplishment in approximately six years.
6. Their stardom eclipsed their husbands who faded into relative obscurity.
7. They campaigned with their spouses in an era when that was very unusual.
8. As children, they showed early signs of an independent spirit.
9. Both played piano.
10. Horsewomen who enjoyed outdoorsy activities from their farm upbringing.
11. Each became First Ladies, then used that as platform to develop an individual identity apart from spouse.
12. Their happiest and most painful life experiences coexisted within the same time frame.
13. Both uninformed about their own health issues—concealed from them by spouses.
14. Lurleen died ON election day. Evita died a few days after election day, but voted from her literal death bed.

15. Both championed women voting and seeking public office at a time when this was considered a revolutionary thought.
16. Each died a ghastly death of untreated uterine cancer.
17. During their lifetimes they became so beloved by their constituencies, that they were mourned by thousands, (or millions) an affection which continues today.
18. Eerie similarities in dates of major life events.

ACKNOWLEDGMENTS

To my publisher Wild Horse Press, Fort Worth, Texas; my editor Helen Anders; long-time editor Kristy Shuford White, Humanities Chair at Lurleen B. Wallace Community College, Andalusia, Alabama for her inestimable support; Ken Barr, researcher; Cynthia Luckie, Photographs Archivist, Alabama State Archives, Montgomery; Jennie Kemp, Genealogy Librarian, Tuscaloosa Public Library, Tuscaloosa; Tuscaloosa Area Virtual Museum; West Alabama Chamber of Commerce; Julie Saint and Joy Murphy, Office of Enrollment Clerk, Alabama State Legislative Offices; Aroine Irby, docent guide, Alabama State Capitol building; Library of Congress, Digital Reference section; Jamie Leonard and Helen Cauthen, University of Alabama Law School library; Kathy Yarbrough, Director of Development, College of Arts & Sciences, University of Alabama; Donna Adcock, Director of Publicity, University Libraries, University of Alabama; Kim Giles, By Design, Waco, Texas for American Evita cover and interior design; husband Donald O. Jansen, Assistant General Counsel, University of Texas Systems; Judge Maria Casanova and Sergio Villafuerte, who assisted with the Spanish translations of the Evita chapter titles; U.S. Rep. John Culberson and his staffer Ellie Essalih; and Anthony Washington of WAMU 88.5 radio, Washington, D.C. NPR affiliate, who assists with publicity.

Also: George Wallace Jr;, Bobbie Jo Wallace Parsons, Peggy Wallace Kennedy, Al Steineker, Ed Ewing, Anita Smith, Governor Albert Brewer.

SPECIAL ACKNOWLEDGMENT TO:

Kathryn Easey of Bissex & Watson law firm, Austin, Texas who transcribed all the interview tapes and converted the Time Line Chart for computer.

Wei-hsun Tao, also known as "De," a college student with the patience of a saint, who fixes computers, and without whom *American Evita: Lurleen Wallace* would not exist.

Eleanor Louise Murphy, my maternal aunt, the love of my life, God Rest Her Soul.

BIBLIOGRAPHY

In researching and writing *American Evita: Lurleen Wallace*, the following resources, listed alphabetically by author surname, were consulted:

Alabama State Archives, Montgomery

Tuscaloosa Public Library, Tuscaloosa

Tuscaloosa Area Virtual Museum

Library of Congress, Digital Reference Section, Recorded Sound Reference Center, recording of Lurleen's voice, American Liberty Records

University of Alabama, Law School Library

Evita First Lady, a Biography of Evita Perón by John Barnes (1978, Grove Press)

An Intimate Portrait of Eva Perón, (1997, Edited by Tomas de Elia and Juan Pablo Queiroz)

Evita The Real Life of Evita Perón by Nicholas Fraser and Marysa Navarro (1996, 1980 W.W. Norton & Company)

Stand Up for Alabama Governor George Wallace by Jeff Frederick (2007, University of Alabama Press)

Lady of Courage The Story of Lurleen Burns Wallace by Jack House (1969, League Press, Montgomery)

George Wallace, American Populist by Stephen Lesher (1994, Addison-Wesley Publishing, Reading Massachusetts)

Evita In My Own Words by Joseph A. Page (1996, The New Press, New York)

Evita The Life of Eva Perón by Charles River Editors (undated)
The Intimate Story of Lurleen Wallace Her Crusade of Courage by Anita Smith, edited by Ron Gibson (1969, Communications Unlimited, Montgomery)
Governor George Wallace, The Man You Never Knew by George Wallace Jr. (2011, Wallace Productions LLC)
Nurturing Spirits, Edited by Kristy Shuford White (undated W.W. Norton & Company, New York)
Lurleen B. Wallace, Alabama's First Woman Governor by Alice Yeager (2003, Seacoast Publishing Birmingham)

TIME LINE

YEAR	GEORGE	JUAN
1895		• Born 10-8-1895
1911		• Entered Superior War College
1912		• Boxing and Fencing
1913		• Graduated Superior War College
1919	• Born 8-25-1919	• Military Career
1929		• Married Aurelia 1-5-1929
1936		• Military Attaché Chile
1937	• Graduated high school • Entered University of Alabama	
1938	• Boxing	• Aurelia died 9-10-1938 • Left Chile
1939	• Entered University of Alabama Law School	• Military Observer in 7 countries in Europe
1941		• Left Europe
1942	• Graduated law school • Met Lurleen 7-1942 • Truck Driver • Army Air Corp 10-20-1942	
1943	• Married Lurleen 5-21-1943	• Secretary of Labor
1944	• Bobbie born 10-1944 • Pacific Theatre	• Met Eva 1-22-1944 • Vice President Argentina
1945	• WWII ended 8-15-1945 • Out of Army 12-8-1945	• Married Eva 10-18-1945 • Left Secretary of Labor and Vice President
1946	• Assistant Alabama Attorney General	• President Argentina 6-4-1946
1947	• Entered Alabama Legislature	
1950	• Peggy born • Re-elected Alabama Legislature	
1951	• George III born	• Re-elected President
1952	• Elected Circuit Judge	• Took office as President of Argentina 6-4-1952
1953	• Became Circuit Judge	
1955		• Deposed as President 9-21-1955
1958	• Lost for Alabama Governor	
1961	• Lee born	• Married Isabel 11-15-1961
1962	• Elected Alabama Governor	
1963	• Took office as Alabama Governor 1-14-1963	
1964	• Lost Democratic Presidential Primary	
1968	• Lost President on American Independent Party Ticket	
1970	• Elected Alabama Governor	
1971	• Married Cornelia 1-4-1971 • Took office as Alabama Governor 1-18-1971	
1972	• Lost Democratic Presidential Nomination • Shot 5-15-1972	
1973		• President Argentina 10-12-1973
1974	• Re-Elected Alabama Governor	• Died 7-2-1974
1975	• Took office as Alabama Governor	
1976	• Lost Democratic Presidential Primary	
1978	• Divorced Cornelia	
1979	• Left office as Alabama Governor	
1981	• Married Lisa 9-9-1981	
1982	• Elected Alabama Governor	
1983	• Took office as Alabama Governor 1-17-1983	
1987	• Left office as Alabama Governor • Divorced Lisa	
1998	• Died 9-13-1998	

TIME LINE

YEAR	LURLEEN	EVA
1919		• Born 5-7-1919
1926	• Born 9-19-1926	
1934		• Moved to Buenos Aires
1937		• Actress
1942	• Left high school • Met George 7-1942 • She was 15, George was 22	• Economic Stability in Radio
1943	• Married George 5-21-1943	
1944	• Bobbie born 10-1944	• Met Juan 1-22-1944 • She was 24, Juan was 48
1945		• Married Juan 10-18-1945
1946	• Agricultural Department Clayton Clerk	• Campaigned for Juan
1947	• Enrolling Clerk Alabama Legislature • Back to Agricultural Department Clerk	• European Tour • Women's Suffrage Law Passes • Purchased Newspaper
1948		• President Eva Peron Foundation
1949	• Leg. Alabama Clerk • Back to Agricultural Department Clerk	• President Female Peronist Party
1950	• Peggy born	• First cancer surgery 1-12-1950
1951	• George III born	• Second cancer surgery 11-6-1951
1952		• Spiritual leader • Died 7-26-1952
1961	• Lee born • Pre-cancer	
1965	• Diagnosed with cancer • Radiation treatment	
1966	• Cancer surgery 1-1966 • Elected Alabama Governor 11-1966	
1967	• Took office as Alabama Governor 1-16-1967 • Cancer diagnosed 6-1967 • First cancer surgery 7-10-1967	
1968	• Second cancer surgery 3-1968 • Died 5-7-1968	

Donald O. Jansen and Kathryn Easey prepared this chart.

ABOUT THE AUTHOR:
JUDGE JANICE LAW

JANICE LAW

Narrative nonfiction *American Evita: Lurleen Wallace*, is Judge Janice Law's sixth book.

She aspires to adapting American Evita into a musical theater production featuring Governor Lurleen, patterned after the Broadway musical "Evita," but featuring country and western music.

Law is a retired Texas criminal court judge, a 14-year print journalist, a newspaper travel columnist, and the author of six books, one of which was a 2007 nonfiction finalist for the Texas Book Award. Her Short story "The Secrets of a Client Are Inviolate" was a 2011 Honorable Mention in the annual Texas Bar "Write Stuff" competition. www.judgejanicelaw.com

In 2012, Law took a three-year break to found the D.C.–based American Women Writers National Museum, a nonprofit whose mission is to honor America's premier women writers, historical and contemporary. AWWNM continues to grow and do well. www.americanwomenwritersnationalmuseum.org.

Law and her nonfiction books have been featured at prestigious national literary festivals where she served as podium speaker, panelist, or teacher. A partial listing of these venues includes: three consecutive times (2005, 2006, 2007) at the National Press Club's annual Book Fair, one of Washington D.C.'s most prestigious literary events; Library of Congress (2012 podium speaker); St. Peters-burg Times Festival of Reading (2007 podium speaker; twice panelist 2007, 2010); Virginia Festival of Books Charlottesville; C-Span Book TV featured on two short videos aired repeatedly; Texas Book Festival (2007); annual meeting Texas Bar (2006 literary panel); National Association of Women Judges, (2013 panel and speaker), Washington, D.C.

Law and her husband Don Jansen also won two Tellys in 2002 for best music and lyrics. Tellys are statuette awards for television commercials equivalent to Emmys.

Law still sits occasionally in Texas as a visiting judge, for judges who are ill or on vacation.

Law has served as a state and federal prosecutor, a staff attorney to federal judges, and done nine years of indigent criminal defense. She is a member of the bar of the Supreme Court of the United States, and a member of the Florida Bar and Texas Bar.

Contact Information:
www.judgejanicelaw.com
judgejanicelaw@yahoo.com
www.americanwomenwritersnationalmuseum.org

Book design/production provided by
By Design • Waco, Texas • (254) 420-1880 • www.bydesignwaco.com

360

CPSIA information can be obtained at www.ICGtesting.com
Printed in the USA
LVOW10s0318030415

433065LV00003B/3/P

9 781940 130835